NEON NUPTIALS

NEON NUPTIALS

THE COMPLETE GUIDE TO LAS VEGAS WEDDINGS

Ken Van Vechten

HUNTINGTON PRESS
LAS VEGAS, NEVADA

Neon Nuptials: The Complete Guide to Las Vegas Weddings

Published by
Huntington Press
3687 S. Procyon Ave.
Las Vegas, NV 89103
Phone (702) 252-0655
e-mail: books@huntingtonpress.com

ISBN: 0-929712-80-3

Cover Photo: ©2005 Mary Schilpp
Cover Design: Bethany Coffey & Laurie Shaw
Interior Design: Bethany Coffey
Production: Laurie Shaw

Acknowledgments

LOVE AT FIRST SIGHT

Since this is my first book, I don't have the whole author-etiquette thing quite wired, so I'm going to start my thanks with the person who typically occupies the last paragraph in such ramblings, and in my case her name is Teresa. Ours was not a neon nuptial, but our love, abiding friendship, and get-every-joy-out-of-life-together sentiment burn a lot more intensely than that visible-from-space light atop the Luxor. Honey, you are without a doubt *the* singular person on the face of this planet. Will you marry me again, in Vegas, on our 10th anniversary?

This book actually started out as a guide to Las Vegas golf courses. Whether directed by fate or folly, the good folks at Huntington Press looked at my proposal for said book, sensed my addiction to the game, and apparently came to the conclusion, "If this guy voluntarily tees it up in Vegas during August's summer heat, he's nuts enough to take on the scores of love shacks in town." That I'd written a few magazine articles about Las Vegas weddings probably helped too. So to Anthony Curtis, Deke Castleman—whose sense of humor might exceed mine for its impishly *noir* quality—Bethany Coffey, Laurie Shaw, Len Cipkins, the entire gang, and most particularly Wendy Tucker, whose clean-up-that-copy skills are eclipsed only by the wide-eyed wonder with which she approaches the world ... thanks for rolling the dice on me.

Then there's LasVegas Advisor.com, that warm and wacky cyber

Sin City. To the many members with whom I've bandied and bantered for these several years: Viva Las Vegas. I count a lot of buds among you, even if we've never shaken hands in the flesh-and-blood.

And mom and dad ... I did it, didn't I? Woo hoo! Thanks for 44 years of support, guidance, and perhaps above all else, friendship.

Contents

Introduction

FIRST KISS

Grace McGee was Clark County's first bride. And apropos to the times in which she lived, she took her husband's surname, Bright. As in Mr. and Mrs. William C. Bright—a fitting name for a pair of lovebirds married in the city of glitz, glamour, and neon yet to come. The joyous event occurred in July 1909, mere days after the county came into existence. Seven other couples followed suit that year. The rush was on!

In 1945, the county recorded its 100,000th wedding. Fifty years later, Clark County surpassed the threshold of 100,000 weddings *in a year* for the first time, and there's been no retreat since. By the end of 2003, the overall tally reached well in excess of three million weddings on the books. That's nearly 100 weddings each and every day, on average, for 95 years.

Sin City is wedding heaven.

Las Vegas' matrimonial magnetism is easy to understand: affordability, ease, diversity, kitsch, excitement. You can show up on the spur of the moment, get a license, find a chapel, and have it done all in less than an hour, for $100. You can say "I do" on one of several rides set atop the tallest freestanding tower west of the Mississippi. You can have Elvis, of several vintages, belt out "Viva Las Vegas" while you head down the aisle. There's literally something, somewhere, and some just-right way for every bride and groom.

It's a brave new nuptial world from the one experienced by Grace and William Bright. And *Neon Nuptials: The Complete Guide to Las Vegas Weddings* sorts through the tacky, the wacky, the so-so, and the best way to go in Las Vegas weddings to help you get a bright start in Glitter Gulch.

ABOUT THE BOOK

Neon Nuptials is a guidebook to Las Vegas weddings. It does for you, a Las Vegas-interested bride (or groom), what a good travel guide would do for a vacationer: Namely, it sifts through a huge volume of information and suggests how to get the most out of your Las Vegas wedding experience—from a bridal perspective, of course.

You have enough anticipation in your life right now, so the first section, *Courtship*, cuts right to the altar with some suggestions as to the best in outdoor wedding sites, freestanding chapels, casino-based chapels, chapels you probably want to avoid, honeymoon spots, and, as an added bonus, the one place that represents the best of the best.

Married life begins at the altar; weddings start much earlier. So to get you to the "church" on time, Chapter Two outlines how and where to get a license, ceremony options, what to be aware of when choosing a chapel, when to go, and some fun facts and anecdotes about getting married Las Vegas-style. This section is titled *Proposal*.

Fifty-six wedding sites are featured in the next two chapters—*I Do* and *I Do ... Too*. Most are chapels, some are outdoors, many are part of hotel-casinos, and a few defy categorization. Contact information, a quick-reference guide, and a critical review of each chapel or venue are intended to get you behind the obligatory smiling face and cutesy façade that greet you at almost every door. These listings are the heart of the book and are alphabetized within two groupings: freestanding venues and hotel-based.

All chapels are wedding facilities, though not all wedding facilities are chapels. Some wedding facilities are mobile, as in the case of a helicopter or a horse's back. Therefore, I frequently use "venue" to denote a place where weddings are conducted. Chapel, venue, facility, site, whatever ... ultimately, they're all the same—a place to wed in the Wedding Capital of the World.

After you figure out how to get to the altar—and which altar to get to—you might just want some insight into where to stay and eat or what to see and do, and Chapters Five and Six, *Honeymoon in Vegas ... Good Bets in Beds,* and *Honeymoon in Vegas ... Eats and Treats,* touch on some choice selections. The book closes with a select listing of publications and Web resources.

A CAVEAT

Despite the obvious distractions and excesses, when you get off the Strip and into the 'burbs, Las Vegas is a town like any other—a place where people live, work, worship, raise kids, heck, even get married. There are supermarkets, schools, libraries and office complexes, Little League games on the weekend, and trick-or-treaters running amok on October 31. As you and your guy are likely to be tourists as well as newlyweds-in-the-making, with only a few exceptions this book does not look at places at which (mostly) locals wed—churches, country clubs and other private hospitality venues, the Elks Lodge or similar fraternal organizations, or, for that matter, the convention/ballroom facilities that you can expect every hotel to have.

There are two reasons for this. One, such spots don't represent the typical Las Vegas wedding aesthetic that draws 100,000-plus couples to the desert each year. Secondly, a country club's pretty much a country club, and while its members may, you likely don't care how Canyon Gate's facilities measure up to Anthem's; you're not going there. And while I do address some of Las Vegas' more freeform and unusual wedding options, I don't go into any depth about, say, getting hitched in a hot-air balloon, since many chapels—particularly the standalones—offer extreme or adventure packages as standard fare.

In a similar vein, although Sin City might be unparalleled when it comes to putting together a wedding reception—being the Entertainment Capital of the World, with many of the world's largest hotels and a culinary sophistication that's a far cry from the billboards touting $9.95 lobster dinners and two-for-one all-you-can-eat buffets—I don't tackle reception sites or facilities that require a wedding/reception combo. This was a matter of cutting through a lot of unnecessary fluff; any place in town with a room big enough for six and a kitchen can claim to be a wedding-and-reception site and that's not what most fly-in/drive-in brides want from their neon nuptial. If a dance-and-dinner-type reception is your ticket, talk to your wedding coordinator. Or call on any of the town's gazillion great eateries. Finally, I pass right by wedding-related service providers. There are too many limos, too many tux rental shops, too many

DJs, too many hair salons—that come and go with the wind—to do them, or you, any justice.

Anyway, you're here to get married, then quickly run off to eat at Emeril's, see *Mystère*, and hit the blackjack tables.

GETTING DOWN THE "AISLE"

As you read through the book, you'll notice a format to the chapel and venue reviews. Each opens with boilerplate information—name, address, phone number, and Web site—and closes with a narrative review (a few places are so, well, yucky that the narratives are purposely terse). In between is a "snapshot" of the place, and the following is an explanation for each part of the image.

Kitsch Factor: One, two, three, four, or five little Las Vegas signs signify the relative "cheese" factor of the venue. They tell you in an instant if the place screams Las Vegas, whether that's because you can dress up like Guinèvere and Arthur or because someone went berserk with lace and a can of pink spray paint. High kitsch does not necessarily mean déclassé; if you choose a ceremony overlooking the fountains of Bellagio with the Eiffel Tower in the background, how much more cool *and* prototypically Las Vegas could that be? High kitsch also doesn't necessarily mean a reason to get married at a particular place.

Romance Quotient: Now it's a heart , and if three are lined up, it's a nice kiss; five and the flames are scorching. (One? You don't really need an explanation, do you?)

Fresh Test: One bar of soap tells you the place is two bars short of passing the freshly scrubbed test and four below perfectly prim and tidy. This also takes into account the fit-and-finish of the chapel: Are the carpets clean or worn? Is the paint peeling? Are the acoustical tiles stained? Is stuff scattered everywhere?

Comfy/Cozy Rating: This is an assessment of how well the whole package works. If the chapel is garish for the sake of being garish, if the employees are lovelorn and cranky, if people are flying about and weddings are stacked up back to back, if you're required to navigate rows of slots and the kid's arcade just to get to the door of the chapel, you won't feel very comfortable. And what signifies comfy and cozy more than a welcome mat ? There's your icon.

The *One* Way to Go: If the chapel offers a superlative, unique, or even wacky ceremony—or if there really isn't a service that is anything out of the ordinary, yet you still *need* to get hitched there because the place is just so cool or cozy—it's highlighted here.

In a Nutshell: This is the venue encapsulated in one paragraph that pretty much tells you what you'd need to know about the wedding facilities and services if you only had seconds to decide how and where to take the plunge.

Cost: Prices are presented in U.S. dollars and represent the range of fees (before tax and gratuity, if applicable) for wedding packages at the time this book went to print. Add-ons and up-grades are always available—from an extra boutonnière or a jazzy video to Caesar and Cleopatra as attendants—although given the many options, I haven't listed the prices. And be aware that many "complete" packages don't include the cost of a minister; a rabbi usually comes with an upcharge. Want a unity candle? It could be 50 bucks. Want to light it? Shell out a few more bills. The moral? Ask a lot of questions and take good notes.

Number of Weddings Performed Annually: The wedding in-dustry, as a whole, is tight-lipped. Some chapel proprietors aren't worried about over-inflating their numbers; some won't disclose any at all. Therefore, these figures represent best guesstimates for each chapel. Take them for what they're worth, which to me is a telltale sign of popularity, affordability, or good geography. And if the number is big and it portends trouble—such as rapid-fire nuptials—I'll tell you.

Hours: When the love masters are on duty. This is really only important to the drop-in-without-a-reservation crowd, an approach that precludes nuptials at some of the bigger fancier establish-ments.

Ceremonies: "Nonreligious" means a minister officiates, but doesn't use the G-word.

Languages: If ceremonies can be performed in languages other than English, those languages are listed here.

Bride/Groom Rooms: Everything from nothing at all to dress-ing areas with bathrooms that would put some homes to shame. The thing to remember here is that broom closets are often passed off as bridal rooms. In any case, most chapels with rooms, however trashy or lavish, ask that you arrive with hair and makeup done, although many allow you to change into your dress.

Commitment: Whether the place offers same-sex commitment ceremonies.

Location: Downtown, north Strip, edge of the valley, etc.

The review that follows the boilerplate information is an unbiased, no-holds-barred critique of the chapel (venue, garden, wedding site). If it's the kind of place where you could anticipate meeting a cockroach, the review spells that out—and that's exactly what happened at one chapel ... stay tuned. If the staff copped an attitude when I asked a ton of questions or if the chapel gives off a warm-fuzzy feel, you'll know. Because it's so difficult to plan a wedding from faraway—relying on Web depictions, brochures, or Cousin Louie's hazy recollection of a wedding he attended between bouts of blackjack and bourbon in '97—*Neon Nuptials* is your eyes and ears. (And please note the absence of advertising; this is a guidebook, not a glossy throwaway paid for by the chapels.)

I visited every venue, often with my wife. I snapped pics, took notes, caught a few weddings here and there, pored over flyers, brochures, and Web sites—in fact, it's buyer beware when it comes to how some chapels represent themselves—checked out the neighbors, and developed a rash caused by excessive exposure to Doric columns twined in faux ivy, mauve wall trim, forest-green carpet, and twinkle-light-bedecked trellises. I talked to breathy doe-eyed coordinator after doe-eyed breathy coordinator, was growled at a few times, and was frequently felled in anticipation of the unequaled bliss that doubtless would ensue if I were to marry at the Tiny Chapel of Exquisite Love ... and no place else. Yes, I stifled more than a few laughs. And I believe I captured it all in the pages that follow—the good, the bad, and the excessively cherubic.

Few places in the world can compete with Las Vegas when it comes to entertainment, nightlife, food, accommodations, and electricity. Toss in gambling and it's hardly a match. Add an altar and there are no other suitors.

But enough with the flirtation. Let's get on with the courtship.

COURTSHIP 1

BEST OF ...

Readers love best-of lists, writers love best-of lists, and so that none of us is disappointed, here are the *Neon Nuptial* best-of-Vegas award winners. These lists suggest some of the best and, yes, least-best choices in places and ways for a wedding in Las Vegas, from chapels that wear kitsch like a badge of honor to tying the knot in the great outdoors. As a wedding is logically followed by a honeymoon, I also offer up the five best choices, overall, for your glitzy getaway. And as "best" can't exist in a vacuum, I list five places that just wouldn't make the cut if my wife, Terri, and I were to do it all over again.

THE ONE SPOT

If you and your guy were just beamed in from a spaceship without having a clue about the diversity of the neon-nuptial experience, materializing at this place would give you the single best chance to figure out exactly how you wanted to proceed, and then not have to leave—except to get that license—to find it.

Caesars Palace. There's a gorgeous chapel, and pool, garden, or by-the-Strip outdoor venues. Not enough? Cleopatra, Caesar, Praetorian guards, and handmaidens dressed as vestal virgins are all available as attendants. Like Rome in its heyday, it's all there.

YOU WANT VEGAS? THIS IS VEGAS!

So the *only* way for the two of you to start your wedded life together is with high kitsch and a prototypically neon nuptial? This is your list.

1. Sirens' Cove at TI. The "Enchantment" wedding puts you on the deck of the sailing vessel, *Song,* moored in Sirens' Cove, with a pirate officiating. If that's not enough camp, you can add pirates for the effect or even have one descend from the crow's nest to present your rings. Guests view the show from the "dock" of TI's seaside village.

2. Drive-thru. Aesthetics don't matter much here, so you can go with any of the three chapels that offer the service: A Special Memory, Chapel of Love, and A Little White Wedding Chapel.

3. Sam's Town. Sam's Town's Mystic Falls Park is the great outdoors, only indoors: a towering atrium filled with the sights and sounds of a Western American mountainscape, put together in perfect theme-park-like fashion. Weddings are conducted on a second-floor balcony overlooking robotic critters, rushing waters, and trees and glades in this romantic and kitschy wonderland.

4. Elvis. One guy, Norm Jones, is both parson and Presley, the rest are performers, and all can put a hunka hunka burnin' love in your ceremony.

5. Gondola at the Venetian. Perhaps the highest-per-foot-traveled cost you'll ever incur for a boat ride, but a beautiful priceless memory and a heck of a tale to tell.

This listing initially included Viva Las Vegas Wedding Chapel. The place is Kitsch Central and in my experience a wacky and wonderful place to take the plunge. However, the chapel—see "The Business of Better Business," page 4, and further discussion below—has an unsatisfactory rating from the local Better Business Bureau.

WEDDING AL FRESCO

Stunning topography, little rain, and two full seasons of nearly perfect weather, coupled with two half seasons of weather that might be considered perfect in other parts of the country, combine to make Sin City a great spot for an outdoor wedding.

1. Lake Las Vegas. Lake Las Vegas is the 300-plus-acre centerpiece of a lifestyles-of-the-rich-and-famous resort and residential development located on the edge of Henderson, near Lake Mead. Two luxe hotels, Ritz-Carlton and Hyatt Regency, and the mixed-use MonteLago Village offer multiple outdoor venues overlooking gardens, the lake, golf courses, and the calico-hued mountains. A wedding here also gives you the chance to flick a hand toward Celine Dion's house, as if you dine there so often you're surprised *everyone* doesn't know where she lives.

2. Flamingo. The Flamingo Garden Chapel—actually, a chapel and several outdoor venues—is one of the most attractive, comfortable, and tasteful "palaces of pink," set within the hotel's famous tropical oasis of pools, palms, waterways, and exotic-bird habitats. This is a category driven more by feel than ratings, but I particularly like the ceremony where the bridal procession takes you behind a waterfall. As with any outdoor wedding, expect some intrusion; foot traffic, spectators around the periphery, and playtime noise in and around the nearby pools are unavoidable, but the scenery makes up for that and the staff keeps the curious at a discreet distance.

3. Bellagio. The Terrace of Dreams ceremony puts you on a private balcony overlooking the lake with the City of Light just beyond. The terrace is located along the Via Bellagio shopping arcade, above Picasso and Prime (two of Las Vegas' best restaurants).

4. Las Vegas Weddings at the Grove. It's a bit of a haul out from the Strip and Glitter Gulch, and the residential development that's swallowing most of the valley is starting to encroach on all sides. Once "inside," however, it's like having your own private park with a brook, meandering walkways, rolling lawns, and big, friendly trees.

5. Caesars Palace. Sin City's first fully themed resort, and its most enduring, has five outdoors venues, ranging from poolside to Strip-side.

THIS IS LAS VEGAS: STANDALONE CHAPELS

I've not done any scientific polling, but I think most couples who come to Vegas to say "I do" have a vision of one and only one form of wedding—a Las Vegas "chapel" wedding. You know, the places where celebrities with a spur-of-the-moment urge get married, the spots whose images appear as Sin City avatars, symbols emblematic of the "Las Vegas" depicted in movies and television shows. These are the chapels that stand the greatest chance of being dredged in fake flowers, the red part of the color spectrum, vivid murals, and altars made of columns both Ionic and Corinthian. Your wish is their command.

1. Victoria's Wedding Chapel. I know this venue didn't pop out of the pink-and-perky mold and it *would* look right at home inside one of the nice new hotel-casinos, but it is a standalone chapel ... and a standout.

2. Vegas Wedding Chapel. There really isn't much to say about this rather Vegas-atypical outfit, which in the chapel racket can speak volumes.

3. A Special Memory Wedding Chapel. It looks like a church on the outside, runs like an efficient factory on the inside, and takes care of the legal "I do" stuff for the Star Trek attraction at the Las Vegas Hilton.

4. Little Church of the West. If you want a wedding that oozes Vegas history, this little hunk of the Ponderosa pinched between the Strip and McCarran International is your ticket.

5. Graceland Wedding Chapel. If the name doesn't say it all, perhaps you're in the wrong town.

THE BUSINESS OF ...

The Better Business Bureau of Southern Nevada provides its members with standards for behavior and consumer relations. The association also serves as a facilitator for consumer complaints against businesses, and it rates nonmember businesses, too.

Listed below are the wedding chapels that, as of October 2004, received unsatisfactory ratings from the BBB:

Chapel of Dreams—two or more complaints
Cupid's Wedding Chapel
Elvis Chapel—two or more complaints
A Las Vegas Garden of Love—two or more complaints
Little Chapel of the Flowers
Mon Bel Ami—two or more complaints
Princess Wedding Chapel
    (the BBB lists it as La Dolce Vita Wedding Chapel)
Shalimar Wedding Chapel—two or more complaints
Viva Las Vegas Wedding Chapel—two or more complaints
Wee Kirk o' the Heather

Businesses receive unsatisfactory ratings when they don't respond to consumer complaints. Obviously, all businesses receive complaints and not all complaints are legitimate (we all know people who bitch just because they like to). So, having received a negative rating from

The same thing that tripped up Viva Las Vegas befell three choices in this category—bad scores from the Better Business Bureau. The Little Chapel of the Flowers, Mon Bel Ami Wedding Chapel, and Wee Kirk o' the Heather are commendable chapels and I still feel comfortable recommending all three—and Viva Las Vegas—based on their aesthetics, uniqueness of services, personnel, and/or a high level of consumer care evidenced toward me when I dropped by. However, now it is with a caveat. As you will note throughout this book, I significantly downgrade a number of chapels because they refused to respond to my inquiries, and being mute—and in a few cases downright rude—in the service industry isn't good business. It is only right that chapels that ignore consumer complaints filed with a leading business-consumer advocacy organization face some repercussions.

... BETTER BUSINESS

the BBB does not necessarily mean that the complaint is legitimate. But that, of course, gets me scratching my head and wondering: Then why not respond? Why not, indeed.

Here's how the process works: A bride complains to the BBB—she didn't get the right amount of pictures, the flowers were dead, the limo never showed up, whatever—and the complaint is forwarded to the chapel. The chapel responds, agreeing to redress the problem or rejecting the claim and spelling out why. The response is sent to the complainant. If the bride's not happy with the response, she can pursue the matter through the usual legal channels or she (and the chapel) can submit to arbitration. At that point, the matter is resolved as far as the BBB is concerned. If the chapel refuses arbitration—if the matter gets that far—or if it ignores the initial complaint, it receives a black mark.

Other than Princess, which is in the small Greek Isles hotel-casino just off the Strip, not a single chapel on this list is part of a major Las Vegas resort. None are members of the BBB, either (at least as of last October).

Better Business Bureau of Southern Nevada
2301 Palomino Lane
Las Vegas, NV 89107
www.vegasbbb.org
(Please note: The BBB doesn't return long-distance phone calls.)

JUST CAN'T SEEM TO LEAVE THE CASINO, EH?

Comparing *most* of the standalone chapels to *most* of the resort-based chapels is somewhat like comparing a pickup truck to a luxury sedan; both can get you to exactly the same place, but given the refinements and capabilities specific to each, the journeys can be quite dissimilar. Resort-based chapels tend to be less gaudy, more refined, newer, and more expensive. Neither experience is superior, just different.

1. MGM. Forget the emerald blaze with which the exterior of this largest-in-Vegas hotel sears the desert air, the two chapels inside are warm, inviting, and comfortably luxurious.

2. Bellagio. Bellagio is a double winner as the beautifully ornate chapels score here like the outdoor terrace mentioned earlier.

3. Luxor. The attention to appealing aesthetics that went into the layout and design of this venue speaks to the advantage of being more recently designed and constructed.

4. Texas Station. Surprisingly, Texas Station has one of the most beautiful "chapels" around and there isn't another like it in town. No pixies, fake ivy, or pastels-gone-riotous pastoral scenes painted on the walls, the look is tastefully Southwestern ranch, without a steer horn or horseshoe in sight. And my wife agrees.

5. Stratosphere. The chapels are on the 103rd floor of the Stratosphere Tower, so they could be wallpapered in burlap and carpeted in blue-green shag and still make the list. A few places tallied higher scores; this one's *all* about the view.

IT'S A CHURCH—WELL, ALMOST

Some Las Vegas chapels want you to think they're churches; it's a bit like casinos *earnestly* wishing you the best of luck. Discussed below are two chapels that come close. You walk in and that's it. The pews are pews, not dinette seats. The ceilings vault rather than stop at the height of a top hat. They're churches without the religious trappings.

1. The Little Church of the West. The look of the American West at the south end of Sin City.

2. Candlelight Wedding Chapel. Weddings churn through this place like $20 bills through slots, yet it's cute and cozy. **Note:** Shortly before this book was published, Candlelight closed its doors and started construction on a slightly larger look-alike facility downtown. Assuming the historic pattern is replicated, the chapel should warrant continued inclusion on this list. Until then, I suggest paying a visit to *A Special Memory Wedding Chapel*, which has a churchly countenance that could have fallen right out of a Hawthorne novel, albeit one dressed up with a little Sin City flavor.

HONEYMOON HABITATION ... ENJOY YOUR STAY

This was the hardest part of writing this book. Chapter 5, "Honeymoon in Vegas ... Good Bets in Beds," featuring the 10 best resorts (and 12 best hotels), was rather easy to compile, although it did require winnowing out some great resorts. But getting down to five was tough, because I had to leave two of my favorites, the JW Marriott and Mirage, off the list.

1. Bellagio. It excels in every way.

2. Ritz-Carlton Lake Las Vegas. The location and setting, design of the resort, and amenities and service make the Ritz-Carlton a winning Southwestern desert resort, not just a winning Las Vegas resort. Relative isolation and comparatively limited dining and entertainment options ultimately cost it the #1 ranking.

3. Caesars Palace. I would not be surprised if in a few years Caesars Palace tops this and other lists. Though the effect of the proposed acquisition of Caesars (and its sister hotel-casinos) by Harrah's can't be predicted, there is seemingly no let up in current management's desire to make this both the best and the best-themed experience in Las Vegas, as it was for years. New construction, continued overhauls of the "historic" parts of the property, culinary diversity, and great commitment to entertainment as witnessed by the signing of Elton John and Celine Dion all add up to a Caesars Palace renaissance. Keep an eye out.

4. Mandalay Bay et al. There's a built-in advantage on this amenity-rich parcel of land: three distinct hotels—Mandalay Bay proper, THEhotel at Mandalay Bay, and the Four Seasons.

5. Paris Las Vegas. Paris triumphed over more famous properties that have better accommodations, entertainment, or restaurants, because Paris does a very good job at everything it needs to do and this is a book about *amour*, after all. The kitschy theme, Champagne bar with live jazz, architecture, street performers, crêperie, cobbled streets, and Eiffel Tower replica all say "be mine, forever."

QUICK, LEGALLY BINDING, LOW-COST, BUT ...

There may be no *worst* place to get married in Las Vegas, because I honestly feel that getting married in and of itself is one of the best things you can do in life. But all chapels are not conceived, designed, constructed, decorated, and staffed—in short, created—equally.

Life is about choices, however, and I'd choose otherwise.

1. & 2. Monaco Wedding Chapel/Hitching Post Wedding Chapel (tie). Sister properties side by side in the same rundown complex next to an XXX-rated motel. Monaco offers a carnival-house-of-mirrors look and a Web site that takes the cake for the most liberal depiction of wishful thinking versus reality in the neon nuptial world. Hitching Post is tired, dirty, and chintzy just to be chintzy.

3. A Las Vegas Garden of Love. Bad carpets, bad décor, and employees in jeans, T-shirts, and strange stretchy fabrics don't really put a chapel's best foot forward.

4. Shalimar Wedding Chapel. Despite some shouldn't-make-this-list numbers in several rating categories, Shalimar's here nonetheless solely on the basis of rudeness.

5. Sweetheart's Wedding Chapel. This one definitely will be revisited in future editions of this book, because maybe by then the obviously well-fed cockroach standing vigil in the lobby will pack up and leave. (Without the roach, however, Sweetheart's Wedding Chapel wouldn't be on this list.)

PROPOSAL   2

VIVA VOWS VEGAS:
TYING THE KNOT, SIN CITY-STYLE

Las Vegas' wedding roster reads like a who's who of first-namers: Sammy, Bing, Demi, Frank, Elvis, Michael, Ann-Margret. Biggies. And then there are those celebrities who are no less great but require both, or all three, names—Joan Crawford, Mary Tyler Moore, Richard Gere, and of course Britney Spears, of oops-I didn't-mean-to-get-married fame. If you want to walk down the same aisle walked by Angelina Jolie, have at it, but don't walk in her path, 'cause she and Billy Bob didn't last too long. Better to emulate Paul Newman and Joanne Woodward, whose neon nuptial is still racing along after more than 45 years.

A LICENSE TO WED

Aside from a groom—or bride if there are any love-struck guys in the audience—the first thing you'll need for your all-star wedding is a license. You can get a license at the County Clerk's office of any Nevada county, which can be used anywhere in the state. Licenses must be used within one year of issuance, although once used, there's no expiration date, which is the point, after all. Weddings must be performed by a state-licensed minister or civil marriage commissioner. If you're just dying to have your minister from back home perform your ceremony, he can get a temporary minister's license from the county. However, wedding chapels exist to marry people and make money, so don't count on Reverend

Hitchman being welcomed in to perform the deed at most places. It's probably best to have him say a few words, then let the locals handle the legal part of the ceremony.

The Clark County Clerk's Marriage Bureau dispenses licenses downtown at 200 South 3rd Street, behind the Four Queens and across Casino Center from the Golden Nugget's valet parking garage and South Tower (walk around to the far side of the building for the entrance, which faces 3rd Street). The bureau's phone number is 702/455-4415.

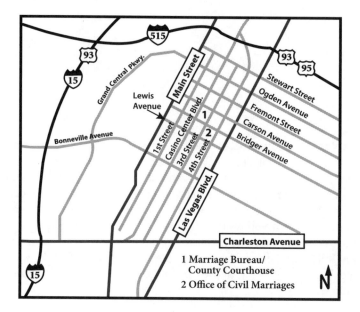

1 Marriage Bureau/
County Courthouse
2 Office of Civil Marriages

RUNAWAY BRIDE ... GROOM
AND WEDDING BUREAU

Sometime in 2005, the Marriage Bureau will relocate to its new digs in the swank Clark County Regional Justice Center at 200 Lewis Avenue. That's about two blocks south of the current location. If you're taking the plunge later in the year, call ahead so you don't go to the wrong building; I'll just assume that those arriving via chapel-provided limo won't need to give the driver directions.

Not too many rules are attached to securing a Nevada wedding license. There's no blood test and no waiting period. Pursuant to state law, applicants must be "a Male and a Female"; 18 years of age or older; single, divorced, or otherwise without a living spouse; and no more closely related than second cousins. (There are additional provisions for 16- and 17-year-old applicants.) You'll have to prove your identity by providing a driver's license or state-issued identification card, original or certified copy of your birth certificate, passport, military ID, or a resident alien card, and provide your Social Security Number (although the actual card is not required). Divorcées, widows/widowers, and those who have had marriages annulled—Britney Spears comes to mind—need to know when and where their former marriage(s) ended, although original documentation is not required. (If you were previously married and/or divorced in Clark County, this information is available online on the Clark County Clerk's Web site at **http://www.co.clark. nv.us/clerk/clerkhome.htm.**) And you'll need a witness. It can be a friend or family member along for the party, a chapel employee (inquire about this in advance), or even a total stranger who gets a charge out of weddings or a passerby who has a few minutes to burn—pretty much anyone but your spouse-to-be.

The Marriage Bureau is open midweek from 8 a.m. to midnight, Monday through Thursday. It opens at 8 a.m. on Friday and stays open through the stroke of midnight on Sunday night. It's also open around the clock on holidays. (The county issues licenses at its offices in Mesquite and Laughlin as well.)

A license costs $55—cash, traveler's check, or cashier's check for the exact amount—and if you want to get a jumpstart, an application with instructions can be downloaded on the Web and filled out in advance, but you still need to bring it in to the office because the application cannot be submitted electronically or by mail. Go to **www.accessclarkcounty.com/clerk/Marriage_License_Applications_online.htm.** Getting ahead of the crowd isn't a bad idea, as a lengthy line does form at times. The record wait was probably set on Valentine's Day 1998, reaching five hours at one point, and the line stretched from the county building to the Golden Nugget. Since then, the county's been on a bit of a public-information campaign to get couples to plan ahead. It's working, but multiple-hour waits can still occur. If you plan to wed on a holiday or weekend, budget ample time prior to your ceremony, or better yet, get your license a day or more in advance of your wedding date. And remember, if your wedding package includes limousine service to get your license, you could lose your ride if the wait's too long.

After you're married, the officiate has up to 10 days to record the marriage certificate with the county, and certified copies of the certificate are available the day after recording for $10 each. Assuming you received your license in Clark County—marriage certificates are recorded in the issuing Nevada county, not where the ceremony was held—a copy or copies can be ordered over the Internet using a major credit card at **www.accessclarkcounty.com/recorder/certs. htm**; in person at the Recorder's Office, 500 South Grand Central Parkway, second floor; or through the mail with a check or money order in U.S. dollars drawn on a U.S. bank made payable to: Clark County Recorder Copies, P.O. Box 551510, Las Vegas, Nevada 89155-1510. The Recorder's telephone number is 702/455-4336.

NOT FROM THESE HERE PARTS

Some 15% of weddings statewide and more than 20% in Clark County involve couples from other countries. Toss out Californians—who account for more than half the marriages—and folks from the four corners of the globe nearly equal the number of state residents who take a walk down a Nevada aisle.

License requirements for foreign nationals are identical, with the obvious exception that they don't need a Social Security Number, although whatever is used to establish identity and age must be in English, and if that's a birth certificate, it must also be notarized. After the ceremony, couples will need to take home with them—or request as outlined above—a certified copy of the marriage certificate (again, available from the County Recorder no later than 11 days after the ceremony), an Apostille, and in some instances a certified copy of the license application. An Apostille is further authentication of the marriage provided by the Nevada Secretary of State pursuant to international treaty. Please note that these are general guidelines and in all such matters, couples are advised to check with authorities back home regarding the documentation required for recognition of their neon nuptial.

The Marriage Bureau's Web site offers instructions and downloadable applications in English, German, French, Spanish, and Italian at **www.accessclarkcounty.com/clerk/Marriage_License_Applications_online.htm**. (Instructions are also available in Japanese.) For more information about Apostilles, consult the state at 800/922-0900, extension 5708, or online at **www.sos.**

state.nv.us/notary/apostille.htm. (The Recorder's Web site also contains helpful information at **www.accessclarkcounty.com/recorder/APOST.HTM**.)

ANOTHER ROUND AND A WEDDING BY ANY OTHER NAME

However they were married the first time around, couples are flocking to Las Vegas to say "I do" all over again in vow-renewal ceremonies. Although renewals aren't weddings and the state doesn't grant them any recognition in law, many couples think the sequel is as good as the original. And as Las Vegas wedding chapels love green almost as much as pink, any scheme hatched for people to get "married" again is fair game. Other than hauling along a copy of your marriage certificate—some chapels ask to see it—the only thing required is to show up with your lawful spouse and reaffirm the best decision you ever made in your life.

Less common but becoming more popular are commitment ceremonies for same-sex lovebirds who aren't afforded the chance to lawfully wed. These are a bit more dicey, as a large number of chapels do not offer such services, which seems both Puritanical and hypocritical given legal sex-for-sale just across the county line, strip clubs on every other corner, and Las Vegas' recent "What happens in Vegas stays in Vegas" marketing campaign. Nevertheless, it comes down to a business decision and many enlightened chapels are happy to oblige.

CEREMONY 101

Perhaps the simplest way to tie the knot in Las Vegas is to walk a half-block from the Marriage Bureau to the Office of Civil Marriages, plunk down $50—traveler's check *in the exact amount* or cash—and have your ceremony executed by a Commissioner of Civil Marriages; think of him or her as a modern-day justice of the peace. In, out, quick, easy, you're married. In a typical month, 600 to 700 couples choose this route, which is down from a few years ago due to reduced hours of operation and cut-rate wedding prices available at nearby chapels.

Civil marriages are performed from 8 a.m. to 10 p.m. each and every day of the year. The commissioner's office is located at 309 South 3rd Street. You will still need a witness (county personnel do not perform this function). Most couples without one simply ask another bride or groom to provide the obligatory eyeball and John Hancock, returning the favor should the original favor-givers need a witness of their own. Additional information can be found on the Internet at **www.accessclarkcounty.com/clerk/Civil_Marriage.htm** or by calling 702/455-4415.

If a justice of the peace ceremony has too much of an I-could've-done-that-back-home quality or if you're in Las Vegas for kitsch or something completely over the top (or even a touch of class), then you're in the market for a wedding chapel. And there's no shortage of nuptial palaces from which to choose—almost 60 between chapels and similar venues. Of course, there are hundreds and hundreds of churches, country clubs, private membership halls, restaurants, parks—you name it—in which to wed. There's even the seemingly endless expanse of the great outdoors—the desert, the mountains, Lake Mead, and that blue desert sky above. The latter are unique ways to wed and warrant some discussion, but because the vast majority of the Las Vegas wedding-bound opt for chapels and the like, these venues are the highlight of this book.

GOIN' TO THE CHAPEL

Most of the establishments discussed in this book are "chapels" in the sense that they're buildings or rooms designed to look like a church, mimicking the pop-fictional idealization of what a hall of matrimony should entail. Of course, we're not exactly talking consecrated ground here, since it's unlikely that a functioning church served as the model for the Hot Dice and Burning Bush Temple of Blessed Love. Just over half (54%) are freestanding and the rest

A CHURCH IN THE DESERT

If you're Catholic, yet still want a Sin City wedding, consider a ceremony at one of the two dozen or so churches in the Las Vegas Valley. You'll need to start by choosing a parish; each church and parish priest determines if Catholics from outside the Diocese of Las Vegas can be accommodated. Once you've made your selection, contact the parish at least seven months before your wedding date.

Your preparatory instruction and counseling will be conducted at your home parish. When completed, the necessary documentation will be transmitted from diocese to diocese, and then down to the parish in Las Vegas, allowing you to enjoy the Sacrament of Marriage and a neon nuptial.

But don't forget that marriage license.

For more information consult the Diocese of Las Vegas online at www.lasvegas-diocese.org.

are part of a hotel-casino. Some actually look nice; many don't. The Strip's resort-based chapels are generally newer and more expensive than the freestanding ones, but not always. Wherever they're located, they all have commonalities.

1. The "typical" chapel. There isn't one. Some venues look like churches, some are in strip shopping centers, some are contained within billion-dollar resorts, and some have beautiful park-like settings. Most are clean, many are gorgeous, and a handful, unfortunately, don't warrant consideration as a place for such a memorable event. The closest thing to typicality is an abundance of fake flowers, imitation stained-glass, pastoral murals with myriad iterations of the color pink, and cherubs, lots and lots of cherubs (especially at freestanding chapels). Sizes vary from just big enough for the couple, minister, and a witness to however much room is required; Caesars Palace has a spot out by one of its pools that appears capable of accommodating a Roman Legion or two. (Back-home-style weddings of 100, 200, or more are rare—excluding locals—because of the logistics of getting everyone to town and, more importantly, the preponderance of couples who are in Glitter Gulch for the express purpose of *avoiding* something big and traditional; 50 guests is huge for a typical Las Vegas wedding.) All but a few outdoor venues have places for guests to sit, whether it be pews, benches, chairs, or concrete garden seats.

2. It's Las Vegas. This means normal conventions are thrown out the window. You might be dressed to the nines, while the next couple's decked out in Goth. Some will choose to exchange vows on a thrill ride atop the Stratosphere Tower and others will go poolside at the luxo-supreme Ritz-Carlton Lake Las Vegas. One couple got married at a drive-thru on motorscooters, dressed as woodland creatures, with attendants and friends similarly clad. It doesn't matter. Every couple is doing it in a way that would make Sinatra proud.

3. What you get. Most ceremonies run 30 minutes, split about evenly between the nuptial stuff and photos: You get married, you get some pictures. Las Vegas wedding venues are as smorgasbord-inclined and bottom-line-oriented as any hotel-casino, so you'll have a range of floral, photo/video, and related options from which to choose, and in some cases, the ability for both a Webcast of the ceremony and a period of time within which people can visit the chapel's Web site to view the archived clip. You can opt for a limo to pick you up from and return you to your hotel or take you downtown to get your license. You can buy extra chapel time. You can be attended by Elvis, Austin Powers, or a Klingon. You can fly to the Grand Canyon. Packages run the gamut from no frills with borrowed plastic boutonnière and bouquet to five-figure or higher extravaganzas, although it's not hard to figure out that more couples opt for the former than the latter.

4. What you don't get. A hunk of latitude within the confines of your time and package. This simply means that Aunt Loretta will be allowed to snap a few pictures from the pew, but don't expect to bring in your own videographer. And in only rare cases can you provide your own flowers. As stated previously, even if you know someone licensed—or capable of being licensed—to perform weddings in Nevada, most chapels want you to use their ministers; it's both a matter of profitability and of timing because their ministers know the in-and-out routine. On the busiest days of the year, wed-

BEEN THERE, DONE THAT ...

More than three million couples have walked the aisle—cruised the drive-thru lane, stood poolside, boarded a pirate ship ... you name it—in Sin City. That's a load of vows and even more dreams. Here are some tips to help those dreams come true and stay alive, from those most in the know: real live neon nupitalists.

Gene and Lisa Bennett had the quintessentially "Vegas" wedding at the drive-thru lane at A Little White Wedding Chapel, a setting and environment far removed from their Puget Sound-area home. That was in October 1997. But Gene has 20 years "in the yoke" as he likes to quip, and has known both the abject heartache and the unbridled hope of matters of the heart. He lost his first wife only to find love again, so who better to tender advice?

1. Know your spouse-to-be well enough to know you want to spend the rest of your life with him or her. (Unlike Britney Spears.)

2. Know that life isn't going to be like the first month over the years. The passion waxes and wanes for a myriad of reasons, and sometimes for no reason at all.

3. Accept that you will both change over time: Your interests will change, your souls will change, your bodies will change.

4. Humor, humor, humor.

5. Never go to bed mad at each other.

6. Accept that some arguments will never be settled and drop them. Perfectly sane, reasonable people can hold differing opinions.

7. Say "I love you" at least once a day, and mean it.

dings stack up back to back. Brides almost always need to show up dressed, or at least with hair and makeup done. Finally, you won't get much privacy during the ceremony or afterward as a good number of the prime wedding and photo spots are along Las Vegas Boulevard or next to a resort's pool.

5. Your wedding is #1. Every chapel will say your wedding is the most important ever conducted. It *is* ... to you. You will, of course, marry the one you love, for a lot less than you would likely spend elsewhere, in a place that's vibrant, edgy, quirky, and full of great food, hotels, and gambling; plus, you'll have one heck of a tale to tell your grandkids. But weddings are a business, a *very big business*. Big enough that a year or two ago, local authorities tried, albeit half-heartedly, to prevent overzealous chapels from soliciting couples outside the county building using tactics more akin to

---

... YOU BETTER LISTEN UP

Chicagoans Eileen and Wes Shapiro's Sin City nuptial was in 1988. They "faked" a wedding with friends and family back home, then formally sealed the deal at the Chapel of Love, chosen because Wes refused to be married in a shopping center and that chapel was the first freestanding one they came across. Remaining close, to each other and Vegas, is at the center of their success in marriage. And if it's not already apparent, so is a great sense of humor.

1. Remember the significance within the minister's last words—"I now pronounce you Mr. and Mrs."—even if he forgets your names, as he did with us.

2. Keep your special memories sacred between you.

3. Live by the neon rule: "What happens in Vegas stays in Vegas."

4. Don't question your partner's motives.

5. Maintain three separate bank accounts; in other words, "her" gambling fund, "his" gambling fund, and "our" gambling fund.

6. Apologize sincerely when you make a mistake.

7. Don't stand in the way of your partner's strong convictions.

8. Be nonjudgmental and satisfied with modest successes.

9. Respect your spouse's needs.

10. Take time periodically to reflect on how you started and where you are going together. (When you return to Vegas, drive by "your" chapel and reflect on your special moment; then get out of that seedy part of town and head for the Bellagio fountains.)

strike-breaking than match-making. So when your chapel time is up, it's up ... and the next bride and groom roll right in.

6. Location, location, location. It's everything in real estate, though apparently something far less in Las Vegas nuptials. Casino-based chapels don't have to contend with the neighboring tattoo parlors, by-the-hour motels, strip joints, adult bookstores, gas stations, and other signs of urban life that surround so many freestanding chapels, although on the inside, some of the former look like many of the latter. As is to be expected, most truly ratty chapels are located in some rather ratty buildings, yet real gems pop up in the most unexpected places, so perhaps it's best not to judge a book by its cover, or the other volumes with which it shares the shelves. Be somewhat wary of Web and printed-advertising depictions and descriptions of chapels and their surroundings, as well. As with the novelty photo vendors who can put your face on the body of Jennifer Lopez, it's not too difficult to take a wedding venue out of its physical context.

Is this a totally jaded view of the experience? Far from it. If you're contemplating a Las Vegas wedding, you already anticipate a ceremony with a twist. You know it isn't your church back home, dad's country club, or the park by the river where you've played since childhood. It's Sin City and that means searing neon and hot dice, sevens lining up on the reels, and all-nighters. Yet somewhere in the middle of it all, you'll find yourself in a chapel that caught your eye, with your betrothed. Any chapel can provide the props; you create the magic. And it never hurts that Las Vegas has a bit of enchantment of its own.

CHAPEL ALTERNATIVES

Wedding options don't begin and end at the wedding commissioner's office or the 56 chapels highlighted in this book, so if you're interested in a ceremony that's more like being back home, yet still Las Vegas, you have tons of options. For one thing, Sin City has places of worship, real ones, covering every faith and denomination. There are reception halls, ballrooms, meeting rooms, and convention spaces in most hotels and resorts, restaurants, public parks, and more than five dozen golf courses with clubhouses; pretty much any place where a bride, groom, officiate, and witness can congregate can be a wedding venue.

If you're looking for something middle-ground, consider a facility, resort, or hotel that offers wedding services, even if there's

COMMON COURTESY—THE COMMITMENT CEREMONY

In the land where major corporations push skin, alcohol, gambling, and naughtiness, and legalized prostitution is only one county away, a surprisingly high number of chapels—in fact, the majority—will not perform commitment ceremonies for gay and lesbian couples. In a sense, it's the Old West, where individualism and freedom rule ... but only so far.

I didn't dock any chapels for not offering commitment ceremonies (which occurs most often at standalone chapels); some chapel owners have religious predispositions against gay and lesbian marriages and the legally moot variant known as a commitment ceremony, and it's not my place to challenge others' spiritual beliefs. However, a few chapels—Viva Las Vegas, for instance—received at least some boost in the ratings because of their acceptance and openness.

If you're looking for a place that will honor your relationship as a gay or lesbian couple or if you just like inclusiveness, here are your chapels.

Standalone Chapels
Chapel of Love
Cupid's Wedding Chapel
Hitching Post Wedding Chapel
Las Vegas Weddings at the Grove
Monaco Wedding Chapel
Mon Bel Ami Wedding Chapel
San Francisco Sally's Victorian Wedding Chapel
The Secret Garden at the Las Vegas Racquet Club
Viva Las Vegas Wedding Chapel
Wee Kirk o' the Heather

Casino-Based Chapels
Bellagio
Boardwalk
Caesars Palace
Excalibur—Canterbury Wedding Chapels
Four Seasons
Lake Las Vegas Resorts—Ritz-Carlton and Hyatt Regency
Las Vegas Hilton —Star Trek: The Experience
Luxor—The Chapel at Luxor
MGM Grand—Forever Grand Wedding Chapel
Monte Carlo—The Wedding Chapel at Monte Carlo
Paris Las Vegas—The Wedding Chapels at Paris Las Vegas
Rio—The Wedding Chapels at the Rio
Riviera—Riviera Royale Wedding Chapel
Stratosphere—Chapel in the Clouds
Texas Station—The Wedding Chapels at Texas Station
TI—The Wedding Chapels at Treasure Island

no chapel, per se, and perhaps not even a single defined location where ceremonies are performed. The two resorts at Lake Las Vegas, Hyatt Regency and Ritz-Carlton, can accommodate weddings at many gorgeous locations around the hotels and the 320-acre lake, or even on a yacht out on the lake. The Four Seasons doesn't have a chapel, but it does have indoor and outdoor wedding sites. Places like TI, Caesars, Paris, and the Flamingo have chapels *and* outdoor sites. Recommended as a place to stay but not reviewed as a wedding venue because it requires a wedding and a reception, Green Valley Ranch has wonderful gardens and a vineyard in which to wed, and both serve up faraway views of the Strip. If you're married, so to speak, to the idea of a sit-down dinner and a ceremony at a gorgeous resort, also consider the JW Marriott in Summerlin.

And the resorts don't have this market cornered. At least a dozen facilities are designed specifically to give you a place for a wedding and reception—Sunset Gardens and Rainbow Gardens being two of the most popular. I *really* like Emerald Gardens, a courtyard-and-gazebo setting like few in town: Raised planting beds, palms, a trickling stream, and twinkle-light-adorned oaks set this place apart. The immediate backdrop is a portion of Badlands Golf Club and the arroyo within which it sits, with Red Rock Canyon and the Spring Mountains in the distance. Unbelievable dressing facilities too. Emerald Gardens does too few standalone weddings, however, to classify it as other than a reception-and-wedding site.

If there's a hotel you like and it's not reviewed as a wedding site, don't fret. Almost every hotel in Las Vegas can host a wedding, either somewhere on the grounds or, more likely, within a convention space. Summerlin's Suncoast comes to mind. Although it has an attractive gazebo setting overlooking a golf course and the resort's pool, most of the 50 or so couples who wed there each year choose to do so indoors. Nevertheless, that's not really the neon nuptial for which most couples are looking. So, rather than fill up page after page with droll descriptions of look-alike meeting spaces, I've purposely limited discussion to what I define as properties with a significant commitment to weddings, rather than catering and sales folks with a minister on the side.

You'll also note the word "garden" in the name of a handful of wedding venues—not just reception sites—and in *some* instances the connotation is warranted. As with the "chapels," the caveats outlined above hold true for these other types of wedding venues.

On the other hand, if you're traveling halfway across the continent or the globe to get married in the middle of a desert sporting replicas of a Caribbean seaport and the canals of Venice, and having your ceremony in a turreted castle with 4,000 rooms or with "Elvis" cooing just isn't wild or wacky enough, don't despair. Las Vegas will come through for you. There are as many unique ways to craft a neon nuptial as there are brains conjuring up such schemes.

Helicopters and horseback are two of the most popular ways to push the already-stretched Las Vegas wedding envelope. I once interviewed a couple who took their vows and were then launched skyward on the Stratosphere's Big Shot ride. You can take the plunge while jetskiing on the waters of Lake Mead. You can marry your nuptials and a love for speed with a ceremony and some fast laps around the Las Vegas Motor Speedway.

The only limitation, literally, is whether your soon-to-be spouse, minister, and witness are willing to go along with whatever it is you choose to do. And if that's exchanging vows on the roller coaster at New York-New York, so be it. Or if you want to experience a wild rush and return to *terra firma* for the formalities, no one's going to say you weren't actually married while in mid-fall bungee jumping in front of Circus Circus.

WHERE IS IT?

For 99% of all visitors, Las Vegas is "Las Vegas," that mass of glittery urbanity sprawling across Southern Nevada. But this mountain-ringed valley harboring all the frolic and fun actually includes three cities—Las Vegas, Henderson, and North Las Vegas—and the region's most famous area, the Strip, isn't part of any. The area from the Sahara southward to Mandalay Bay (and beyond) falls under the jurisdiction of Clark County, although you need not be concerned with how the political lines are drawn in the desert sand. In other words, it's perfectly acceptable to stand at the corner of Tropicana Avenue and the Strip and scream to everyone and no one, "I love Las Vegas!" because even if they lack the same level of unbridled adoration, pretty much everyone thinks of it all as Las Vegas too.

Yet for ease of orientation, I've broken the larger valley into eight regions and in the review of each chapel, there's a place that denotes in which region you'll find that particular love shack. The eight designations are:

Downtown: Glitter Gulch, Fremont Street, old Las Vegas (and many would argue the real Las Vegas). This is the historic heart of the City of Las Vegas, home to the highest concentration of chapels in the valley and perhaps anywhere in the world. "Downtown" includes all chapels north of the Stratosphere, even if they're a few miles south of downtown.

The Strip—North, Center, and South: Typically divided north, center, and south, the Strip is where you'll find the biggest hotel-casinos, a large percentage of which have chapels.

North Strip largely extends from Sahara Avenue (moving southward) to the new Wynn Las Vegas on the site of the late great Desert Inn. And although it's just north of Sahara, and hence not technically on the Strip, the Stratosphere is grouped with the north Strip properties. This is where you'll find many of the town's *grande dames*—the Sahara, Riviera, and Stardust, for example—and a few standalone chapels.

Center Strip gets you from TI at Spring Mountain Road to the Caesars/Bally's/Bellagio cluster at Flamingo Road.

South Strip takes you southerly from there, encompassing Paris and Aladdin on through to Mandalay Bay and beyond; there's a lone chapel at the far, far end.

Henderson and Lake Las Vegas: Henderson sits on the south/southeast side of the valley. This city offers some of the best golf in the area and several popular "locals" casinos—neighborhood casinos geared toward local residents drawn by ease of access, more favorable gambling odds, good slot-club rewards, extensive and often inexpensive food offerings, movie theaters, and even bowling alleys or an ice rink. There are no freestanding chapels in Henderson, though Green Valley Ranch has some wonderful outdoor locations throughout the property that are suitable for ceremonies (however, as mentioned before, a reception is required). Lake Las Vegas is a high-end residential and resort development that sits about 17 miles southeast of the Strip. It has two beautiful hotels, the Ritz-Carlton and Hyatt Regency, both of which sport classy outdoor wedding venues.

West Las Vegas: A good portion of Las Vegas' growth is occurring to the west, where the valley meets the Spring Mountains. You'll find a top-notch resort out there, the JW Marriott Las Vegas, and to the north, one of the *Neon Nuptials'* top spots for an outdoor wedding, Las Vegas Weddings at the Grove. Farther past the west side of town, although officially beyond "town," you'll find a number of alternative wedding options, from horseback riding at Bonnie Springs to an outdoor ceremony at Red Rock Canyon.

East Las Vegas/Boulder Highway: Largely developed years

ago, this side of the valley lacks much of the homogenized look and newness of the western part of the valley. Notable sites are Sunset Gardens, a reception facility that does not perform standalone weddings, and Sam's Town, home to a Top-5 venue.

Rancho Strip: A busy commercial corridor (Rancho Drive) that extends through the northwest part of the valley. Of the several good-sized hotel-casinos out this way, only Texas Station has a dedicated wedding facility (it's also one of the most attractive to be found, and one of the handful of noteworthy nuptial spots).

TIMING IS EVERYTHING

Given that some chapels are open round the clock, is there an off time to tie the knot in Las Vegas? No. November and December are the slowest months. But slow in Las Vegas still equates to 7,000 to 8,000 couples getting married each month. New Year's provides a spike, as does Valentine's Day, the most popular one of the year (two couples short of *5,000* got hitched on February 14, 2004). And by the time spring is in full bloom, so too are brides and grooms. Perhaps surprisingly, the numbers climb into summer, eclipsing 11,000 weddings per month with July usually being the most popular. (What about June brides? My best guess is that more people get vacation time in July.) It doesn't cool down again until after Halloween.

If you like crowds, book a weekend. If you like huge crowds, choose a long holiday weekend. Another hot choice is a same-numbered date, as in May 5, 2005, or August 8, 2008. These will remain popular into 2012, after which they'll disappear for a very long time ... try New Year's Day 3001. Weekend and holiday ceremonies often command slightly higher prices. However, unlike Las Vegas room prices and airfare, wedding costs neither nosedive nor skyrocket in reaction to seasonal variations in the travel market. If you want to save some cash, Las Vegas room prices are at some of their lowest levels in December, between the beginning-of-the-month National Finals Rodeo and Christmas Eve. Fall is reasonable too. Summer shows some pricing weakness, but don't expect to find rooms at Bellagio for $99 per night; summertime hotel occupancy can run in excess of 90%.

Weather might be something to consider, though given summer's popularity, it doesn't seem to deter many couples. Southern Nevada effectively has three seasons: lousy, good, and great. Spring and fall are great—warm days, refreshing evenings, even less chance of rain in a place that gets next to none. Good and lousy are inter-changeable, and which is which is largely a matter of perspective and experience. If you're from the upper Midwest, Las Vegas' high-of-50-degree winter days might seem tropical, so winter will look quite good to you, while someone from Phoenix might prefer the relative cool of Las Vegas' low-three-digit summers.

	High (°F)	Low (°F)	Record High (°F)	Record Low (°F)	Precipitation (in inches)
January	57.1	36.8	77	8	0.59
February	63.0	41.4	87	16	0.69
March	69.5	47.0	92	19	0.59
April	78.1	53.9	99	31	0.15
May	87.8	62.9	109	38	0.24
June	98.9	72.3	116	48	0.08
July	104.1	78.2	117	56	0.44
August	101.8	76.7	116	54	0.45
September	93.8	68.8	113	43	0.31
October	80.8	56.5	103	26	0.24
November	66.0	44.0	87	15	0.31
December	57.3	36.6	78	11	0.40

Data provided by the National Weather Service. Monthly averages and precipita-tion are over the 30-year period ending in 2000.

The *how* of a neon nuptial is about as quick and easy as it gets: two people in love, legal age, unmarried, sober, not too closely related, with some form of ID and $55 ... voilà, marriage license. What makes it interesting is *where*. From a tropical lagoon to the bridge of the *Starship Enterprise*, from the Big Apple to Paris, from the waters of Lake Mead to the alpine cool of Mt. Charleston, when it comes to a Las Vegas wedding, the only limit is your imagina-tion. For every bride with a dream, Sin City has a reality. Let's go look for it.

I DO 3

TACKY, WACKY, OR FIT FOR JACKIE: STANDALONE CHAPELS AND VENUES

These are the neon nuptials of legend, vows exchanged in wannabe churches, beneath trellises bound in fake ivy and orchids and roses and tulips and daisies, with an Elvis impersonator marching you down the aisle and your post-vow getaway in a pink Caddy convertible. This is the world of the Las Vegas wedding chapel.

Reviewed in this chapter are 30 standalone chapels and venues, so designated because they aren't within a hotel-casino. Most of them are arrayed along Las Vegas Boulevard, between Stratosphere and Fremont Street or scattered about downtown. Included are some of Sin City's oldest chapels, some of its most quaint, a smattering of real disasters, and a few surprising gems. Taken together they serve up more representations of angels than the Vatican and enough pink to dye every ball of cotton candy from Seattle to Key West, making it easy to forget that Nevada is dubbed the Silver State.

WHAT WEDDING INDUSTRY?

When I started researching this book, I went looking for what seemed to me the logical starting place: the Association of Las Vegas Wedding Chapels, or some such trade organization.

Boy, was I off base.

Although there's an extremely large and active network of chapel operators and related service providers in Las Vegas, considering it as a unified industry is a stretch at best. This is the domain of hard-driving individualists, so after all my research, it's no wonder that I still haven't found anything approaching a functioning, unified, let's-all-pull-together, wedding-trade association.

While the majority of operators are good-hearted and honest people, some are eerily paranoid and secretive, and I've had more than one badmouth a competitor in a schoolyard-reminiscent way. And do you recall the chapels that were implicated a few years back in an aggressive and sometimes even violent campaign of "couple-mining"? No? Well, representatives from competing chapels would hang outside the county building trying to dissuade brides and grooms from going to Chapel A because Chapel Z (their own) was far superior/duly licensed/not run by a Satanic cult/you fill in the blank.

Suffice it to say, there's not a lot of love within the love industry.

But I will give the "industry" credit for apparently seeing eye-to-eye on one thing: overestimating the number of plunges taking place. In a bit of sleight-of-hand worthy of Penn & Teller, the venues listed in this book claim to have performed more weddings than occur annually, based on public records, in all of Clark County—and there are a lot of non-chapel locations, independent ministers, churches, and the like that are busy marrying a whole lot of folks, too, yet I've not even accounted for them in this book.

Oh well. The only association that counts is yours and the only number that truly matters is two.

ALWAYS AND FOREVER WEDDING CHAPEL
3003 Rigel Avenue
800/259-2978; 702/318-5683
www.alwaysandforeverweddings.com

Kitsch Factor: 3	
Romance Quotient: 3	
Fresh Test: 4	
Comfy/Cozy Test: 3	

The chapel's nice and the people are quite friendly, but I'm pretty sure you drive by a taxidermist on the way there.

The *One* Way to Go: The chapel's cute, but you might want to try one of the off-site venues.

In a Nutshell: New clean chapel in an office/commercial center. The full name is Always and Forever Wedding Chapel & Destination Weddings: The latter designation indicates that they can take you to places like Lake Las Vegas, Red Rock Canyon, Valley of Fire, etc., or places the minister can find you, like your hotel. (This service isn't unique to Always and Forever, but it is an integral part of its operation and worth pointing out.)

Costs: $75 to $798 for chapel services; prices vary for off-site weddings.

Yearly Weddings: 1,500 (in the chapel).

Hours: 8 a.m. to midnight daily.

Ceremonies: Non-religious and non-denominational Christian; rabbi available.

Languages: Spanish

Bride's Room: Yes, dressing room only (restroom down the hall).

Groom's Room: No (Actually, the men's room is rather large. He can change there if coming in late off the links.)

Commitment: No

Location: West Las Vegas.

Always and Forever is located in an office/commercial complex a couple miles north of the Rio on the west side of I-15. Scandia Family Fun Center is just around the corner and the area to the west is given over to service-commercial and light-industrial uses—auto-body repair, sheet-metal fabrication, RV and boat storage, etc.

The chapel opened in 2002 and the newness shows in a tidy crisp look. There's an assembly area outside the chapel's twin doors, which are within a partial wall framed into the building shell. Silk trees, garden benches, and a small fountain brighten the foyer and ivy tumbles down from the top of the wall. The chapel is carpeted in green, with pink faux finish on the walls and columns, and the altar is a raised platform flanked by a half-circle of columns twined with draping fabric, silk greenery, and flowers. A pastel mural of a high mountain valley backs the altar. Seats for 60 are of the high-back white-composite style that I seem to remember seeing at a lot of Indian restaurants, upholstered in a floral pattern.

All in all it's a modern twist on the tried-and-true chapel look with the advantage of youth (recent construction) and friendly people.

CAVEAT EMPTOR

While surfing the Internet for the multitude of Vegas wedding resources (so to speak), I stumbled across a link to "The Complete Guide to Las Vegas Weddings." As anxious as a guy can get when he's not in the presence of his first heartthrob, I plunked down $8.95 to discover who was trying to seduce my dearly beloved.

It certainly wasn't Brad Pitt.

"'The secret to a perfect Las Vegas Wedding ...'" turned out to be five pages of online content that had boilerplate, and not altogether accurate, info about how to get married in Sin City and links to wedding brokers and a few chapel-specific Web sites. No analysis, no critical reviews, every link in essence an advertisement, and miles and miles short of being an exhaustive survey of what's available; more information can be gleaned from free sites—the Convention Authority and Clark County, for instance. Even the opening picture depicted a gazebo venue situated such that it is a geographic impossibility.

To be fair, the provider immediately refunded my payment when requested. But looking back, I don't know that it was a fair test of what Joan Q. Public would have experienced, as my e-mail signature line included the title of this book and information about its publisher; it was obvious I wasn't just an everyday love-struck consumer.

The moral of this experience is, as it is with any form of commerce: Beware what riches are offered in exchange for your credit card number.

CANDLELIGHT WEDDING CHAPEL
2855 Las Vegas Boulevard South
800/962-1818; 702/735-4179
www.candlelightchapel.com

Kitsch Factor: 4	*(Las Vegas) (Las Vegas) (Las Vegas) (Las Vegas)*
Romance Quotient: 3.5	♥ ♥ ♥ ♥
Fresh Test: 3.5	
Comfy/Cozy Test: 2.5	WELCOME WELCOME WEL
The *One* **Way to Go:** Roll the dice; it's all rather straightforward.	
In a Nutshell: About as close as you can get to a "church" look in Sin City.	
Costs: $189 to $499.	
Yearly Weddings: 9,000 ("One every fifteen minutes, hon," according to a chapel employee whose math is a little off, although her sense of the place's popularity isn't.)	
Hours: 8 a.m. to midnight each and every day.	
Ceremonies: Non-religious, non-denominational Christian, Jewish.	
Languages: French	
Bride's Room: No	
Groom's Room: No	
Commitment: No	
Location: Downtown	

Okay, this is a matrimonial factory—a cute, quaint, perhaps even charming matrimonial factory—but a matrimonial factory nonetheless. Putting it another way, if you want the heart-and-soul of a true neon nuptial, sign up.

It seems like eons that Candlelight Wedding Chapel sat on the north Strip, all pumped up and proud like a proper little church in a neighborhood dominated by the architectural grace of places like the Riviera and Circus Circus. The chapel is white, with a cross-gabled roof and steeple. Inside, you'll find a high-pitched ceiling beamed and clad in wood, plantation shutters on small arched windows, pews seating 50, and an appropriate touch of "greenery" and "flowers." Outside are several trees, a hedge, lawn, Las Vegas Boulevard South, and in all likelihood, another wedding waiting to roll. The pace of weddings here obviously doesn't put anyone off, otherwise there wouldn't be any pace to the weddings. Celebrities too have been caught up in the allure, including Whoopi Goldberg, Ray Liotta—fitting since he plays a good Wiseguy and this is Vegas—Michael Caine, Bette Midler, and for Motor City rock fans, Bob Seger, presumably without the Silver Bullet Band.

I'm pretty confident that some of the photos in the brochure and on the Web site have been doctored—was the Riviera ever white and why does it and other structures seemingly disappear in some shots, replaced by a perfect blue sky? But that's moot now, as the chapel recently closed and a brand-spanking-new version is set to open up downtown on the site of the even-more-historic and soon-to-be-razed (at press time) Wee Kirk o' the Heather. Though updated and slightly expanded, the chapel-to-be should look and operate like it has for years.

A CHAPEL BY THE COURTHOUSE
201 East Bridger Avenue
800/545-8111; 702/384-9099
www.achapelbythecourthouse.com

Kitsch Factor: 3	
Romance Quotient: 1	
Fresh Test: 1	
Comfy/Cozy Test: 1.5	

The *One* Way to Go: If it's gotta be here, take the $40 quickie and get a headstart—financially and time-wise—on your new life together.
In a Nutshell: Tiny dreary chapel right smack dab across from the building where you get your marriage license.
Costs: $40 to $219.
Yearly Weddings: 4,000
Hours: 8 a.m. to midnight daily.
Ceremonies: Non-religious, non-denominational Christian and Jewish.
Languages: Spanish, German, French, and Japanese (translators in some instances).
Bride's Room: No
Groom's Room: No
Commitment: No
Location: Downtown

A Chapel by the Courthouse. It's a chapel. It's by the courthouse. You can get married for $40. What? You need more? Okay, the interior is depressing with red velvety seats and dark mauve carpeting and the building needs repainting.

CHAPEL OF LOVE
1431 Las Vegas Boulevard South
800/922-5683; 702/387-0155
www.vegaschapeloflove.com

Kitsch Factor: 4	⬥ ⬥ ⬥ ⬥
Romance Quotient: 2.5	♥ ♥ ◗
Fresh Test: 2.5	🍞 🍞 🍞
Comfy/Cozy Test: 3	WELCOME WELCOME WELCOME
The *One* Way to Go: Renaissance	
In a Nutshell: Wonderfully gaudy little 15th- and 16th-century Gothic room with "thrones" for the king and queen and seating for up to a dozen, I'd guess; two "standard" Las Vegas chapels seating 30 and 60; gazebo; drive-thru "chapel"; fantasy costumes ranging from Tarzan and Jane to ancient Egyptian.	
Costs: $49 to $1,000, plus something listed on the Web site as "The Ultimate," a package so extraordinary that the promotional material states that I "will not believe it," and since I apparently will not believe it, I've not bothered to inquire.	
Yearly Weddings: 6,500 to 7,000.	
Hours: 10 a.m. to 8 p.m. daily.	
Ceremonies: Non-religious and non-denominational Christian; rabbi available.	
Languages: Spanish	
Bride's Room: Yes, dressing allowed, separate restroom.	
Groom's Room: The same setup.	
Commitment: Yes	
Location: Downtown	

"World Famous"—says so right outside, as if couples young and old, from Paris to Pyongyang, have one and only one thought on their minds: "We're going to Vegas this instant so we can get married at the Chapel of Love." That *has* to be the case.

Chapel of Love offers five places to tie the knot, the best of which, from a kitsch point of view, is the Renaissance Fantasy Chapel, a dark little chamber decked out in the regal reds, blues, and purples of the age of chivalry. Dress up like Henry VIII and whichever of his wives kept her head, plop down in the thrones, and be wed. You might be able to squeeze 10 or 12 members of your court into your royal chamber.

The 30-person Garden Chapel has green carpeting to represent grass, ornate brass-colored garden benches, a fountain in the corner, Edenic murals on the walls, and a stained-glass window with doves, a heart, flowers, and a rainbow (the place drips with so much artificial sentiment that I almost expect a pack of Care Bears to jump out and dispense hugs). Lover's Pathway seats 60 in a more demure atmosphere of abundant floral arrangements with a rose-inset window.

The automotive set can pick from a drive-thru window or lattice-and-lights gazebo set on synthetic turf that resonates with the sounds of cars heading back and forth between the Strip and downtown. And while out there, you can take in the gentlemen's club just down the road, the psychic reader next door, and the Del Mar Hotel to the north, proudly and prominently advertising XXX-rated movies *en suite*.

I'm not being hypercritical here, but instead making a point: Jarring land-use patterns are as common to Las Vegas as dice and booze, and many chapels have less than stellar neighbors. And while Chapel of Love's ornamentation goes over the top and a pass with a dust mop wouldn't hurt, the setting at this chapel, like so many others, is *exactly* the type that beckons much of the neon and nuptial crowd.

CHAPEL OF THE BELLS
2233 Las Vegas Boulevard South
800/233-2391; 702/735-6803
www.chapelofthebellslasvegas.com

Kitsch Factor: 2	
Romance Quotient: 2	
Fresh Test: 4	
Comfy/Cozy Test: 2.5	
The *One* **Way to Go:** Like the name of the video poker game, pick 'em.	
In a Nutshell: Well-kept pretty chapel in a funky building with really ugly neighbors, but that's not unusual for Las Vegas.	
Costs: $115 to $375.	
Yearly Weddings: 2,800	
Hours: 9 a.m. to 10 p.m. Sunday through Thursday; till 1 a.m. Friday and Saturday.	
Ceremonies: Non-religious and non-denominational Christian.	
Languages: Spanish	
Bride's Room: Large restroom for changing only, if necessary.	
Groom's Room: If he needs to and you aren't in there, he can use the restroom too.	
Commitment: No	
Location: Downtown	

Another "world-famous" Sin City wedding chapel, though this one's been around long enough—since 1957—that the designation just might apply. The chapel is simple with high-backed white chairs, a piano, ivory drapes trimmed in gold, and a white altar and arbor laced in silk vines and flowers; and like the foyer/assembly area, it's all clean and tidy. The inviting look and feel help to downplay the adjoining, and tacky, Fun City Motel (and the nearby pawnshop).

INSIDER KNOWLEDGE:
A CHAPEL MANAGER'S TOP TEN TIPS

This book was written to help you pick the best wedding venue for you; I've reviewed pretty much every place to take the plunge, saving you the legwork. But what do you need to watch for after you've decided on a chapel? What are some surefire tips to help you have a smooth and carefree wedding day? Well, here they are from someone who's guided thousands and thousands of couples through the process and on into happy lives together. It's the Neon Nuptials' *Top 10 get-me-to-the-church-on-time-and-then-some tips from* **Kris LaBuda**, *manager of the Flamingo Las Vegas Garden Chapel:*

1. Relax. *Know that unexpected things might happen. You've done all the planning you can, so once you're at the chapel, it's time to sit back and enjoy.*

2. Make your own decisions. *Don't let your friends and family influence your choices, because you'll only be truly happy if things are the way you want them (though your way may mean giving some concessions to others now and then).*

3. Remember your manners. *I see so many brides looking so elegant, yet acting so badly by yelling at their mothers, arriving drunk, tugging at their bodices, and using bad language. To me, the whole event is maximized when you act as good as you look.*

4. Get your dress properly fitted *and don't lose or gain weight after your final fitting; otherwise, your dress, well, won't fit. And make sure your undergarments are the correct size. If your bra is too small, it will cause bulges under your arms that aren't attractive in pictures.*

5. Make sure your shoes are comfortable ... *and bring them to your final fitting.*

6. Be ready and arrive at least 20 minutes before the scheduled wedding. *That way you can cool off a little before walking down the aisle.*

7. Arrive sober—*and it's a good idea for him to have his bachelor party several days before the wedding.*

8. For the groom and groomsmen, look as good as your ladies. *Spend time looking for the right outfit.*

9. Make sure your contract *clearly states the services you'll be getting.*

10. Check in with your venue *before the wedding day.*

Whatever good vibes were engendered by the interior aesthetic were somewhat offset by a staff that was very casually dressed and more interested in our departure when it became apparent we were "surfing" on our visit and not "plunging." However, follow-up calls were handled by busy attendants who nonetheless worked very hard to answer my questions.

CHAPEL OF DREAMS
316 Bridger Avenue
702/471-7729
www.dreamchapel.com

Kitsch Factor: 2	
Romance Quotient: 1	
Fresh Test: 3	
Comfy/Cozy Test: 2	
The *One* **Way to Go:** There's not much differentiation here.	
In a Nutshell: Storefront-style chapel with several low-frills "chapels" within the interior space; bills itself as a ministry providing no-cost services to the poor.	
Costs: $49 to $179; brochure indicates that the chapel will beat any other chapel's "lowest actual price" by 50%.	
Yearly Weddings: 2,000	
Hours: 8 a.m. to midnight daily and by appointment.	
Ceremonies: Non-denominational Christian.	
Languages: Tagalog and Spanish; Thai, Chinese, and German pending.	
Bride's Room: One of the smaller "chapels" can be used for changing when not in use; the restroom is just down the hall.	

Groom's Room: No; okay, technically, what's good for the bride is good for the groom.
Commitment: No
Location: Downtown

This nondescript storefront chapel is located on Bridger Avenue in downtown Las Vegas. The chapel's immediate neighbors in its two-story office-commercial building are a place that makes cash loans, a sandwich shop, and a document-service company; Bank of America is across the street.

The interior space has been divided into several wedding areas with various mural and floral embellishments. While not the most elaborate or imaginative interior scheme ever conceived, the place is clean. Kudos appear to be in order as the chapel claims to run an outreach ministry offering no-cost weddings to the indigent.

CUPID'S WEDDING CHAPEL
827 Las Vegas Boulevard South
800/543-2933; 702/598-4444
www.cupidswedding.com

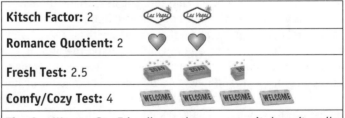

Kitsch Factor: 2	
Romance Quotient: 2	
Fresh Test: 2.5	
Comfy/Cozy Test: 4	
The *One* Way to Go: Friendly employees mean it doesn't really matter.	
In a Nutshell: It's called Cupid's. Doesn't that say it all? Impersonator, theme, and off-site weddings; reception hall; chapel seats about 50.	

Costs: $179 to $1,299.
Yearly Weddings: 4,000
Hours: 10 a.m. to 1 a.m. Tuesday and Wednesday; variable hours Sunday, Monday, and Thursday; around the clock Friday and Saturday.
Ceremonies: Non-religious, non-denominational Christian, Jewish.
Languages: Spanish
Bride's Room: Essentially a changing booth like the ones in department stores.
Groom's Room: Although guys usually show up dressed, your groom can use your booth if necessary.
Commitment: Yes
Location: Downtown

You just knew someone had to grab the most obvious name for a wedding chapel and this is the place that did.

Cupid's is a 50-or-so seat chapel located a handful of blocks from the heart of Glitter Gulch. The facility itself looks rather utilitarian, with a long reach of banquet space extending back from the chapel and an outside that could use a touch of paint, some roof work, and new blacktop for the parking lot. But hey, that's the *outside*, and unless you choose the gazebo, your wedding will be *inside*. The chapel is relatively tame—one wall is covered with mirrors providing the illusion of more space and a window behind the altar is inset with a dove wrapping ribbon around a heart of flowers; the carpeting is deep green, fresh, and new; and the just-right amount of floral arrangements are nicely color complementary—or as my wife commented on the way out, "Phew, it's not overly pink."

The people staffing the utilitarian office just beyond the chapel were amongst the nicest and most accommodating encountered during my great nuptial search. Phones were ringing, a couple arrived for their wedding, several window shoppers were seeking a first-hand look and information, and no one panicked, copped an attitude, or even came close to the crankiness that pervades many Sin City love chapels.

I like the sign outside: a big heart with an arrow through it that hints at the caring atmosphere inside.

ELVIS CHAPEL
727-C South 9th Street
800/452-6081; 702/383-5909
www.elvischapel.com

Kitsch Factor: 2 Without "Elvis"	
Romance Quotient: 2	
Fresh Test: 3	
Comfy/Cozy Test: 3.5	
The *One* Way to Go: With a name like this, what else?	
In a Nutshell: A chapel with a yin-yang home-within-an-office-building look; good people run the place.	
Costs: $179 to $749.	
Yearly Weddings: 1,500	
Hours: 9 a.m. to midnight daily, or as needed.	
Ceremonies: Non-religious, non-denominational Christian, Jewish.	
Languages: English only	
Bride's Room: Yes, with restroom; changing allowed.	
Groom's Room: Ditto	
Commitment: No	
Location: Downtown	

The look here truly is distinct—a flesh-pink stucco office building with green awnings, white wrought-iron fencing, and a desert-landscape palette of saguaro cactus and mesquite trees. Inside, it feels quite a bit like a home, your elderly aunt's perhaps, with a sense of formality coming from an entry filled with nuptial photos, dark wood furniture, and a settee. The chapel down the hall features large, comfortable, peach-colored side chairs, steel-blue carpeting, and what amounts to a small stage for an altar, with columns and a single vault behind it. The chapel comfortably seats 30, which is the number allotted to each wedding package (although additional guests can be accommodated, for a price).

NO DEVIL ...

I have no idea what rises in greater numbers above Sin City, faux steeples or wannabe Elvis pompadours. But there's one thing of which I'm sure: There's only one Norm Jones, the Presley of the pulpit.

You are the only Elvis licensed as a minister, correct?
Yes, I am the only licensed Elvis minister that I know of.

How long have you been doing this—ministering and Elvising?
I've been a minister since 1989, and licensed to perform weddings since 1994. I've been a professional Elvis impersonator since age eighteen.

How long have you been in Las Vegas?
I've been in Las Vegas since 1988. I was born in Salt Lake City. But I left home when I was twelve and moved to Montana, where I lived till I was about eighteen.

You are available through Graceland and which other chapels?
I'm at Graceland, Flamingo Garden Chapel, and Chapel of Love. I also can be booked through Las Vegas Weddings and Weddings Are Us (wedding brokers).

There's quite a road between Salt Lake City through a metaphorical Tupelo, Mississippi, and on to the ministry in Las Vegas. What made you follow that path?
For me, the calling came from the people.

You're a minister and the King. Which is better: rock 'n roll or hitchin' people?
I feel it's great to bring back some memories and make people

As the (first) name implies, Elvis plays a big part in ceremonies here; traditional services are offered too. Unfortunately, I've not seen one King in action and that's not a function of laziness. The people here are among the best when it comes to keeping weddings from stacking up one after another and making sure that your wedding does not become a public event. So the fact that I've never been past the entryway during a ceremony is due to the staff's commitment to ensuring private affairs, and that's a good thing for brides and grooms.

This facility is also known as Las Vegas Wedding Chapel.

... IN THIS DISGUISE

happy. I am an entertainer and I enjoy being a part of peoples' special days. But I am also a Christian man who strongly respects the sanctity of marriage. So, to answer your question, both fill a need I have to make people happy.

How many knots have you tied?

Countless. I've performed so many weddings that I haven't had a chance to stop and count them.

Why are Las Vegas weddings so popular?

They're easy and basically inexpensive compared to big church weddings. Today, the money couples save is often used to help them get a start on their lives together.

What are your most requested songs?

"Can't Help Falling in Love With You" and "Love Me Tender."

I'm sure you've seen a little bit of everything, but what tops your list of wedding tales?

The time I was about to marry a couple and upon looking at their license, I saw the groom had been married twelve times before, and the bride had been married 14 times before. I had to ask about this and I learned they liked to travel and had gotten married to each other twelve times in twelve different states. So, of course, it would be pretty tough for them to get divorced.

What's the best piece of advice you can give to newlyweds?

Two people in love, two people to make the promise, two people to keep the promise, and two people to protect it so no person, place, or thing comes between them.

GRACELAND WEDDING CHAPEL
619 Las Vegas Boulevard South
800/824-5732; 702/382-0091
www.gracelandchapel.com

Kitsch Factor: 3 & 5 With Elvis	
Romance Quotient: 3	
Fresh Test: 3.5	
Comfy/Cozy Test: 3	
The *One* **Way to Go:** Well, it is called *Graceland*.	
In a Nutshell: This Top-5 chapel claims to be the pioneer of the Elvis nuptial and this is one of the handful of places where he actually performs the ceremony; cutesy cozy chapel; next-door neighbor is a crappy old motel that's closed and surrounded by chain-link fencing.	
Costs: $55 to $595; Elvis included on upper-tier packages or as an add-on to any package for $145.	
Yearly Weddings: 4,800	
Hours: 9 a.m. to midnight Sunday through Thursday; till 3 a.m. Friday and Saturday.	
Ceremonies: Nonreligious and nondenominational Christian; a rabbi is available.	
Languages: Spanish	
Bride's Room: Yes, detached bathroom.	
Groom's Room: No, but you can use the large bathroom if/when she vacates.	
Commitment: No	
Location: Downtown	

No, it doesn't look like *that* Graceland. In fact, it looks a heck of a lot like a church on the outside—a white church with blue trim, a hand-railed porch, steeple, stained glass, a big old tree weeping over the top … oh, and a sign out front with Elvis in full thrust announcing that this is the very spot where rocker Jon Bon Jovi took the plunge. Reportedly, this is the place that pioneered the "Elvis wedding," so who can fault a trendsetter for exercising a bit of creative license?

Viva Las Vegas.

Graceland *is* a cute chapel. The garnet-hued carpeting works well with the dark pews and wood paneling. Roses figure prominently in the peaked stained-glass windows and arrangements behind the altar. There's no vault to the ceiling, which in fact helps add to the cozy and comfortable feel. It all seems so quaint, 'til the minister proclaims, "I now pronounce you man and wife … and Elvis must leave the building."

HARTLAND MANSION
525 Park Paseo Drive
702/387-6700
www.vegasweddings.com/hartland

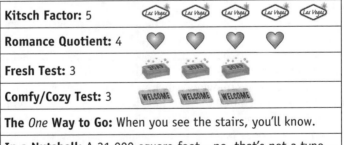

Kitsch Factor: 5					
Romance Quotient: 4					
Fresh Test: 3					
Comfy/Cozy Test: 3					
The *One* Way to Go: When you see the stairs, you'll know.					
In a Nutshell: A 31,000-square-foot—no, that's not a typo—private residence with an architectural treatment straight from the imagination of Walt Disney.					
Costs: $500 for a basic hitch.					
Yearly Weddings: No one seems to keep count, but it won't be a zoo.					

Hours: Vary
Ceremonies: The owner, Dr. Toni Hart, is a minister and performs non-denominational Christian ceremonies; couples can bring in a rabbi or other officiate of their choosing.
Languages: English only provided by chapel, but your ceremony can be conducted in any language for which you can find a licensed officiate.
Bride's Room: Yes, with a restroom; changing allowed.
Groom's Room: No
Commitment: No
Location: Downtown

For years, Hartland Mansion was one of the places where the neon nobility hung out, threw parties, and hosted fundraisers, but now regular folks like you and I can get in for a private bash, reception, or wedding. Most weddings are held in the grand foyer, where dual staircases descend to a perfectly chic floor patterned with big black and white checks. Your grand entry takes you down these stairs, so practice at home with a few blankets pinned to the bottom of your jeans.

The place is kind of funky and kind of kooky, as you'd expect of a private residence that started as two homes now combined into one, with a façade right out of Disneyland. After two fires burned it all to the ground, the Hartland Mansion of today emerged, at more than twice the previous square footage. Good places for a reception or a post-hitch toast include the facility's atrium and the indoor and outdoor pool areas. The historic neighborhood where the mansion resides appears to be making a comeback, but don't expect the surroundings to be buttoned down and spit polished like the Bellagio.

By the way, scenes from the movie *Casino* were filmed here and what could be more Vegas than that?

HEAVENLY BLISS WEDDING CHAPEL
516 South 4th Street
702/477-0789
www.heavenlyblissweddingchapel.com

Kitsch Factor: 4	
Romance Quotient: 3	
Fresh Test: 2 There was something going on in the kitchen.	
Comfy/Cozy Test: 2	

The *One* **Way to Go:** Why not tie the knot with some Hawaiian music, aloha shirts, and leis?

In a Nutshell: Converted residence two blocks from Fremont Street; garden-style chapel (but not too much garden); Hawaiian-themed room; small gazebo out front.

Costs: $40 to $499; reception packages higher.

Yearly Weddings: You know, it's not like I'm asking for the special-sauce recipe from Bob's Big Boy ... what's with these people refusing to answer such mundane questions? Is John Ashcroft now running things in Vegas?

Hours: Ditto

Ceremonies: Non-religious and non-denominational Christian; a rabbi might be available.

Languages: English, Spanish, Chinese, and Tagalog.

Bride's Room: Yes

Groom's Room: Yes

Commitment: I asked, but they didn't tell.

Location: Downtown

Heavenly Bliss occupies a converted arts-and-crafts-style cottage on 4th Street downtown. Office buildings predominate on these blocks, with an occasional residence, and this house-turned-chapel could pass for someone's home if not for the dressed-up gazebo on the lawn and the simple sign over the carport.

Heavenly Garden is the main chapel, a small two-dozen-or-so-seat affair set behind French doors. It is painted in a warm honey-comb-yellow hue with a black ornamental fence and an arbor for the altar. A mural behind the altar continues the effect of moving out and through a tiled patio to a garden beyond. Artificial plants and flowers, representing the Heavenly Garden in the chapel's name, add to the pastoral quality without being overbearing. Another room has been converted into a Polynesian-like hut that "overlooks" a wind- and sea-swept beach, with slender palms standing guard. The altar is kitsched up with tropical flowers and bright birds, and floral-print mats sit on the hardwood floor. It's wholly faux and corny, but cute, and when you see it, you'll understand why it's called "Hawaiian Shores."

During my visit, the person on duty was not unfriendly, but a little cool. I was under my usual cover of being in town on business and using my spare time to check out a list of possible nuptial sites for my at-home fiancée to review. *What, guys don't do this sort of thing?* Judging by her reaction, I guess not. And the building had that morning-after-a-big-dinner-party aroma that wasn't necessarily offensive, but was decidedly noticeable. (The place does have a working kitchen, so perhaps someone was just warming up leftovers for lunch.) A remodeled chapel is scheduled to open in early 2005.

HITCHING POST WEDDING CHAPEL
1737 Las Vegas Boulevard South
888/540-5060; 702/387-5080
www.hitchingpostweddingchapel.com

Kitsch Factor: 5	Las Vegas	Las Vegas	Las Vegas	Las Vegas	Las Vegas
Romance Quotient: 1	♡				
Fresh Test: 1	SOAP				
Comfy/Cozy Test: 1	WELCOME				

The *One* Way to Go: You're on your own here.
In a Nutshell: If you want the perfect caricature of a Vegas wedding, look here (as well as the sister property next door, Monaco Wedding Chapel).
Costs: $48 to $520.
Yearly Weddings: I've asked on several occasions in several manners and the result is always the same: chatter, chatter, chatter, avoid the question, click. Two e-mails were ignored.
Hours: 24/7 (by appointment).
Ceremonies: Non-religious, non-denominational Christian, Jewish.
Languages: French and Spanish (for ceremonies); some staff members reportedly speak Russian and Polish.
Bride's Room: You can use his or the bride's room next door at sister-chapel Monaco.
Groom's Room: Yes, with a restroom.
Commitment: Yes
Location: Downtown

The carpeting is red, worn, and cheap. Pounds of stucco adhere to the walls. Lattice and faux flowers abound like a craft supply store on steroids. The ceiling is given over to a sky treatment that compares to the one at Caesars Palace's Forum Shops as Chef Ronald McDonald does to Emeril Lagasse, and industrial-grade air deodorizer almost knocked both my wife and me off our feet when we visited. The adjoining hotel is named Oasis and it has fantasy rooms available by the hour. By name, it's reportedly the oldest chapel in town, but its current building wasn't around in 1926 when it was founded.

HOLLYWOOD WEDDING CHAPEL
2207 Las Vegas Boulevard South
800/704-0478; 702/731-0678
www.ahollywoodweddingchapel.com

Kitsch Factor: 3	
Romance Quotient: 2	
Fresh Test: 2	
Comfy/Cozy Test: 2	
The *One* Way to Go: The Complete Wedding Package at $225 takes you off the hook for tipping the limo driver and the minister.	
In a Nutshell: Cookie-cutter 30-seat chapel on the site of a former Rat Pack-era nightspot.	
Costs: $125 to $225.	
Yearly Weddings: Refused to disclose	
Hours: 11 a.m. to 7 p.m. Sunday; 10 a.m. to 7 p.m. Monday through Thursday; 10 a.m. to 8 p.m. Friday; and 10 a.m. to 9 p.m. Saturday.	
Ceremonies: Non-religious and non-denominational Christian.	
Languages: Spanish (ring exchange and vows)	
Bride's Room: Yes, with a restroom. Hair, make-up, gown—do what you want as long as you get it done in time for the ceremony.	
Groom's Room: Same as above.	
Commitment: No	
Location: Downtown	

Hollywood Wedding Chapel is another of the flock of syrupy love palaces dispensing quick legal marriages at low cost. The owner once lived in Hollywood, according to a chapel staffer, and apparently thought it would be a good name for a Las Vegas wedding chapel. The other Tinseltown "connection" is movie posters lining a narrow hall coming in from the rear entrance and packages named after famous Hollywood streets. (In a past life, the building was known as the Red Fez, a bygone hangout for the likes of Frank, Dean, Sammy, and other legendary entertainers, or so the story goes.)

Although the carpeting is deep red and yellow faux flowers abound, this is a very white chapel, from the walls and ceilings to the straight-backed chairs. Wedding supplies, everything from jewelry and wine flutes to rings, are displayed in the busy and cluttered lobby. The casually clad attendants are talkative and friendly when not lounging on the couch in the foyer enthralled by a novel or soap on television.

A LAS VEGAS GARDEN OF LOVE
200 W. Sahara Avenue
866/483-5683; 702/385-5683
www.lvgardenoflove.com

Kitsch Factor: 5 Waterfall Chapel	*Las Vegas Las Vegas Las Vegas Las Vegas Las Vegas*
Romance Quotient: 1	♡
Fresh Test: 1	
Comfy/Cozy Test: 1	WELCOME
The *One* **Way to Go:** Perhaps to another chapel discussed in this or the next chapter.	
In a Nutshell: Three chapels with capacity for 20, 50, or 100; reception area; outdoor area that is seldom used.	
Costs: $40 to $999.	
Yearly Weddings: 6,000 to 7,000.	
Hours: 10 a.m. to "whenever" daily.	

Ceremonies: Non-religious, non-denominational Christian, Jewish.	
Languages: Spanish	
Bride's Room: Yes, but desperately in need of new carpet. Restroom down the hall for changing, hair, and make-up.	
Groom's Room: Yes; the restroom is down the hall.	
Commitment: No	
Location: North Strip	

Proving the validity of the adage "there's something for everyone," A Las Vegas Garden of Love is a ramshackle three-chapel-and-a-reception-hall facility located near the corner of the Strip and Sahara Avenue, right behind the "biggest gift shop in the world."

Claiming to do a whopping 7,000 weddings annually after only a few years of operation—that's more than one out of every 20, for Cupid's sake—this place never slows down. The larger chapel is the "Garden" in the name. The indoor-outdoor carpeting is lawn green, there are enough faux flowers and greenery to outfit a look-alike Eden at a plastics convention, and the altar is a wall of rock with a waterfall. This place is pretty much near the top for stereotypical Sin City chapel kitsch. Low ceilings and fluorescent lighting complete the effect, whatever that is. The outdoor garden, dressed up in synthetic turf and white-rock rose-filled planting beds, is seldom used due to the deafening noise from traffic on Sahara and Las Vegas Boulevard. Two other chapels seat 20 and 50 guests.

On two visits, staff members have been very casually attired—spandex, jeans, T-shirts—and put me under a used-car-salesman-like hustle, even though I made it clear I was just dropping by for some literature. The lobby/reception area is cluttered and covered in bric-a-brac and replacing of the mélange of worn carpeting throughout the place should be a top priority. Promo materials, the Web site, and the sign out front tout a #1 chapel rating, though no one at the chapel has been able to pinpoint the exact polling source (it was not the *Las Vegas Review-Journal's* annual best-of edition). Nevertheless, the chapel is conveniently located, inexpensive, and marries thousands of couples each year. And although they couldn't provide all the answers, unlike some chapels they didn't hide from any questions either.

LAS VEGAS WEDDINGS AT THE GROVE
8101 Rachel Street
866/645-5818; 702/645-1094
www.lasvegasweddingsatthegrove.com

Kitsch Factor: 2	
Romance Quotient: 4	
Fresh Test: 4	
Comfy/Cozy Test: 4	
The *One* Way to Go: This place is special in its own right.	
In a Nutshell: A park-like setting on three acres with plentiful shade trees, flowers and shrubs, an old almond grove, a trickling stream and a pond, lots of grass, and a big, comfy gazebo.	
Costs: $299 to $1199.	
Yearly Weddings: 700	
Hours: Flexible	
Ceremonies: Non-religious and non-denominational Christian; Jewish and other religions available (you can bring in your own officiate).	
Languages: Translators based on availability or bring in a (licensed) officiate of your choosing.	
Bride's Room: Yes, changing only, with restroom facilities.	
Groom's Room: Same as above.	
Commitment: Yes	
Location: West Las Vegas, and then quite far north.	

The Grove is a wonderful outdoor setting that, until recently, was set off by itself in the far northwestern corner of Sin City. The residential development that's enveloping Las Vegas is creeping in, and though not yet adjacent, tract homes form a ring around this lovely site. Weddings are performed within a big, solid, open, and airy gazebo dressed in brown to fit in with the site's trees and (manufactured) natural setting; there're no two-by-fours or dove white-colored pre-fab lattice choked with faux ivy and flashing lights here. Guests—up to 50 with the packages, though more can be accommodated—sit comfortably spaced on an expanse of lawn. With meandering walkways, a rock-lined brook and pond, beautiful landscaping, and a grove of almond trees, great photo ops are readily available. The onsite Garden Bistro can take care of any reception needs.

Next door is a bird sanctuary and vacant land that's likely to soon go under the blade of a Cat dozer. And though all of Las Vegas is susceptible to winds, this side of town seems to get more than its fair share. The site is at least 30 minutes from the Strip, more if traffic picks up. These drawbacks are minor when taking into account the Grove's comfortable attractive surroundings. It's a winner … and a best-of recipient.

LITTLE CHAPEL OF THE FLOWERS
1304 Las Vegas Boulevard South
800/843-2410; 702/735-4331
www.littlechapel.com

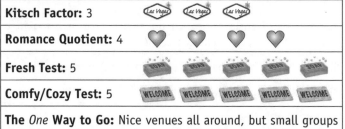

Kitsch Factor: 3	Las Vegas	Las Vegas	Las Vegas		
Romance Quotient: 4	♥	♥	♥	♥	
Fresh Test: 5	SOAP	SOAP	SOAP	SOAP	SOAP
Comfy/Cozy Test: 5	WELCOME	WELCOME	WELCOME	WELCOME	WELCOME

The *One* **Way to Go:** Nice venues all around, but small groups should consider a ceremony in the Magnolia Chapel. If you want

to blow your inheritance, helicopter to Lake Las Vegas and meet up with your wedding party on a yacht.
In a Nutshell: Three chapels seating 20, 30, and 65; gazebo; many classy off-site options; about the nicest people around in what can be, sadly, a cutthroat business.
Costs: $75 to $4,795, to which you can add a $1,650 helicopter upgrade.
Yearly Weddings: 6,000 (1,500 from Great Britain ... those nutty Englanders, Scots, and Welsh).
Hours: 9 a.m. to 9 p.m. Monday through Thursday; till 10:30 p.m. Friday and Saturday; closed Sunday.
Ceremonies: Non-religious, non-denominational Christian, Jewish.
Languages: German, French, Spanish, and Japanese translators, others upon availability.
Bride's Room: Two, one with restroom *en suite*, the other across the hall. Most packages include limo service, so very few brides arrive without being all dolled up.
Groom's Room: Who needs it, right?
Commitment: No
Location: Downtown

This is a sanctuary tucked into a frenzied part of Las Vegas Boulevard, not far south of the heart of downtown, with nice grounds, new limos in the lot, and, once inside, a family-like harmony, and unlike some chapels, I don't mean *that* family (a.k.a. La Cosa Nostra or the Mafia).

I really like the small 20-seat Magnolia Chapel with its blonde pews and tastefully adorned arched altar. The Victorian seats 30, its predominant color is light blue, and windows all around bring in warming light. The largest chapel, previously known as Heritage, was recently redone with an Italianate look; it seats 65. A gazebo on the chapel grounds is set up for eight guests; if you choose it, expect noise intrusion from the world beyond.

Little Chapel of the Flowers is another of the wedding purveyors that has perfected the art of off-site weddings, incorporating helicopters and limos into excursions to Red Rock, the Grand Canyon, a winery, or a yacht at Lake Las Vegas.

It can get darn busy here with the wedding volume, and the list of packages and options reads like a small phone book. But these people are nice and they handle the momentum with focused determination that doesn't come at the cost of a smile, and no one gets worked up over a drop-in look-see visit or a follow-up call with questions involving something other than how much money you're going to commit to them at that exact moment in time. And the place is closed on Sunday, which may have meaning for some.

THE LITTLE CHURCH OF THE WEST
4617 Las Vegas Boulevard South
800/821-2452; 702/739-7971
www.littlechurchlv.com

Kitsch Factor: 5	Las Vegas Las Vegas Las Vegas Las Vegas Las Vegas
Romance Quotient: 4	♥ ♥ ♥ ♥
Fresh Test: 3	SOAP SOAP SOAP
Comfy/Cozy Test: 3	WELCOME WELCOME WELCOME
The _One_ Way to Go: The chapel itself is the story.	
In a Nutshell: 50-seat chapel built in 1942 that's on the National Register of Historic Places; hey, that's a long time out here in the Wild Wild West. It's also a Top-5 pick.	
Costs: $199 to $525.	
Yearly Weddings: Politely declined to disclose. (When I spoke with a chapel representative, he candidly and accurately said that most chapels lie about their numbers. And if he didn't inflate to keep pace, it would look like Little Church just wasn't as popular as it is. So he passed.	

Hours: 8 a.m. to midnight daily.
Ceremonies: Non-religious, non-denominational Christian, Jewish.
Languages: Spanish and French.
Bride's Room: Yes; restroom adjacent.
Groom's Room: No, per se, but restroom is large, if needed.
Commitment: No
Location: South Strip

The Little Church of the West is, to my knowledge, Vegas' second-oldest chapel operating in its original digs. A-framed, shingled, and set on an acre of heavily arbored land, this place is history and a wee bit of an oasis on the Strip.

Like the exterior, the interior is all about wood and more wood—walls, ceiling beams, slat-back pews good for 50 of your closest family and friends, altar, the decorative organ in the corner, even the flooring, which is a far cry from the pedestrian indoor-outdoor carpeting found in so many chapels. The Little Church of the West is particularly attractive at night, all lit up with steeple aglow and a neon cross adding to its allure.

Founded in 1942, this little church has seen its fair share of glitterati pass through it on the way to marital bliss, even if all didn't last, including Richard Gere and Cindy Crawford, Judy Garland, Mickey Rooney (not sure which of his eight times), even Telly Salavas, a.k.a. "Kojak," to name a few.

The Little Church is a perennial favorite, and as often as not, winner of one of the local newspaper's annual best-of surveys. It scores well in my book, too, despite a location bracketed by Las Vegas Boulevard and McCarran International Airport.

A LITTLE WHITE WEDDING CHAPEL
1301 Las Vegas Boulevard South
800/545-8111; 702/382-5943
www.littlewhitechapel.com

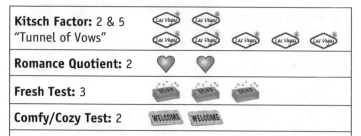

Kitsch Factor: 2 & 5 "Tunnel of Vows"	
Romance Quotient: 2	
Fresh Test: 3	
Comfy/Cozy Test: 2	

The *One* **Way to Go:** A Little White Chapel in the Sky (hot-air balloon).

In a Nutshell: This place is to Las Vegas weddings what Henry Ford was to manufacturing. It encompasses three chapels, so a group of just about any size can be accommodated; drive-thru Tunnel of Vows; gazebo; and hot-air balloon ceremonies. Everything you'd need for a wedding—flowers, photo studio, formal wear, bridal shop, and salon—is right there on site; same owner-operator as the Chapel by the Courthouse.

RED ROCKS ...

Red-flanked purple mountains rise up out of the pale desert to the west of Las Vegas. The effect is, in a word, gorgeous. This is Red Rock Canyon National Conservation Area, 300 wild and often inaccessible square miles of desert-and-range majesty, 30 minutes west of the Strip. The reserve is a magnet for hikers, mountain bikers, rock climbers ... and bridal parties.

Weddings are scheduled in the evening, near sunset, at one of two locations adjoining the main access road (though one requires a short walk in). Sites are available on a first-come first-served basis, and while the agency that runs Red Rock Canyon, the federal Bureau of Land Management, doesn't double-book activities, the two areas remain open to the public. A permit is required and the fee is $160, in addition to what-ever wedding costs you incur (the BLM provides no wedding services). For more information, visit www.redrockcanyon.blm.gov or call 702/515-5350. Most chapels offer Red Rock Canyon wedding packages, with the requisite markup of an industry that embraces cash and Cupid almost equally.

At the southerly end of Red Rock Canyon, on a hunk of ground

Costs: $55 to $799; drive-thru starts at $40; $1,000 for the balloon.
Yearly Weddings: 30,000. (If the claim is at all accurate, this place conducts more than one-quarter of all ceremonies performed annually in Clark County. Wow!)
Hours: 24/7
Ceremonies: Non-religious, nondenominational Christian and Jewish.
Languages: Spanish, German, French, and Japanese (translators in some instances).
Bride's Room: Two, with restrooms available; changing allowed.
Groom's Room: Same
Commitment: No
Location: Downtown

... ROCK

carved out of the larger preserve, sits Bonnie Springs/Old Nevada. This replica Western town—complete with Boot Hill and staged gunfights—is set within a 100-plus-acre ranch. If your nuptial sense runs more toward nostalgia than neon, Old Nevada, the boardwalk-and-clapboard town portion of Bonnie Springs, could be just right for you and your wedding posse. Wedding packages begin at $350 and include use of the period chapel. Add-ons include a horseback ceremony and a barbecue reception; there's even a motel. 702/875-4191; www.bonniesprings.com.

Another outdoor option is Valley of Fire State Park, 55 miles northeast of Las Vegas near Lake Mead, a magical area of canyons and desert flamed red, hence the name. There is presently no permit required for "private weddings." In other words, show up and hitch up, so to speak. (A number of chapels offer Valley of Fire packages if you don't want to go through the hassle of hiring a minister and making your own way out there.) Simply show up, find a place you like, park legally, and exchange I dos. For more information visit www.parks.nv.gov/vf.htm or call 702/397-2088.

I don't know whether anyone has done a poll, but this just might be Las Vegas' most famous chapel; it certainly is the busiest. And although it doesn't have the history of Little Church of the West or Wee Kirk o' the Heather, it *does* have a who's-who roster of famous knot-tiers—Michael Jordan, Mickey Rooney (he nicely spread his business around), Demi and Bruce, and Sinatra—listed on a hard-to-miss marquee as part of the chapel's aggressive marketing campaign.

With three chapels, Sin City's first drive-thru wedding window, a gazebo, and off-site options like a hot-air balloon, there's more than a little buzz to this place. The three chapels can accommodate a petite-sized ceremony up to one that hits the century mark. Each is distinct in look, though wholly Vegas—fake pillars, pews white or velveteen, lots of burgundy and rose and white, draping fabric, and vines. The drive-thru is an elaborate carport, fenced by ornamental white iron with gold-capped white pillars holding up a blue-painted canopy liberally peppered with a chorus of cherubs floating amid wispy clouds and starbursts.

I've been to this chapel during quiet times (which for this place still translates to hundreds of weddings per week) and on the busiest day of the year, Valentine's, and in every case, I saw an edgy coolness and clocklike precision. That makes it efficient, but so are factories. I can't say the same thing for phone service, though, as I've had nearly as many 10-minute waits on hold as unreturned calls. Surely, they must've been busy dispensing love, yet some might think service prior to the point of sale is just as important as when the deal is closed. Nevertheless, Little White has tens of thousands of satisfied perfectly wed customers, which is what it is all about.

MONACO WEDDING CHAPEL
1735 Las Vegas Boulevard South
888/540-5060; 702/796-5060
www.monacoweddingchapel.com

Kitsch Factor: 5	*Las Vegas* *Las Vegas* *Las Vegas* *Las Vegas* *Las Vegas*
Romance Quotient: 1	♥
Fresh Test: 1	SOAP
Comfy/Cozy Test: 1	WELCOME
The *One* Way to Go: There isn't.	
In a Nutshell: An eyesore.	
Costs: $79 to $625; more for Elvis and helicopter nuptials.	
Yearly Weddings: No idea; see entry for Hitching Post Wedding Chapel.	
Hours: 24/7 (by appointment).	
Ceremonies: Non-religious, non-denominational Christian, Jewish.	
Languages: French and Spanish (for ceremonies); staff members at sister chapel Hitching Post reportedly speak Russian and Polish, so I imagine they can walk over and interpret, if needed.	
Bride's Room: Yes; restroom available.	
Groom's Room: No, but if you need some private time, negotiate with the wife-to-be or go next door and use the facilities at the Hitching Post.	
Commitment: Yes	
Location: Downtown	

Monaco Wedding Chapel is to chintz as Santa is to glee, just like Hitching Post, its fraternal twin—you know, same genes, different face—located one storefront over. There are likely enough mirrors here to rival the by-the-hour motel next door, more twinkle lights than Tivoli Garden, and more (plastic) plants than the combined sets of the stage and film versions of that "Little Shop" show. The front windows are covered in peel-and-stick "stained glass." And there's this orange-arch-mirror-twinkle thing about which I'm obviously clueless; I guess it *could* be an altar.

Beware the Flash intro on the Web site depicting a white limo pulling up to a stately castle with fireworks kissing the night sky ... that's not what awaits here.

MON BEL AMI WEDDING CHAPEL
607 Las Vegas Boulevard South
866/503-4400; 702/378-4445
www.monbelami.com

Kitsch Factor: 2	
Romance Quotient: 4	
Fresh Test: 5	
Comfy/Cozy Test: 4	
The *One* Way to Go: It's new, clean, and nice-looking ... that's all you need.	
In a Nutshell: Most packages include a sparkling-wine toast for a set number of guests.	
Costs: $159 to $1,599.	
Yearly Weddings: Would not disclose.	
Hours: 10 a.m. to midnight midweek; till 3 a.m. on Friday and Saturday nights (technically Saturday and Sunday mornings).	
Ceremonies: Non-religious and non-denominational Christian; rabbi available.	
Languages: English only; translators might be available depending on language.	

Bride's Room: Big new bathroom, more than roomy enough for changing.

Groom's Room: Indeed—a score for equal opportunity.

Commitment: Yes

Location: Downtown

It was out with the old as Mon Bel Ami rose anew in 2003. And hidden inside what looks like a well-maintained modest stucco home—albeit, one with a small bell tower—is one of the prettiest chapels this side of Las Vegas' version of the Mason-Dixon Line, Sahara Avenue.

This is a great chapel.

The interior is Mediterranean regal with a gold and honey color scheme accented by green and desert rose. High ceilings rise above comfortably spaced wheat-colored pews. Clean-lined double doors inset with many panes of clear glass open to the chapel. Outside, white-wood fencing has been erected to create defined congregation areas—including a gazebo—around the chapel's grassy flowered yard and to hide some of the adjacent urban clutter, liked the shuttered motel next door.

The classic sign—a lighted steeple above an old-fashioned message board, the kind upon which individual letters are affixed— should be gone by the time you arrive, replaced by one patterned after the elegant yet simple "Beverly Hills" shield used to mark that city's boundaries. Another small piece of Vegas history dies.

SAN FRANCISCO SALLY'S VICTORIAN WEDDING CHAPEL
1304 Las Vegas Boulevard South
800/658-8677; 702/385-7777
Web site pending

Kitsch Factor: 5	
Romance Quotient: 1.5	
Fresh Test: 1.5	
Comfy/Cozy Test: 1.5	

The *One* Way to Go: Donning Western or Victorian garb.

In a Nutshell: Tiny parlor-style chapel that's actually part of a formal-wear rental shop. For the record, the people with whom I've had contact are nice.

Costs: $95 to $370, including the minister's fee, unlike most standalone chapels.

Yearly Weddings: Not many; several per day, but not every day.

Hours: 10 a.m. to 6 p.m. Monday through Thursday; till 9 p.m. Friday and Saturday; till 5 p.m. Sunday.

Ceremonies: Non-religious and non-denominational Christian; it's rarely requested here, but a rabbi can be secured, which adds several hundred dollars to the tab.

Languages: Spanish

Bride's Room: They rent costumes and wedding apparel, so changing rooms are available, as is a restroom.

Groom's Room: Ditto

Commitment: Yes

Location: Downtown

The Victorian Chapel is a tiny poorly lit little room toward the back of San Francisco Sally's Bridal & Formal Wear Rentals. The chapel is set up like a Victorian-era parlor room, with seating for six on period loveseats and chairs and standing-room-only space for an additional dozen in an adjoining anteroom. Pink abounds. So does dust. The shop and chapel are located in an older commercial building about midway between the north end of the Strip and downtown.

This is a rental shop, primarily, so racks and racks of clothes and dusty display cases of accessories fill the main room, which has the look and musty odor of a thrift shop. But for couples traveling without a large retinue who have a penchant for the quaint, this is the only venue of its kind in Sin City. And because it's a rental shop, you can get your nuptial wear—whether modern, traditional, Victorian, or Western—right there.

THE SECRET GARDEN AT THE LAS VEGAS RACQUET CLUB
3333 Raven Avenue
702/361-2202
www.asecretgardenwedding.com

Kitsch Factor: 2	
Romance Quotient: 3	
Fresh Test: 3.5	
Comfy/Cozy Test: 4	
The *One* Way to Go: Rent the horse-drawn carriage.	
In a Nutshell: Indoor/outdoor wedding, reception, and private-function facility located on the site of a former tennis club.	
Costs: $625 to $1,150.	
Yearly Weddings: 150	
Hours: Vary by season.	
Ceremonies: Non-religious, non-denominational, and sectarian Christian, Jewish; outside officiates welcomed.	

Languages: Because you're allowed to bring in your own officiate, who if necessary can obtain the required Nevada (temporary) license, you have total latitude.

Bride's Room: HUGE ... a one-time locker room. Do what you want.

Groom's Room: No discrimination here (and ESPN on the tube).

Commitment: Yes

Location: South Strip—several miles south of Mandalay Bay, west of Interstate 15.

Admittedly, I was skeptical about the Secret Garden at the Las Vegas Racquet Club, as I wasn't caught up by what I saw on the chapel's easy-to-use Web site. And the drive in—take I-15 south; exit west on Blue Diamond; turn south on Industrial, driving around and behind the Silverton, paralleling the freeway for another mile; then turn onto a street settled over the years by people who plopped larger-than-usual homes on larger-than-usual lots in an attempt to get "away" from the urban, suburban, and touristy, yet all the while keeping the comforts of, say, Caesars Palace within an easy 10-minute drive—left me scratching my head. However, while passing through the perimeter pines and Lombardy poplars remaining from the club's earlier days, my outlook changed. By the end of our visit, I was convinced that the place just feels good, and my wife, who was with me, agreed.

The racquet club was founded in 1962, which is medieval if not ancient for Sin City history. The tennis surfaces remain and an indoor court that never saw any play now functions as the reception hall and a place for indoor ceremonies. Now the game is weddings, receptions, parties, and corporate events. Ceremonies are held in an ample gazebo, steps from a swimming pool that has the big, classical, symmetrical look that was popular in the days when outdoor entertaining was more formal, if not more serious. There's effectively no limit on the number of guests, as the entire site covers 10 acres. The owner has a classic-car collection and you can arrive at the aisle in top-down splendor; there's a horse-drawn-carriage option too.

This is a one-wedding-a-day place, so you won't trip over another bride's train as you arrive or depart. Being a former tennis club, the one-time women's locker room serves as your dressing and assembly room—you can even shower if you're so inclined—and it comes with everything from an iron and board to blow dryers. The old pro shop has been converted into a bridal shop where you can borrow from hundreds of wedding accoutrements, from ring pillows to feather pens. Given the nature of the facility, most ceremonies are held near dusk or in the evening on Friday, Saturday, or Sunday, although ceremonies at other times and days of the week are allowed. Many couples choose from several reception options, ranging from hors d'œuvres and a toast to a multi-course meal served indoors or outside on the verandah.

The Secret Garden isn't perfectly pristine and it's not for everyone; it is a former athletic club and the time-worn courts remain across the wedding lawn. A private residence anchors a corner of the facility and the interstate sits not far away. But for an outdoor venue that is private, spacious, and reasonably priced, it's hard to beat.

SHALIMAR WEDDING CHAPEL
1401 Las Vegas Boulevard South
800/255-9633; 702/382-7372
www.shalimarweddingchapel.com

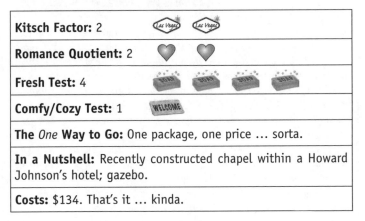

Kitsch Factor: 2	
Romance Quotient: 2	
Fresh Test: 4	
Comfy/Cozy Test: 1	
The *One* Way to Go: One package, one price ... sorta.	
In a Nutshell: Recently constructed chapel within a Howard Johnson's hotel; gazebo.	
Costs: $134. That's it ... kinda.	

Yearly Weddings: During a phone interview, the chapel proprietor chose not to answer any questions and hung up on me; multiple faxed and e-mailed inquiries were ignored.	
Hours: Ditto	
Ceremonies: Ditto	
Languages: Ditto	
Bride's Room: Ditto	
Groom's Room: Ditto	
Commitment: Ditto	
Location: Downtown	

You'll find Valentine's-red carpet, white pews, and standard chapel flower arrangements at Shalimar ... and that's about it—except for the great Cuban restaurant on the other side of the lobby. This

THE FINAL BELL

What's the one sure bet in Vegas? Tens of thousands of neon nuptialists showing up year in and year out. Yet despite the certainty of the matrimonial market, wedding chapels do occasionally go out of business.

One of the most recent to meet its demise was Wedding Bells Chapel on the north Strip. In the grand scheme of things, this chapel's disappearance should be greeted as a blessing, however. It committed perhaps the most egregious bit of Web misrepresentation with a photo of an alluring gazebo backed by an all-along-the-Strip view that was a physical impossibility in this or any other dimension, and the whole shebang was housed in a rundown albeit historic motor inn. Another casualty in 2004 was Westminster Chapel, an attractive facility that perhaps just couldn't overcome its surroundings in a somewhat eerie commercial-residential complex set in a dreary corner of downtown. And even popular stalwarts move around, as in the case of Candlelight Wedding Chapel, and disappear, as is the case with the soon-to-be-razed (at press time) Wee Kirk o' the Heather.

Vegas is forever changing. So if places like the Sands and Dunes bid adieu, it shouldn't come as a surprise that chapels do too.

is a turnkey neon nuptial, with a flat rate of $134, not including tax, minister donation, or limo-driver tip. (Why do ministers receive donations while drivers are tipped?) Returning from my philosophical musing, also included in the price are a 12-frame roll of film that they shoot and you process, a witness if you came without one, a bridal garter, a loaner bouquet and boutonnière, and a video.

This simple, almost boring, chapel is located in the lobby of a Howard Johnson's hotel along that stretch of Las Vegas Boulevard between the Strip and downtown that's just peppered with love palaces. Shalimar is clean and tidy, a benefit of its recent construction. But there's just something not right about a service-oriented business that refuses to answer questions about its service and if I had been inclined to allow rudeness alone to dictate a chapel's placement on the list of infamy in the first chapter, this place would have been so designated. Oh, that's right, I have that latitude. So be it.

A SPECIAL MEMORY WEDDING CHAPEL
800 South Fourth Street
800/962-7798; 702/384-2211
www.aspecialmemory.com

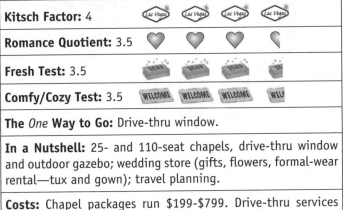

Kitsch Factor: 4	🎰🎰🎰🎰
Romance Quotient: 3.5	♥♥♥◗
Fresh Test: 3.5	🍞🍞🍞🍞
Comfy/Cozy Test: 3.5	WELCOME WELCOME WELCOME WEL

The *One* Way to Go: Drive-thru window.

In a Nutshell: 25- and 110-seat chapels, drive-thru window and outdoor gazebo; wedding store (gifts, flowers, formal-wear rental—tux and gown); travel planning.

Costs: Chapel packages run $199-$799. Drive-thru services start at $25, not including the minister's gratuity. This chapel provides officiates for ceremonies at Star Trek: The Experience at the Las Vegas Hilton.

Yearly Weddings: 5,000 (including 900 at the window).	
Hours: 8 a.m. to 10 p.m. Sunday through Thursday; till midnight Friday and Saturday.	
Ceremonies: Non-religious, non-denominational Christian, Jewish.	
Languages: Spanish, French, German, and Japanese; translators can be provided for other languages, including American Sign Language.	
Bride's Room: Two, not huge, with detached bathroom—arrive with hair and makeup done.	
Groom's Room: One, detached bathroom.	
Commitment: No	
Location: Downtown	

A Special Memory is a quaint clapboarded and steepled retreat amid the urban clutter near downtown. The nearly decade-old facility features small and large chapels and a gazebo; flowers, cakes, rings, and gifts for sale; formal wear to rent; and coordinators who can set up almost anything from bachelorette parties to childcare or an off-site ceremony astride horses or amongst Klingons and Ferengi. And if you're in a hurry (because you just can't wait a minute longer to compromise that well-guarded virtue), A Special Memory is mere blocks from the license bureau. But the highlight of the place is out back, where *Lovers Lane* (marked with street sign and all) takes the nuptial-bound past the menu complete with services, prices, and side orders (flowers, etc.)—"Honey, what should we order?"—to the drive-up window, one of a handful in town; it's depicted on the cover.

This place sees a *ton* of business, so expect lots of company on weekends and the big days—Valentine's, New Year's, and through 2012, as noted in Chapter 2, dates with repeating numbers (for example, 05/05/05). With two chapels, a drive-thru window, and a gazebo, you might be part of separate yet simultaneous ceremonies, and on busy days, services can be stacked back to back. Nevertheless, it scores a *Neon Nuptials* commendation as a best-of chapel.

A good portion of the lobby is lined with display cases housing some of the aforementioned wedding memorabilia and the main counter can be a hive of activity with people filling out paperwork and staff members fielding questions and handling the phones. New retail and office space should be completed some time in 2005, reducing a lot of the buzz.

THE STAINED GLASS WEDDING CHAPEL
901 E. Ogden Avenue
702/384-4340
www.stainedglasschapel.com

Kitsch Factor: 4	*(Las Vegas icons x4)*
Romance Quotient: 3	♥ ♥ ♥
Fresh Test: 2	*(dice x2)*
Comfy/Cozy Test: 1	WELCOME
The *One* Way to Go: I don't think it makes a difference.	
In a Nutshell: Funky twin chapels in a funky historic house situated past the point where downtown goes from showy to seedy. One chapel should comfortably seat a dozen-plus and the second can take 20 or so guests; another larger chapel is being constructed. The name comes from period glass that the antique-collecting owners have picked up over the years. Most of the panes themselves are not inset, but instead affixed over the house's existing windows. Receptions are offered.	
Costs: $175 to $599; Internet specials offered at times.	
Yearly Weddings: Wouldn't reveal during a phone conversation, but asked that I e-mail the question. I e-mailed twice and was ignored twice. If this were the Olympics, there'd be a decided deduction in style points.	
Hours: 24/7 ... by appointment.	

Ceremonies: Non-religious and non-denominational Christian.	
Languages: Spanish	
Bride's Room: Yes, and it's small.	
Groom's Room: Yes, and it's tiny.	
Commitment: Yes	
Location: Downtown	

The walls of this historic-house-turned-chapel are a mish-mash of rocks, some etched with fossils and pictographs, and minerals mortared together—the kind of construction once seen throughout the West. It's really quite cool. (The house reputedly was built by a former Clark County Sheriff who employed prison labor to construct it.) Too bad the time warp—an effect already skewed by a swimming pool in the corner of the shaded courtyard—doesn't extend to the surrounding urban squalor that is downtown Sin City just several blocks removed from Glitter Gulch and the Fremont Street Experience. Looking at the neighborhood, it becomes obvious why the entire facility is enclosed by a high fence; the area would be a "thrill" at night and that's the reason why the Comfy/Cozy rating is what it is.

The larger Stained Glass Chapel features a 17th-century pulpit behind the altar and an antique organ. The chapel's pocket-sized dressing rooms are located just down an adjoining hall. The Crystal Cathedral Chapel feels like a cabin given its beamed porch and working fireplace. There's a kitchen off this small chapel and the distinctive and not wholly pleasant odors from someone preparing lunch came barreling through the day Terri and I visited; I assume no one stews up cabbage during a ceremony. As the name implies, there's a good amount of stained glass in the two chapels. And although it might not be enough to choose Stained Glass as your wedding venue, the people who run this outfit are approachable and earnest ... to a point.

SWEETHEART'S WEDDING CHAPEL
1155 Las Vegas Boulevard South
800/444-2932; 702/385-7785
www.sweetheartschapel.com

Kitsch Factor: 1	
Romance Quotient: 1	
Fresh Test: 1	
Comfy/Cozy Test: 1	
The *One* Way to Go: With a can of Raid.	
In a Nutshell: Small 20-guest family-run chapel that's part of the Rose Eren Bridal Boutique offering gowns for sale or rent, tuxedo rentals, veils and headpieces, shoes, and other accessories; the bridal boutique/chapel shares an old commercial building with an adult bookstore.	
Costs: $85 to $499; $175 to add Elvis, who'll sing three songs, walk you down the aisle, and leave behind a satin scarf to add to your memories.	
Yearly Weddings: 2,000+	
Hours: 10 a.m. to 8 p.m. daily.	
Ceremonies: Non-religious and non-denominational Christian.	
Languages: Spanish	
Bride's Room: One changing room, restroom available.	
Groom's Room: If you want to share, it's okay with the owner.	
Commitment: Okay, I've been told yes and no by two different people, so roll the dice.	
Location: Downtown	

Whoever said first impressions last forever was right: I'll never get past the greeter at the door, because official or not, it's hard to forget a big fat Sin City cockroach. And it was still standing its ground when my wife and I left five or so minutes later, shining golden in the afternoon Mojave sun. Ugh!

True story, I'm afraid, although I've not been back to check on the current condition of the place. Reportedly, the décor is changed every year; during our visit, the chapel, effectively a portion of the larger shop, consisted of a simple altar rather tastefully prepared with white silk flowers, white chairs for up to 20, and gold lamé valances on white walls. If not for the "doorman" and an impertinent employee/coordinator who really seemed put off by our presence (perhaps she suspected that we weren't who we said we were), the place would work in a low-key no-frill way, and you wouldn't see a string of "1s" in the rating. But it doesn't work, because while all buildings have bugs, this is the spot where a big one came out.

VEGAS WEDDING CHAPEL
320 South 3rd Street
800/823-4095; 702/933-3464
www.702wedding.com

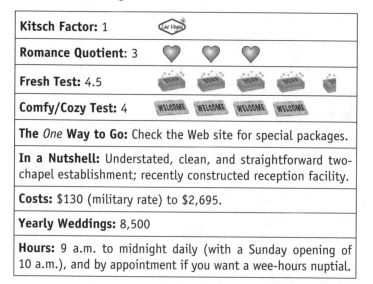

Kitsch Factor: 1	
Romance Quotient: 3	
Fresh Test: 4.5	
Comfy/Cozy Test: 4	

The *One* Way to Go: Check the Web site for special packages.

In a Nutshell: Understated, clean, and straightforward two-chapel establishment; recently constructed reception facility.

Costs: $130 (military rate) to $2,695.

Yearly Weddings: 8,500

Hours: 9 a.m. to midnight daily (with a Sunday opening of 10 a.m.), and by appointment if you want a wee-hours nuptial.

Ceremonies: Whatever you need, they'll provide.
Languages: Spanish
Bride's Room: Yes, with a restroom.
Groom's Room: Same for you, big guy.
Commitment: No
Location: Downtown

This chapel is located in the heart of downtown inside a relatively common-looking commercial building sporting "Las Vegas Wedding Bureau" painted on two sides and a subtle Mediterranean-reminiscent mural on the front. The larger chapel, Wedding Garden, seats 40-plus guests. The room is white, with large Mexican-style tile floors and a terra cotta-colored fountain behind a column-and-balustrade altar. Ornate white metal chairs, flower arrangements, potted plants, and Italian cypress unify the garden look.

The almost-too-simple Traditional Chapel seats less than 20 in formal straight-backed chairs sitting on wine-colored carpeting. Tapestries adorn the walls and the altar; a semicircular table of metal and glass, upon which sits a candle-and-flower arrangement, is subtle and straightforward. Light-colored draperies, several potted ferns, and large tasteful white-flower arrangements complete a look that is anything but traditional in a Sin City sense.

When I visited, no one growled or tried to get me to sign a contract and I was allowed to look around at my leisure. Nice place and a worthy Top 5.

WALTER'S PAD

Just south of Tropicana, not far east of the airport, sits what can only be described as a shrine to the opulence or gaudiness—and perhaps both—that comes with wealth and success: the Las Vegas home of the late Wladziu (Walter) Valentino Liberace.

Operated today as Las Vegas Villa, the glitter master's 20,000-square-foot former abode—actually two residences combined into one with a connecting "Eternal Hallway" of Greco pillars and etched mirrors—is a favored spot for corporate get-togethers, dinner parties, and some neon nuptials.

If Las Vegas Villa is a piano, and corporate events and private dinners are the white ivories, then weddings tally up like the black keys, and are typically followed by a reception. Although I've primarily passed by wedding venues that cater to the vow-and-chow crowd, this place is just too wholly Vegas to ignore.

The villa seemingly contains enough gilt, frescoes—one a replica of what's on the ceiling of the Sistine Chapel—marble, columns, chandeliers, copper-inlaid tile, wall after wall of etched glass, and the aforementioned mirrors to outfit three Louvres, two Hermitages, and the Nashville mansion of a country singer left without supervision when it came time to decorate. Hyperbole? Sure. Yet the words ornate, flamboyant, and ostentatious can't adequately capture the degree of kitsch in this place.

I'm not being catty here. This isn't just Vegasiana, this is Americana at its pinnacle: An Italian-Polish son of the heartland becomes one of the most adored entertainers of all times, redefines showmanship and popular entertainment, and builds over-the-top homes with his multi-million-dollar wealth ... and this is one that you can rent for the eve. If you've always dreamt of raising high the flame of love at a place that features a $65,000 marble tub housed in a Romanesque temple, with his (Liberace's that is) likeness painted on the ceiling, this is your candelabra. (This is the same tub that figured in Liberace's bubble-bath scene from his television specials.) The staff was accommodating when I toured the villa, but as of press time, have not responded to my follow-up questions; that's just not right.

Wedding-only packages start at $550 and run through $1,200.

Las Vegas Villa
4982 Shirley Street
800/259-2978; 702/318-5683
www.lasvegasvilla.com

VICTORIA'S WEDDING CHAPEL
2800 W. Sahara Avenue
800/344-5683; 702/252-4565
www.avictorias.com

Kitsch Factor: 2	
Romance Quotient: 3.5	
Fresh Test: 5	
Comfy/Cozy Test: 4	
The *One* Way to Go: This is a good-looking chapel, so you need only concern yourself with which package suits you.	
In a Nutshell: An attractive purposeful chapel—and reception venue—built into what otherwise looks like a nice office-commercial center on Sahara Avenue about a mile west of the freeway. The chapel accommodates up to 150 guests. And it's the top Top-5 selection.	
Costs: $90 to $856.	
Yearly Weddings: 600	
Hours: 10 a.m. until whenever a bride and groom desire.	
Ceremonies: Non-religious, non-denominational Christian, Jewish.	
Languages: Spanish, German, Russian, and French.	
Bride's Room: Yes	
Groom's Room: No	
Commitment: Yes	
Location: West Las Vegas	

Victoria's Wedding Chapel is muted and subtle, with light oak pews, floral-patterned carpeting, and a clouded sky on the ceiling and behind gilt arches that comprise the altar; in Sin City that's subtle. An oversized bridal room adjoins the chapel, and because there's a connecting door, brides need to be conscious that their conversations can be heard. (It's not good form to let out a little kiss-and-tell gossip right before the big event.) Despite the door, your procession takes you outside, down the walk, and around the corner to doors that both enter the chapel and front busy Sahara Avenue; that's an advisory more than it is a slam (few standalone chapels don't have some land-use compatibility challenge). Early arriving guests can congregate in a landscaped courtyard behind the chapel to get away from the buzz of one of Las Vegas' most traveled thoroughfares. In a nuptial world marked by a large number of chapels that run from dour to nearly dilapidated, Victoria's has a bit of a radiant shine.

Victoria's is part of a much larger wedding empire that includes several reception or ceremony-with-a-reception sites. Most of the facilities are arrayed around Victoria's, but sister facility El Caribe is on the east side of town near Boulder Highway. If you opt for a reception at El Caribe, make sure to tell your friends and family members to plan ahead for taxi service. My wife and I attended an event there once and we ended up shuttling a number of friends back to the Strip because we weren't warned that it could take up to an hour for a taxi to arrive.

VIVA LAS VEGAS WEDDING CHAPEL
1205 Las Vegas Boulevard South
800/574-4450; 702/384-0771
www.vivalasvegasweddings.com

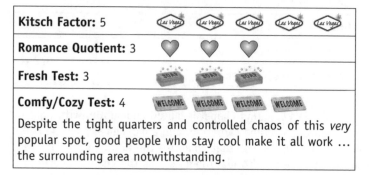

Kitsch Factor: 5	Las Vegas Las Vegas Las Vegas Las Vegas Las Vegas
Romance Quotient: 3	♥ ♥ ♥
Fresh Test: 3	SOAP SOAP SOAP
Comfy/Cozy Test: 4	WELCOME WELCOME WELCOME WELCOME

Despite the tight quarters and controlled chaos of this *very* popular spot, good people who stay cool make it all work ... the surrounding area notwithstanding.

The *One* Way to Go: Wearing blue suede shoes, of course.
In a Nutshell: There's more theme in the weddings here than Disney has characters; three chapels for groups from two to 100; gazebo; three-story motel, Viva Las Vegas Villas, with enough corn to fill a silo in Iowa; extreme and adventure weddings off-site.
Costs: $189 to $1,595; accommodation/reception packages go higher.
Yearly Weddings: 4,000+
Hours: Office opens at 9 a.m. daily; weddings typically begin at 10:30 a.m. and run through 10 p.m. or so.
Ceremonies: Non-religious, non-denominational Christian, Jewish.
Languages: English-only in-house, but you're allowed to bring an officiate who speaks the language of your choice.
Bride's Room: Yes, nice traditional look, with restroom, although the chapel prefers that you come prepared.
Groom's Room: Yes, but it's really just a staging area in the '50s diner behind the main chapel, which is available when the diner's not being used for a ceremony.
Commitment: Yes—Viva Las Vegas also does business as the Gay Chapel of Las Vegas.
Location: Downtown

I almost ran out of breath just trying to figure out where to start with this beehive of a place. The business model looks simple enough—wedding venues for groups of 20, 36, and 100. Yet the available choices are almost endless: Elvis, Blue Hawaii Elvis, Elvis in a pink Cadillac, Elvis in a pink Cadillac with Priscilla, young Elvis, height-of-his-career Las Vegas Elvis but not fat Elvis; Tom Jones, James Bond, or Liberace; Gothic or graveyard; Phantom, gangster, Egyptian, Western, Intergalactic ... ah, you get the picture. They even offer something called a "traditional" wedding, whatever *that* is.

Viva Las Vegas is the brainchild of long-time Sin City entertainer Ron Decar, who parlayed talent and a pretty good Elvis impersonation into a smorgasbord of campy mimicry, and couples love it. (Decar performs and the legal stuff takes place afterwards with a minister.)

The complex has a fairly prototypical 36-seat chapel rolled up in burgundy and ivory and a small eatery straight from the '50s, Decar's Diner, which serves as a place for motel guests to pick up a continental breakfast and a time-warp neon-nuptial spot complete with soda fountain, jukebox, black-and-white tile floor, neon advertisements, and vinyl-and-chrome dinettes. The main chapel is faintly Mission Revivalesque in appearance. The flooring consists of Spanish tile and heavy wood beams lead to a high vault and stained-glass clerestory windows; it's a unique effect for Sin City chapels. Double doors lead from the chapel where you, a newly married couple, turn around to see your names in lights ... right there on Las Vegas Boulevard.

There's also the mandatory gazebo, myriad options for ceremonies in the great outdoors, and that reworked motel out back, Viva Las Vegas Villas, with rooms and suites to match pretty much any theme that can be conjured up in the chapels.

Where some chapels fumble with the question—"Do you offer commitment ceremonies?"—and others respond with a cold terse negative, this is a place that treats commitment ceremonies with the same respect as state-recognized weddings, albeit without all the legalese. Viva Las Vegas also does business as the Gay Chapel of Las Vegas—for more details go to www.gaychapeloflasvegas.com—making it the most commitment-ceremony-committed venue in town.

WEE KIRK O' THE HEATHER
231 Las Vegas Boulevard South
800/843-5266; 702/382-9830
www.weekirk.com

Kitsch Factor: 5 It's reputed to be the oldest continuously operated chapel in town.	
Romance Quotient: 3	
Fresh Test: 3.5	
Comfy/Cozy Test: 4	

The *One* Way to Go: Any ceremony you choose, because this is the original Las Vegas chapel and it's perfect for the nostalgic set and history buffs.

In a Nutshell: The one that started it all, Las Vegas' first wedding chapel, or at least the oldest one still standing (at press time) and continuously operated; small, 16-seat, parlor-like chapel.

Costs: $189 to $649.

Yearly Weddings: 2,500

Hours: 9 a.m. to midnight daily.

Ceremonies: Nonreligious, nondenominational, Jewish.

Languages: Spanish.

Bride's Room: Yes, large and fully equipped, with a restroom.

Groom's Room: Be a dearie and give him a wee nip o' Scotch while he waits in the limo.

Commitment: Yes

Location: Downtown

Situated in a converted pre-war Craftsman bungalow on a downtown corner that the urban world has overtaken, history alone almost dictates that you consider a Wee Kirk o' the Heather neon nuptial.

But do it quickly, as this place is giving way, if it hasn't already, to the new-and-should-be-improved Candlelight Wedding Chapel.

The cute and tiny chapel inside the house feels like a parlor, or perhaps more correctly, a cozy living room, since "parlor" connotes an excess of Tiffany lighting, lace, and velvet. The pews seat 16 and are white, simple, and have bows on the ends. The altar is likewise simple, surrounded by candles and nice (but artificial, of course) floral arrangements on tall columnar stands. The doors to the adjoining anteroom can be kept open for larger standing-room-only groups. At night, the exterior is twinkled with lights and the starburst atop the steeple reminds you where you are. Wee Kirk is not elaborate, fancy, cluttered, stuffy, musty, or perfectly modern. It is what it is—a commendable quaint Las Vegas wedding chapel that opened way back in 1940.

The name is Scottish, which according to my research translates to "little chapel of the small-flowered shrub," but the folks at Wee Kirk say they are the "little chapel of lucky flowers." Hmm ... luck ... marriage ... Vegas. Coincidence?

I DO ... TOO 4

CRAP TABLES AND A FATHER'S SHOTGUN: CASINO WEDDINGS

Las Vegas wedding chapels have been around, at least in the form held up as the "standard," since the early 1940s, two of which are still going strong. You know the type: a small chapel with a façade like a church and, failing that, at least lace on the windows, red velvet on the seats, and a five-minute speech that renders you wife and husband. Over time, more and more chapels started to pop up, although it wasn't until the mid-1960s that a chapel appeared as part of one of the new themed big-for-that-time hotels and casinos.

The honor of being the first went to Circus Circus. (And although the original chapel is no longer around, you still can get hitched in the hotel that first introduced kids and corn to Sin City.)

Having a chapel is now almost mandatory, and in the land of the megaresorts, from Mandalay Bay to Wynn Las Vegas, only New York-New York, Bally's, Harrah's, and Mirage don't offer wedding services. The hotel-casino chapel game is dichotomously both very similar to and wholly distinct from what's played at the independent chapels around town. It's similar in that you can find all the cherubs and pink your heart desires. You can keep it simple with a small bouquet, one boutonnière, two "I dos," and a kiss. Elvis can officiate. The price can be kept in the low three-figures.

But if that's not quite the neon nuptial you want to look back upon, the resorts are the places that can *deliver*, from sailing ships, thrill rides, and a soaring atrium with mountains and streams to a luxurious garden within the courtyard of a Tuscan villa.

Reviewed in this chapter are 26 resorts that offer weddings and renewals (without requiring a reception). Most are along the

THE TOP 10 THINGS TO KNOW ...

1. Money Is Important. *But so is your wedding. Unless you truly want to make it nothing more than legal at a rock-bottom price, seriously consider the big or little things that would make your special day special for you ... without causing dire financial consequences. By the same token, don't be upsold on stuff you don't want or need.*

2. Money Is Important, Part II. *Know what you're getting before you get it. For instance, the school-cafeteria mystery-meat equivalent in the Las Vegas wedding industry is the minister's fee. Will you need to dig for 50 bucks to tip the "free" minister right after you say "I do"? Fully comprehend what's in your nuptial package and get it all in writing.*

3. Beauty Is in the Eye of the Beholder. *The vast majority of neon newlyweds take the plunge without seeing their love palace beforehand. This puts them at the mercy of what's depicted on chapel Web sites and brochures and what they hear secondhand. (On the other hand, I've had cyber chats with brides married in some of the ugliest, filthiest chapels in town and they thought they'd witnessed Eden. Love is blind, indeed.) Luckily, you now have this book. I have neither an axe to grind nor a stake in any chapel, so I call 'em like I see 'em.*

4. This Is a Service Industry? *I was dumbstruck that some chapel folks had to be prodded and prodded and prodded to answer even the most basic questions. You know, real subversive stuff like, "How many weddings do you perform?" or "Can I get that in Spanish?" Some never responded. I tried every approach: from pretending to be a guy helping his fiancée pick a wedding site to admitting that I was a journalist who had some follow-up questions after an anonymous visit. I even used my wife's e-mail identity to pose questions as a prospective bride. Like I said: This is a service industry? Luckily for you, such behavior is the exception, not the rule, and the most egregious offenders are identified in the chapel reviews—and elsewhere—as are those who run too fast and loose with Web and brochure photos.*

5. Tick-Tock. *All weddings are orchestrated, whether back home in your church or with two Klingons in Vegas. The pace with the latter,*

Strip, a few are scattered about the valley, and one is downtown. Although not all hotel-casinos have chapels, most do—some with multiple venues, both inside and out ... and a host of iterations of the neon-nuptial experience awaits.

... ABOUT A NEON NUPTIAL

however, will be more like the "Minute Waltz" than anything by Wagner. Thirty minutes is the standard block of time, with assembly/fidgeting around, service, and pics about evenly spaced. You can buy more chapel or photo time, but why? Unless you've chosen a service poolside at Bellagio or something similarly elaborate, you'll probably want to quickly get married, clear out the chapel for the next bride and groom, and hit Vegas.

6. This Is B-I-G Business. *Sure, there're a lot of hearts and cherubs on display, but the dollar is as important to the chapels as your happiness is to you. That's not an indictment (though some in the industry are decidedly despicable). It's a reminder, rather, that your neon nuptial is one of more than 100,000 performed annually; the wedding business is one of the Silver State's largest industries.*

7. Plan Ahead. *This goes for you and your guests. Las Vegas is a lot bigger than it looks on maps and TV shows and there are a whole lot of ways to get distracted. I almost missed the start of a friend's wedding at the JW Marriott because I was waiting for a handpay in the casino. No joke. Another time I had friends show up late for a get-together at New York-New York because they thought the little caricatured map in the entertainment magazine made it look like the resort was only a few-minute walk from the Venetian. So build some extra time into getting wherever you're going, whether by foot, car, cab, limo, bus, motorcycle, or monorail.*

8. Go Get That License. *There are times when the license bureau turns into a zoo, particularly on holidays and weekends. Download the form from the Internet as outlined in Chapter 2, fill it out at home, and when you hit town, go get your license as far in advance of your wedding as possible.*

9. Read the Whole Book. *You already bought it; you might as well get full benefit out of what's in it—which is the most in-depth and unbiased look at the crazy world of the Las Vegas wedding chapel and the neon nuptial.*

10. Enjoy. *'Nuff said.*

BELLAGIO
3600 Las Vegas Boulevard South
888/464-4436; 702/693-7700
www.bellagio.com

Kitsch Factor: 5	Las Vegas	Las Vegas	Las Vegas	Las Vegas	Las Vegas
If married on the terrace.					
Romance Quotient: 5	♥	♥	♥	♥	♥
Fresh Test: 5	SOAP	SOAP	SOAP	SOAP	SOAP
Comfy/Cozy Rating: 5	WELCOME	WELCOME	WELCOME	WELCOME	WELCOME

The *One* **Way to Go:** *Terrazza di Sogno* ... Terrace of Dreams.

In a Nutshell: Two gorgeous ornate chapels, perhaps the most eye-catching around, suitable for weddings of 30 and 130.

A WYNNER EVERY TIME ...
OR SO I ONLY CAN ASSUME

He turned a bingo hall into downtown's best resort, spawned new Vegas with the Mirage, changed the paradigm again with Treasure Island, then absolutely broke the mold with Bellagio. At press time, Steve Wynn's magnum opus is about to open—the coyly named Wynn Las Vegas.

The resort has two wedding chapels (or salons in Wynn parlance). One seats 65 and the other handles 120. A foyer fronts each salon, giving guests a place to mingle. An outdoor courtyard, the Primrose Court, is also available for pre- or post-ceremony functions. It's too early to tell what it's like inside—it's easier to pry a bucket of nickels from granny's hot little hands than it was getting pre-opening info out of Wynn's PR people—but I'll accept on faith that it will be opulent, tasteful, and wow-inducing; Wynn rarely screws up.

It'll be expensive too, as in five grand ... to start. But ceremonies are booked in two-hour blocks, so unlike Little Cherub's Assembly Line of Love Chapel, you won't be faced with a best-pal-for-15-minutes wedding coordinator shoving you out the door at minute 16.

Sometimes you get what you pay for.

The Wedding Salons at Wynn Las Vegas
www.wynnlasvegas.com
866/770-7116

Terrazza di Sogno upgrade—lakeside ceremony, the Eiffel Tower in the background, and a little something at the end that's just perfect; spectacular settings for photos around the lake, by the pool, or within the conservatory, where you'll doubtless upstage the garden's beauty. A double best-of selection.

Costs: $1,000 to $15,000 for wedding packages; $800 for a renewal. The Terrace of Dreams upgrade is an additional $1,800.

Yearly Weddings: 1,000

Hours: 10 a.m. to 7 p.m. Sunday through Thursday; 9 a.m. to midnight Friday and Saturday. (Office hours are 8 a.m. to 6 p.m. daily.)

Ceremonies: Non-religious, non-denominational Christian, Jewish.

Languages: Spanish, Italian, German, French, and Japanese based on availability of officiate.

Bride's Room: Two, with restrooms, in the chapel area; changing allowed.

Groom's Room: No

Commitment: Yes

Location: Center Strip.

As would be expected of the most beautiful resort along the Strip, Bellagio weddings are elegant romantic affairs. The resort's two chapels—prosaically named South and East, seating 130 and 30, respectively—are cast in gentle soothing tones of wheat, gold, peach, and green; draperies frame the altars and stained-glass windows; and Italian-made chandeliers radiate a warm glow. Located toward the back of the property within the hotel's banquet and meeting area, the chapels are isolated from the bustle of the casino, and the world just beyond those draped windows is Bellagio's Mediterranean villa-reminiscent pool and garden complex.

As an added touch, the foyer and assembly area is closed to the public during ceremonies—so you won't have nosey people like me poking around looking for a brochure—and the service plays on video monitors if the kids get restless or grandpa can't quite sit still after his great run of blackjack. And since only one chapel is in use at any time, you and the girls can access both bridal rooms if needed. All in all, these are gorgeous spaces that rank at the bottom for kitsch and at the top for romance.

A best-of selection, the *Terrazza di Sogno* (Terrace of Dreams) package is the ticket for those who want their nuptials to include a touch of elegance and a pure dose of Las Vegas, in an outdoor setting. The terrace is located off Via Bellagio, the resort's shopping promenade, and it features a two-tiered private balcony overlooking the lake, with Planet Hollywood and Paris Las Vegas beyond. If you're timid, it's a long walk out to the terrace, but once there, it's all yours. The happy couple gets the lower level and up to 34 guests can stand (literally) witness from above. Right after you both say "I do," the Fountains of Bellagio shoot skyward, accompanied by music, at your first kiss.

Day or night—I like the latter—that's hard to beat.

BOARDWALK
3750 Las Vegas Boulevard South
702/735-2400—resort; 702/730-3126—chapel
www.boardwalklv.com

Kitsch Factor: 2			
Romance Quotient: 2			
Fresh Test: 2.5			
Comfy/Cozy Rating: 1			
Chapels aren't cozy when they ignore people.			
The *One* Way to Go: I recommend the gazebo. Good thing, too, since it's the only option.			
In a Nutshell: Gazebo on the lawn near the pool of the ugly-duckling sibling of some of the Strip's biggest and brightest.			

Costs: $160 to $440; $195 renewal.
Yearly Weddings: The chapel proprietor refused to answer specific questions. (Hey, at least she called me back.) The resort's PR person ignored *multiple* fax and phone inquiries.
Hours: Let's see, the hours are ... did I mention that the PR person ignored multiple inquiries, both fax and phone?
Ceremonies: Non-religious, non-denominational Christian, Jewish.
Languages: See above.
Bride's room: See above.
Groom's room: See above.
Commitment: Yes
Location: South Strip.

If you want a legally binding frill-free low-cost outdoor wedding on the Strip, Boardwalk is your place. Weddings are held in a gazebo surrounded by a nice green lawn not far from the hotel's utilitarian pool area; seating is seemingly infinite, so bring in guests by the busload.

The Boardwalk, the former Holiday Inn with the Coney Island look, sits not far north of Monte Carlo. By virtue of adoptive parents, it's related to Bellagio, TI, and the other MGM MIRAGE properties. Any commonalities end there.

CAESARS PALACE
3570 Las Vegas Boulevard South
877/279-3334; 702/731-7422
www.caesars.com/Caesars/LasVegas

Kitsch Factor: Up to 5 *Las Vegas* *Las Vegas* *Las Vegas* *Las Vegas* *Las Vegas*	
The chapel's rather tame, though in a warm beautiful way.	
Romance Quotient: 5 ♥ ♥ ♥ ♥ ♥	
Fresh Test: 5 SOAP SOAP SOAP SOAP SOAP	
Comfy/Cozy Rating: 5 WELCOME WELCOME WELCOME WELCOME WELCOME	

The *One* **Way to Go:** Outside, at the new Roman Plaza at the corner of Flamingo and the Strip, with Caesar and Cleopatra attending and a few centurions for added effect.

In a Nutshell: Five outdoor venues—three in the Garden of Gods (pool and garden) complex and two Strip-side in the Roman Plaza—and a tasteful indoor chapel in the Palace Tower; package add-ons run from spa services to having the emperor and the Queen of the Nile in attendance during your vows; one of the best line-ups of restaurants, lounges, and entertainment venues in Las Vegas for assured good times before and after. The best of the best, overall.

If you've read the first chapter, you know this is my pick for the most representative and get-the-best-of-all-worlds wedding spot in Sin City. If you want a refined chapel wedding, come to Caesars. Poolside or in a garden, come to Caesars. Outside in a plaza by the liveliest intersection in Las Vegas, come to Caesars. Need a centurion or Julius himself tagging along (for the ceremony, not the honeymoon), come to Caesars. It's all at the Palace.

There are three venues within the Garden of the Gods, Caesars' pool and garden complex. The Intimate Garden seats up to 100 people and is very secluded. Ceremonies take place beneath a Roman-style temple and the area is lighted for night services. If you've ever eaten at Café Lago, the Intimate Garden is just outside the window at the rear of this surprisingly culinarily rich "café." The Terrazza Lawn accommodates 50 and it too features a little temple

Costs: $500 to "Look out, Daddy!" Okay, the high end's only $2,500, but that's before adding the Rainman Suite, eight limos, cases of Veuve Cliquot Champagne, and a host of Praetorian Guards in full regalia to precede you down the aisle.

Yearly Weddings: 1,400

Hours: 10 a.m. to 6 p.m. daily and till 7 p.m. on Saturday for ceremonies. The office is open from 9 a.m. to 6 p.m. Monday through Friday.

Ceremonies: Non-religious and non-denominational Christian; a Jewish service is offered as a standard package.

Languages: Rome controlled a good hunk of the world during its prime and you can still hear many tongues in today's version of the empire. Just kidding: Spanish and French, with other languages based on availability.

Bride's Room: Yes, but only in the chapel (not available for the outdoor venues).

Groom's Room: No, and not really necessary if he remembers to get up from the blackjack table in a timely manner.

Commitment: Yes

Location: Center Strip.

and lights. Although ringed with shrubs, this area is relatively open to the festivities around Caesars' active pools. Really big weddings, from 125 up to 1,000, are accommodated just off the south side of the main pool. The area is huge, with hardscape and lawn, Italian cypress, colonnades, and Romanesque treatments around the pools just beyond. Members of the wedding party are staged in a nearby cabana awaiting the grand entry.

The wedding chapel is located in the Palace Tower, which rises above the Garden of the Gods. Windows let in ample light, and as expected of Caesars and other high-end properties, the chapel's tawdry/gaudy rating is nonexistent. The chapel will seat 70 comfortably and includes a bride's waiting room—arrive ready to go—just off to the side.

Caesars' newest venues are at the front of the resort within the

Roman Plaza, an outdoor playground for dining, shopping, catching a performance within its open-air auditorium and as it turns out getting married. The plaza sits at the corner of Flamingo and the Strip, across from the Flamingo, Barbary Coast, Bally's, and Bellagio; not a bad address. A portion of the plaza is available for private

---

FIVE FOR ...

Attention: *Weddings are bizarre events. This doesn't mean that they're not fun or heart-warming; they are. But weddings aren't like anything else on the face of this planet. And you're in Vegas, for heaven's sake, so you'll have the typical spectacle of happy people bawling their eyes out and a white-leather-and-rhinestone-clad Elvis singing you down the aisle.*

In the interest of helping you get to that exact point in the cosmos with the minimal amount of potential disruption, here are five sure-fire Neon Nuptial tips for you, the groom.

1. It's her day. *That's not as bad as it sounds, or seems. But weddings are largely designed around and for women. The good thing is she picked you. Smile and go with the flow. (Nightfall's approaching ... wink.)*

2. I absolutely enraged a few friends by not having a traditional bachelor party, *especially one in particular, who felt I'd cheated him out of his birthright to get drunk, act stupid, and leer at scantily clad women. Terri and I planned a weekend getaway with friends and family instead. The guys had a little golf tourney, the ladies had a shower and lunch reception, and that night we hosted the gang at a cocktail party in our suite. The rest of the time, people did what they wanted to do—hung out, gambled (we were in Laughlin), caught the nightly comedy act, partied. It was killer.*

It worked perfectly for us, but it might not for you; it's what we wanted to do.

And that's the point I'm trying to get across. There are now two of you, even before it's legally binding, so be considerate of her needs and feelings. If going to a strip club really runs counter to her sentiments, if she really doesn't see the need for you to get away over the weekend for one "last" time, then really think about doing something else. You aren't losing your freedom; you're starting a great new adventure with your best

functions with up to 230 guests This is a lively active spot and a prime location for a wedding and years of great storytelling.

Whichever of the many venues you choose, at Caesars Palace you are empress and emperor. If you want your wedding to include a harpist or handmaidens in waiting, just pass down the edict.

... THE GUYS

friend and the woman you love. Why make your first step a misstep?

3. If she wants your input, decline. *If she asks again, decline. If there's a third request, she really means it, so participate. We planned every aspect of our wedding together, from invitations and menus to colors and flowers. If that sounds like a bore, just remember that you're having a neon nuptial, so the biggest decision you two face is choosing a chapel. Yes, you'll have to pick out some music and how many pictures you want, but Vegas chapel weddings are largely turnkey. So if she wants your opinion about a chapel or a hotel (whether it's the third request or the first), don't act like you don't give a rip. And whatever you do, make sure you let her know if there's anything you simply cannot go along with.*

4. The matrimonial act—*no, not that one—probably means more to her than you, so be considerate. If she really wants a fancy dress and for you not to look like you're watching Monday Night Football, don't give her any grief. She's going to get all fixed up, so make sure you tell her how pretty she is. Let her know how her eyes are sparkling. You'll want to do this stuff anyway—trust me—but we're guys and reminders of such things aren't without merit.*

5. Be prepared. *If everything's not prepaid, make sure you know how much you owe and have ready a form of payment accepted by the chapel. Depending on where you get married, you might need to tip the minister (you know, the all-inclusive package often excludes the "all" part). A typical gratuity is fifty bucks, but find out for sure before you're standing there fumbling around with the change in your pocket. Same for the limo driver, who needs to be toked, and $20 to $30 is the starting point. Make sure you have your license. Arriving early is preferable to late. Oh, and make sure you're sober too.*

That's it, Nuptials 101 for the Guys. And please remember one more thing: Your future mother-in-law is all-knowing, all-seeing. Accept that now and you'll have a much easier transition into your new life. Trust me. (I have two of them.)

CIRCUS CIRCUS—CHAPEL OF THE FOUNTAIN
2880 Las Vegas Boulevard South
800/634-6717; 702/794-3777
www.circuscircus.com

Kitsch Factor: 3	
Romance Quotient: 2.5	
Fresh Test: 3	
Comfy/Cozy Rating: 2	
The *One* Way to Go: In the Adventuredome (not on the regular menu, but available by special order).	
In a Nutshell: Reportedly Las Vegas' first wedding chapel in a hotel-casino, though the original venue no longer exists; seating for 50.	
Costs: $135 to $875; prices vary for Adventuredome ceremonies.	
Yearly Weddings: 2,400	
Hours: 10 a.m. to 6 p.m. Sunday through Thursday, till 8 p.m. Friday and Saturday; may vary seasonally.	
Ceremonies: Non-religious, non-denominational Christian and Jewish.	
Languages: English only.	
Bride's Room: One, changing only; restroom adjacent.	
Groom's Room: No	
Commitment: No	
Location: North Strip.	

Circus Circus, you know the place: trapeze artists performing over the table games, midway for the rugrats, under-the-big top décor *everywhere*, the nation's largest indoor amusement park, and out in front of it all, the biggest clown you'll ever see. Yet come time for a Circus Circus neon nuptial and the only big feet will be on the guys in the wedding party and the only bright-red noses the result of tears of joy.

Chapel of the Fountain is a classic Las Vegas love den. An anteroom leads to the chapel, with double glass doors inlaid with rose stems set within a peaked arch, providing a sense of transition. Inside, the pews—with seating for 50—are white, upholstered, and adorned with lace and greenery, and vine-like swags and silk-flower arrangements deliver a garden-like feel. Behind the altar sits a babbling fountain, from which the chapel derives its name; it's Vegasly cheesy. The chapel entrance is across from the buffet, up a flight of stairs. And although this frenetic, rabbit-warren-like casino teems with kids, the din dies down quickly upon ascent.

Circus Circus' wedding coordinators can also set you up with a nuptial inside the Adventuredome, the resort's five-acre indoor theme park. If you opt for an "I do" on the log ride or coaster, the this-is-Vegas (kitsch) factor surely will rise. Add some grease paint and a squirting boutonnière ... and it's through the roof.

EXCALIBUR—CANTERBURY WEDDING CHAPELS
3850 Las Vegas Boulevard South
800/811-4320; 702/597-7278
www.excaliburcasino.com

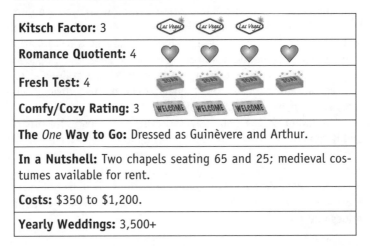

Kitsch Factor: 3	*Las Vegas*	*Las Vegas*	*Las Vegas*	
Romance Quotient: 4	♡	♡	♡	♥
Fresh Test: 4	SOAP	SOAP	SOAP	SOAP
Comfy/Cozy Rating: 3	WELCOME	WELCOME	WELCOME	
The *One* Way to Go: Dressed as Guinèvere and Arthur.				
In a Nutshell: Two chapels seating 65 and 25; medieval costumes available for rent.				
Costs: $350 to $1,200.				
Yearly Weddings: 3,500+				

Hours: 9 a.m. to 7 p.m. daily, till midnight on Saturday.
Ceremonies: Non-religious, non-denominational and sectarian Christian, Jewish; one of the few places that actively advertises that couples can bring in an outside (licensed) officiate of their choice.
Languages: Spanish interpreters are usually available; inquire about other languages; since couples can provide a minister of their choosing, they can tailor their language preferences too.
Bride's Room: Yes. The bride and one attendant can arrive 15 minutes prior to ceremony, ready to go. The bride's room includes a restroom.
Groom's Room: Nope.
Commitment: Yes
Location: South Strip.

Forget whatever preconceived notions you have about Excalibur—the massive white castle capped in red, blue, and gold turrets across the street from New York-New York—because the Canterbury Wedding Chapels are an oasis in a sea of some of the—let's be honest—worst décor in Las Vegas. It's okay, really, because you and your guy leave Merlin the Magician far behind when you step into the chapels' tasteful fireplace-warmed lobby and assembly area, then on to the chapels proper, where the look finishes the transformation from battlements, heraldic banners, and a color palette monopolized by the primary portion of the spectrum to classy stained glass, vaulted cathedralesque ceilings, chandeliers, burnished wood, and tans, soft greens, and light coral hues.

The larger of the two chapels is the more posh and ornate, and it can comfortably seat up to 65 in upholstered armchairs. The smaller chapel is just right for 20-25 in similar, although downsized, surroundings. If you caught the Camelot bug on the way in, period costumes are available for rent. And don't think you'll be going this route alone, as it's the add-on of choice for one-quarter of Excalibur's brides and grooms.

So what's with Excalibur's kitsch rating of three? Why isn't it higher? Even if you don the garb of 14th century nobility, it's just not that campy, because the chapels are so elegantly romantic. The cozy rating is attributable to the large number of weddings performed—the staff is friendly and accommodating, but 100+ weddings per day on the busiest days is really moving 'em in and out—and the route to the chapels, which is through the hotel's frenzied second-floor Medieval Village filled with shops, fast-food joints, kids, and kiddie activities.

FLAMINGO LAS VEGAS—FLAMINGO GARDEN CHAPEL
3555 Las Vegas Boulevard South
800/933-7993; 702/733-3232
www.caesars.com/Flamingo/LasVegas

Kitsch Factor: 4	Las Vegas Las Vegas Las Vegas Las Vegas
Romance Quotient: 4	♡ ♡ ♡ ♡
Fresh Test: 4	SOAP SOAP SOAP SOAP
Comfy/Cozy Rating: 4	WELCOME WELCOME WELCOME WELCOME

As with all outdoor weddings, you accept the consequences of onlookers, the weather, and, with the layout here, the potential for drunken frat boys.

The *One* Way to Go: Crescendo Package—poolside procession takes you behind a waterfall.

In a Nutshell: Octagonal indoor Garden Chapel accommodates 60 guests; four outdoor venues accommodating groups from eight to 125—poolside, Rose Trellis, Gazebo Chapel, and a semi-private lawn area; fun photo ops as the grounds are about as decked out in pools, foliage, meandering paths, and water features as any resort in town; and, of course, the Flamingo has habitats for the same-named birds and penguins; very friendly chapel folks.

Costs: $519 to $1700; $359 for renewal.
Yearly Weddings: 2,100
Hours: Summer—9 a.m. to 8 p.m. Monday through Friday, till 10 p.m. Saturday and 7 p.m. Sunday; winter—9 a.m. to 7 p.m. Sunday through Friday, till 9 p.m. Saturday.
Ceremonies: Non-religious, non-denominational Christian, Jewish.
Languages: Spanish
Bride's Room: Waiting rooms for the Gazebo and Garden chapels; West Lawn brides can wait in the nearby health spa.
Groom's Room: He looks like a penguin, so have him go chat them up for a while.
Commitment: No
Location: Center Strip.

The Flamingo is probably as famous for its lush grounds as its Mob beginnings. And while the wiseguys are gone, the greenery remains to tickle the fancy of brides and grooms. At 15 acres, the Flamingo's pool and garden complex is one of the largest and the most verdant in town. Waterfalls drop over rocky outcroppings and pines and palms soar skyward; penguins and flamingoes hang out in their own little habitats; pools glisten under the desert sun—and right in the middle sits the Flamingo Garden Chapel.

Four outdoor wedding sites and a traditional chapel are offered. The most relaxed setting is the Rose Trellis, set before the main chapel. The trellis is suitable for small services—likely no more than eight people—and it's only available Monday through Thursday. The West Lawn is a semi-secluded area, adjacent to the hotel and lined with trees, shrubs, and a white picket fence. Ceremonies are within a traditional gazebo, and if you're traveling with an entourage, this spot can accommodate up to 125 people. The third outdoor option is the Gazebo Chapel, a solid purpose-built structure capped with red tile, grown over in ivy, and backed by trees and shrubs. Up to 100 guests can be seated in folding chairs on the lawn before the chapel. The "Crescendo" wedding takes place within an alcove by the resort's Lagoon Pool. The bridal procession passes behind a waterfall and around a portion of the pool; how cool is that? Shy brides should note that the walk is relatively lengthy, and as the focal point, you'll be even more center stage than usual. This area also accommodates up to 100 guests and is used only during the off season—late October through the end of May. Lastly, there's the indoor octagonal Garden Chapel, capped by a star-shaped ceiling and chandelier. Fittingly, variations of pink and flesh tones prevail, although unlike so many places in town, it has an inviting comfortable feel, with tasteful permanent (artificial) floral arrangements standing in for the usual lace and cherubs.

All in all, this is a great place to get married; it's tidy and well-run and the staff is *very* friendly. If you choose an indoor wedding, the kitsch factor might only rate a three, but you still get the tropical surroundings and the wonderful spots for photos. That the Flamingo dropped a notch in the comfy rating stems solely from the fact that outdoor wedding venues are by nature somewhat public places and these are some of the most public in town. So, while the layout and coordinators do a great job of keeping spectators at bay, you can expect foot traffic and sound in the background. But it can't be that bad; otherwise the Flamingo wouldn't rate a *Neon Nuptial* Top 5.

FOUR SEASONS
3960 Las Vegas Boulevard South
702/632-5000
www.fourseasons.com/lasvegas

Kitsch Factor: 1					
Romance Quotient: 4	♥	♥	♥	♥	
Fresh Test: 5					
Comfy/Cozy Rating: 5	WELCOME	WELCOME	WELCOME	WELCOME	WELCOME
The *One* **Way to Go:** On the Fountain Terrace.					

In a Nutshell: Outdoor oasis-like setting seating 150; clubby indoor venue perfect for 90 or fewer guests; slightly smaller Desert Willow function room that dresses up as beautifully as any chapel; balcony ceremonies; standalone ceremonies cannot be booked at peak times, particularly Saturdays; kosher kitchen; AAA Five Diamond resort tucked away, but far from isolated, within the confines of Mandalay Bay.

Costs: All weddings are custom designed, starting at a base price of $3,000.

Yearly Weddings: 225

Hours: This is a full-service signature resort, so you just tell them when.

Ceremonies: Non-religious, non-denominational and sectarian Christian, Jewish.

Languages: If it's spoken in town, the Four Seasons will find it.

Bride's Room: Pre-function rooms available for bridal-party preparation and assembly.

Groom's Room: Same

Commitment: Yes

Location: South Strip.

The Four Seasons is within Mandalay Bay, but in a sense, it's a world away. Occupying five floors of the MBay tower, the resort's rooms are serviced by their own set of dedicated elevators. Although the resort has its own entry, valet, lobby, restaurants, and a guest-only pool, spa, and gym, Four Seasonians can also stroll over to the Mandalay Bay side of the house and crash its pool, as well as have access to all the bars, eats, and the like over there. The look here is much more subtle than Mandalay Bay's, a decidedly European spin on a tropical retreat, rather than unabashed temple and jungle. And the service is one notch above what's already some of the best in town; it *is* a Four Seasons.

The resort offers several wedding venues, the most requested

FLOWER OF POWER

A red rose signifies passionate love; white means purity. Yet a yellow chrysanthemum is the last thing you want to see in your groom's boutonnière; the flower's indicative of a secret admirer.

Or so it goes in flower lore.

Like most everything else associated with a wedding—and Las Vegas for that matter—flowers carry with them connotations that go back ... way way back. We might be more sophisticated and less superstitious in this wi-fi modern world; heck, it was the last century, no, the last millennium when we landed on the moon. But why take a chance with one of the most important days in your life?

The Society of American Florists has compiled a list (to which I've added a healthy dose of comments, some of which might even be a little facetious) of some popular flowers and blossoms, along with what they meant to our grandparents and great-grandparents—and indeed a lot of good folks here today. Following are some perfect neon-nuptial blooms and a few that are just good for a chuckle. For more, visit AboutFlowers.com.

The "Good"

Baby's Breath: Festivity	*Is that why it's in every bouquet?*
Calla Lily: Regal	*Every bride is a princess.*
Carnation (pink): Gratitude	*Thank you, indeed.*
Tulip (pink): Caring	*The heart of love.*

The "Bad"

Carnation (striped): Refusal	*Ring. License. Minister. No way.*
Lavender: Distrust	*You didn't make him sign a pre-nup, did you?*
Poppy: Consolation	*Consolation? Hah. You're at the altar, girl.*
Rhododendron: Beware	*Of Uncle Guido, if your guy's smart.*

The "Funny"

Bachelor Button: Anticipation	*Go ahead, make him wait.*
Begonia: Deep thoughts	*You see kids, he sees "hubba hubba."*
Lisianthus: Calming	*And what exactly is wrong with Prozac?*
Nasturtium: Patriotism	*That's all good, but this is Vegas, not D.C.*

What about my wedding? Terri and I went with alstroemeria (aspiring) of the amaryllis (dramatic) family.

Wow, that's deep, because "perfection" works nicely for both ... and our marriage.

being the outdoor Fountain Terrace and the Palm Room, seating groups up to 150 and 90, respectively. (The Fountain Terrace is the immediate view from the huge windows past the birds and aquarium in Mandalay Bay's reception area.) The terrace, flanked by statuary lizards and protected by a winged dragon, is a palm- and semi-tropical tree-shaded courtyard with a cascading fountain and azure tiles. No, it's not some role-playing fantasy game gone riotous or one of those faux leaded-glass love-chapel treatments with unicorns prancing through beds of tulips. Rather, Four Seasons' well-conceived grounds depict art and water working in harmony, while maintaining a taste of the Southeast Asian theme of the larger Mandalay Bay project. And it works, especially when the crew brings in the huge arbor that serves as your altar.

The Palm Room is just off the Four Seasons' lobby. Its cream walls have clean lines, etched with high arches and accented with amber sconces. Simple chandeliers hang from ceiling recesses and windows bring in light from the resort's porte-cochère. Class and coziness join forces here. The adjoining Palm Lounge can be brought into play for a reception. And although the 60-seat Desert Willow usually functions as meeting space, the resort's wedding magicians can cast a spell over it that sings sophistication and romance.

A number of other meeting and convention spaces are also available if you're going for a wedding and reception combo; my favorite is Mesquite, cloaked in plantation white, with inviting windows and a balcony overlooking the resorts' lush "backyard" that, luckily for you, can be used as the backdrop for a ceremony.

GREEK ISLES—PRINCESS AND LA DOLCE VITA CHAPELS
305 Convention Center Drive
800/823-3435; 702/967-0045
www.greekislesvegas.com

Kitsch Factor: 5	*Las Vegas*	*Las Vegas*	*Las Vegas*	*Las Vegas*	*Las Vegas*
Romance Quotient: 3	♥	♥	♥		
Fresh Test: 3	SOAP	SOAP	SOAP		
Comfy/Cozy Rating: 2.5	WELCOME	WELCOME	WEL		

The *One* Way to Go: Just finding this place is a pleasant surprise.

In a Nutshell: Very attractive, ornate chapels with seating capacities of 65 and 50; the usual off-site and adventure ceremonies; poolside gazebo weddings; although just steps from the Strip, not many tourists know about this place, but couples do ... or do they?

Costs: $199 to $2,200.

Yearly Weddings: 4,500

Hours: 7 a.m. to 8 p.m., or as needed, daily.

Ceremonies: Non-religious, non-denominational Christian, Jewish.

Languages: Spanish

Bride's Room: Down the hall; preferred that you arrive prepared.

Groom's Room: No

Commitment: No

Location: North Strip.

Greek Isles deserves a Hidden-Gem award for these two chapels. And anyone who actually finds the chapels gets the Odysseus Navigation Award. Ever since Debbie Reynolds took her name off the front and sold it to the World Wrestling Federation (in an attempt at operating a casino that paralleled the organization's prowess with professional football), this small hotel-casino (which is no longer owned by the WWF) hasn't exactly been anywhere near most Las Vegas visitors' radar screen. Admittedly, I'm quite dubious of the number of weddings claimed by the proprietor.

The Princess and La Dolce Vita chapels are wholly elaborate and ornate, yet not chintzy. Princess, the larger of the two, has a multi-paneled mural depicting an idyllic Mediterranean world and the nearly temple-like altar sits in front of a hand-painted veranda looking out to a perfect sea and sky watched over by trumpeting angels. This is high camp. Columns, a few candelabra, warm-colored tile flooring, fake ficus trees, and blond-wood armchairs (the ones along the aisle are adorned with bows) wrap it all up. La Dolce Vita is more post-Renaissance Italianate than Greco-Roman. The walls are monochromatic fleshy-rose with marshmallow-white wood accents. Twin columns at the altar give way to a painted portico shouldered by alcoves freshened with floral arrangements and more ficus. If anyone wants a lesson in how to do an over-the-top, fresco-happy, quintessentially Sin City chapel—and do it right—this is it.

The hotel itself is compact and dated, and the chapels aren't far from the casino. Yanni's Greek restaurant is only steps away and the Star Theater box office is literally next door. Expect some foot traffic when the nighttime shows kick off.

IMPERIAL PALACE—IMPERIAL PALACE WEDDING CHAPEL
3535 Las Vegas Boulevard South
866/228-0918; 702/697-8500
www.imperialpalace.com

Kitsch Factor: 2	🔶 🔶
Romance Quotient: 3	🤍 🤍 🤍
Fresh Test: 5	🧼 🧼 🧼 🧼 🧼
Comfy/Cozy Rating: 3	WELCOME WELCOME WELCOME
Although new, it's still inside Imperial Palace.	

The *One* **Way to Go:** Let your wallet dictate.
In a Nutshell: 15- and 100-seat chapels, basically brand new after a top-to-bottom much-needed makeover.
Costs: $300 to $1,800.
Yearly Weddings: Opened in 2004, so figures not yet available.
Hours: 10 a.m. to 6 p.m. daily.
Ceremonies: Non-religious, non-denominational Christian, Jewish.
Languages: Spanish; French using an interpreter.
Bride's Room: Yes; new, fresh, and with a restroom; changing only.
Groom's Room: No
Commitment: No
Location: Center Strip.

In 2004, Imperial Palace took control of its wedding chapels from a long-time contract operator and set about on a complete overhaul of the facility. And oh, what a difference an interior designer with an eye for aesthetics and new paint, carpeting, and fixtures can make; out with the burgundy and pink, tired carpeting, and torn wallpaper, and in with cream, wheat, and gold, clean lines, and (in the larger of the two chapels) a behind-the-altar big-screen-sized high-definition photograph of a garden or the Strip. (Future plans include the scanning of personal photos, allowing each couple to customize the "backdrop.") The second chapel seats 15 and replicates the classy new look, *sans* the photo thingy.

Nevertheless, this chapel is still within Imperial Palace, which is a little rundown and rather long in the tooth when compared with its neighbors on the Strip. And getting to the upstairs chapels requires a rather serpentine journey if you choose the wrong set of elevators: right, left, left, right, right, right, successive lefts, right, spin around twice, then just go 'round the corner when you hit the sports book. Yet if the top-to-bottom makeover of the chapel is any indication of changes in store elsewhere in this Asian-themed resort, then this vintage property might just rise from the ashes like a phoenix.

LAKE LAS VEGAS RESORT
RITZ-CARLTON LAKE LAS VEGAS
1610 Lake Las Vegas Parkway
702/567-4700
www.ritzcarlton.com/resorts/lake_las_vegas
www.lakelasvegas.com

HYATT REGENCY LAKE LAS VEGAS
101 MonteLago Boulevard
702/567-1234, extension 4421
www.lakelasvegas.hyatt.com
www.lakelasvegas.com

Kitsch Factor: 1	
Romance Quotient: 5	
Fresh Test: 5	
Comfy/Cozy Rating: 5	
The *One* Way to Go: Please, don't make me pick.	
In a Nutshell: Multiple gorgeous outdoor venues ... a *Neon Nuptial* chart topper.	
Costs: $1,000 to bring-along-every-charge–card-you-have rates.	
Yearly Weddings: Several hundred.	
Hours: Your wedding, you decide.	
Ceremonies: Whatever you wish.	
Languages: The United Nations of Las Vegas.	

Bride's Room: Varies depending on venue.
Groom's Room: Same
Commitment: Yes
Location: Henderson

Not too many neon newlyweds will make the journey to Lake Las Vegas to take the plunge, and that's unfortunate. The 320-acre man-made lake is the centerpiece of this master-planned high-end residential resort development located 17 miles east/southeast of the Strip, near Lake Mead. One of Las Vegas' finest and most exclusive and attractive developments, Lake Las Vegas brings together luxury living, fantastic golf, shopping, a wee spot of gambling, and two dynamite getaway resorts all oriented around the eponymous lake.

The Ritz-Carlton, Hyatt Regency, and the larger lake environs provide nearly a dozen of the most fetching outdoor wedding venues in greater Sin City. On the Ritz-Carlton side, you can get married poolside, lakeside, beachside, within the intimate Tuscany Courtyard, or surrounded by the exquisite Florentine Garden (Lake Las Vegas' outdoor equivalent to Bellagio's conservatory).

The Moorish/Moroccan-inspired Hyatt Regency offers two gorgeous spots for a neon nuptial. The Andalusian Gardens is a tiered grass amphitheater and gazebo overlooking the lake, gardens, arching palms, and Reflection Bay golf course. Lotus Court is a terrace behind the resort's beautiful step-down atrium where water flows through tiled pools and cascades over waterfalls, fireplaces take the chill off the cool desert evening air, and the lake laps gently below. (Reflection Bay Golf Club serves up one of the best courses anywhere and a private beach club for a toes-in-the-sand wedding, though it requires a reception.) If being on the water is Cupid's call, book either of the resorts' private yachts.

There is nothing cookie-cutter about a Lake Las Vegas wedding, and your imagination is the only limitation on ways to wed in this most alluring spot for an outdoor nuptial. Packages at the Ritz-Carlton begin at $3,500. The starting point is $1,000 at the Hyatt Regency, which doesn't include an officiate as you are free to bring in whomever you please (the resort will make recommendations on request). Both resorts are world-class hospitality providers,

so whatever you want—as long as it's legal—you largely can have
... for a price. Depending on the venue, seating accommodates
anywhere from a handful to hundreds of guests. The Hyatt Regency
offers changing facilities in the resort's Spa Moulay locker facilities
and accommodations are included in Ritz-Carlton nuptial packages,
so the prep thing is covered.

About half the ceremonies performed at Lake Las Vegas are
for out-of-town couples; considering the setting and the amenities, it can be a more easily accessible and affordable option over
traditional getaway destinations, like Hawaii, plus you can gamble
here. And although you can have only a ceremony, most brides
and grooms avail themselves of the resorts' and golf clubs' culinary
prowess, pairing a reception with the wedding. Receptions run
from Champagne and hors d'œuvres on a yacht to seven courses
and silver on the shore.

Lake Las Vegas is removed from the action of Glitter Gulch
and the Strip, a 30-minute drive away if all of Southern California
hasn't descended upon Las Vegas at once, gridlocking the road
system. So go ahead, make it a wed-and-stay getaway; it's a fun
and magical place.

LAS VEGAS HILTON—STAR TREK: THE EXPERIENCE
3000 Paradise Road
702/697-8750
www.startrekexp.com

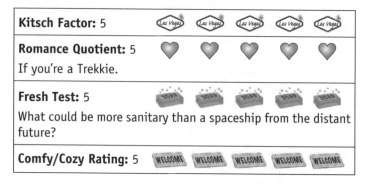

Kitsch Factor: 5					
Romance Quotient: 5 If you're a Trekkie.					
Fresh Test: 5 What could be more sanitary than a spaceship from the distant future?					
Comfy/Cozy Rating: 5					

The *One* Way to Go: The only way to go for diehard fans.
In a Nutshell: Ceremony on the bridge of a starship, with Star Fleet officer officiate and options for all sorts of extraterrestrials to attend; accommodates groups of five to 30. The setting and ratings are such that it should warrant a Top 5. But it's an attraction, not part of a larger theme like at TI or Sam's Town, and it's just too niche.
Costs: $500 to $3,000.
Yearly Weddings: 120
Hours: 11 a.m. to 11 p.m. daily.
Ceremonies: Non-religious, non-denominational Christian, Jewish.
Languages: Spanish, French, German, and Japanese; interpreters can be provided for other languages.
Bride's Room: No
Groom's Room: No
Commitment: Yes
Location: North Strip (one big block to the east on Paradise Road).

The ceremony is marked by truly high kitsch, perhaps more Hollywood or Orlando than Vegas, yet if you want Klingons and Ferengi attending, this is your ticket. Weddings take place on the "bridge" of the *U.S.S. Enterprise 1701-D*. Upper-tier packages add various numbers of other alien characters or additional Star Fleet officers if Klingon odor or Ferengi greed offends. Your wedding date is forever commemorated on a plaque in Quark's Bar & Restaurant, the spot for an out-of-this-world reception.

Fun stuff, just don't expect to hear Pachelbel or Mendelssohn playing when you walk down the aisle.

LUXOR—THE CHAPEL AT LUXOR
3900 Las Vegas Boulevard South
866/I-LUV-YOU; 702/730-LOVE
www.luxor.com

Kitsch Factor: 1	*(Las Vegas icon)*
Romance Quotient: 5	♡ ♡ ♡ ♡ ♡
Fresh Test: 5	*(soap icons ×5)*
Comfy/Cozy Rating: 4	*(Welcome icons ×4)*
The *One* Way to Go: Beautiful chapels, limited options; take your pick.	
In a Nutshell: Two chapels with capacities of 60 and 100, with few peers when it comes to décor, particularly as it pertains to its inviting assembly area; weddings are held simultaneously, although offset by 15 minutes.	
Costs: $625 to $1,400.	
Yearly Weddings: 1,500	
Hours: 9 a.m. to 7 p.m. daily; may change seasonally.	
Ceremonies: Non-religious, non-denominational Christian, Jewish.	
Languages: English only.	
Bride's Room: Two, very large, and each with restroom and full-length angled mirrors; changing only.	
Groom's Room: Two—yes, two—amply sized and with restrooms.	
Commitment: Yes	
Location: South Strip.	

Luxor is a late arrival to the marriage game; its two chapels opened in 2003. Nevertheless, having waited gives the pyramid people a leg up on a lot of the competition, because everything is new, the style is fresh and timely, and there's no hint of the typical

Las Vegas chapel lineage (cherubs, cotton-candy-pink walls, lace applied by the bolt, etc.).

The Chapel at Luxor is located on the mezzanine level of the resort, where you'll find quick eats and arcade-style attractions. Perhaps because there are several ways to get to this level—allowing you to avoid yard-long-margarita-hunting guests—the locale isn't overly jarring. And once behind the first set of doors, the rest of the world starts fading away.

Past the reception area, you'll find a stone-lined foyer that gives way to a come-hither hall with rich wood paneling, inlaid carpeting, and a vaulted ceiling. The hall leads to a massive waiting area with couches, seats, flower arrangements, inset ceiling, more paneling, and molding—its Great Hall appellation is deserved.

The larger of the two chapels is adjacent, with upholstered sidechairs for 100. The palette hues toward honey and gold, offset against the colors of the setting sun; soffit, wall, and chandelier lighting works with backlit "windows" for illumination; a semicircular draped canopy adorns the altar. The 60-seat chapel is closer to the entry foyer and replicates the ambience and look of the larger chapel.

Comfortable, attractive, tasteful ... a Top-5 selection.

MANDALAY BAY—CHAPEL BY THE BAY
3950 Las Vegas Boulevard South
877/632-7701; 702/632-7490
www.mandalaybay.com

Kitsch Factor: 1	Las Vegas
Romance Quotient: 4	♥ ♥ ♥ ♥
Fresh Test: 4.5	SOAP SOAP SOAP SOAP SOAP
Comfy/Cozy Rating: 4	WELCOME WELCOME WELCOME WELCOME

The *One* Way to Go: The most popular package, "Platinum Skies," is incidentally the most expensive.

In a Nutshell: Two identical 50-seat chapels that can be combined into a single chapel—for a $500 upcharge—if you're traveling with an entourage or just want extra room to roam; chapel is self-contained, oh so attractive, and sits on the edge of (yet is discreetly removed from) Mandalay Beach, the resort's massive pool complex.

Costs: $675 to $1,955.

Yearly Weddings: 2,400

Hours: 9 a.m. to 7 p.m. Sunday through Friday; till 10 p.m. Saturday.

Ceremonies: Non-religious, non-denominational Christian, Jewish.

Languages: English only.

Bride's Room: Huge, well appointed, and restroom equipped. You are strongly encouraged to come dressed and ready.

Groom's Room: Same as above, but not as large.

Commitment: No

Location: South Strip.

Mandalay Bay's Chapel by the Bay is a rarity for a casino chapel in that it sits off by itself in a dedicated building, the lines of which hint at the Southeast Asian roots of the property's overall theme. The chapel is set within a grove of trees beyond the statue-guarded Four Seasons pool and the entrance to Mandalay Beach, the spectacular pool complex. Nearing the chapel, a fountain sits before a walled enclosure and iron gates, which open to a courtyard and the chapel beyond. It's a bit of a walk.

Chapel by the Bay has two identical chapels, each suitable for a group of 50. The interior wall can be moved to create a single chapel for couples who have many attendants or just desire more space. Parallel sets of double doors lead from the main reception area down wide halls ending at the chapels' doors. The setup allows for an elegant and traditional procession. Natural light filters into the chapels through sheer-draped windows behind the altars and the

I DO ... TOO • 111

ceilings reach to sufficient heights to comfort any claustrophobe. Though you might see another wedding party on your way in and out, ceremonies are not held simultaneously.

Las Vegas has chapels that are more beautiful than Mandalay's, yet a good number of those come loaded with cheese. But the combination here—elegance, amenities, setting (even the long walk to the chapel isn't a detriment because it's so pretty), and service—makes for a great nuptial experience.

MGM GRAND—FOREVER GRAND WEDDING CHAPEL
3799 Las Vegas Boulevard South
800/646-5530; 702/891-7984
www.mgmgrand.com

Kitsch Factor: 1	
Romance Quotient: 5	
Fresh Test: 5	
Comfy/Cozy Rating: 5	

The *One* Way to Go: Any way you decide to go is the way to go in this classy facility.

In a Nutshell: Legacy Chapel for 50-55 guests, Cherish Chapel for 25-30; wedding packages named after movies; extremely inviting assembly area; poolside weddings are available, but they require a reception. My #1 pick.

Costs: $699, $899, and $1099; $499 for a renewal.

Yearly Weddings: 1,600

Hours: 11 a.m. to 5 p.m. Sunday through Thursday; till 8 p.m. Friday and Saturday.

Ceremonies: Non-religious, non-denominational Christian, Jewish, "New Age."

Languages: Spanish. Other languages depending on availability of interpreters.
Bride's Room: Two with full-length mirrors, restroom; changing allowed but dressing beforehand is preferred.
Groom's Room: Two with restrooms and, atypically, direct chapel access.
Commitment: Yes
Location: South Strip.

Forever Grand is a Top 5; in fact, it is the #1 selection for casino-based chapels. From the Moorish-style cathedral façade reminiscent of Seville to the supremely inviting assembly area cast in the streamlined art-deco moderne style made famous and chic by Hollywood in the '30s and '40s, this is one of *the* places to get married in Las Vegas. High ceilings, rich wood trim, bright floral arrangements, black-and-white photos of Hollywood greats, and scenes from the silver screen ... classy.

The Legacy and Cherish chapels are like finely finished screening rooms, a fitting arrangement with your guests comfortably seated in upholstered armchairs, arrayed so that they can catch the opening credits to the movie of your new life. Light wall treatments and floor coverings share the space with the wood accents of the foyer and a recess in the ceiling radiates soft reflective light accented by a single large chandelier. Whether you're booked into the 55-seat Legacy or the half-that-size Cherish, there's no trade-off between these chapels large and small, as the refined and welcoming look is shared.

MGM's wedding facility is set toward the back of Studio Walk, not far from the spa, which is a perfect get-me-away-from-it-all spot in the midst of Sin City's, and the world's, largest hotel. Studio Walk is a promenade of great eateries and shops that leads from the casino to the pool and concert/event venues, and you will take more than a few steps getting there. Yet when you pass through the glass-and-iron doors within that arch, stepping into a setting straight from Hollywood's greatest era, you might just feel like Rick and Ilsa—during their Paris days, of course—even if you've opted for the "An Affair to Remember" package and not the "Casablanca."

MONTE CARLO—THE WEDDING CHAPEL AT MONTE CARLO
3770 Las Vegas Boulevard South
800/822-8651; 702/730-7575
www.monte-carlo.com

Kitsch Factor: 2	(Las Vegas) (Las Vegas)
Romance Quotient: 3	♥ ♥ ♥
Fresh Test: 4	SOAP SOAP SOAP SOAP
Comfy/Cozy Rating: 3	WELCOME WELCOME WELCOME
The *One* Way to Go: It's a toss-up.	
In a Nutshell: Rather straightforward like the resort itself, the lone attractive chapel is free from excessive embellishment and performs the service it was designed to perform. Just steps away are the Monte Carlo's spa and salon, and André's, at the front of the casino, is one of the best restaurants in town (as discussed in Chapter 6).	
Costs: $375 to $1,350.	
Yearly Weddings: 1,900	
Hours: 10 a.m. to 6 p.m. Sunday through Thursday; till 7 p.m. Friday and 10 p.m. Saturday.	
Ceremonies: Non-religious, non-denominational Christian, Jewish.	
Languages: Spanish and Japanese.	
Bride's Room: Yes, with a restroom, although you must arrive dressed and ready to go.	
Groom's Room: No	
Commitment: Yes	
Location: South Strip.	

Monte Carlo has earned a reputation for offering a quality product, visual appeal, style without sensationalism, and a fair price. That same level of hospitality carries forward to weddings. The 95-

seat chapel is warm, with upholstered side chairs and a brighter look after a recent freshening that brought in new carpeting—sage colored with a pink floral contrast. Multiple pairs of French doors encircle the chapel and behind each are murals of vivid gardens, while silk floral arrangements and magnolias add some "natural" contrast, offsetting what is a low ceiling for a major Strip chapel. The staff is organized and friendly, which is essential, since Monte Carlo is extremely popular and has just a single chapel, forcing all nuptial traffic through one spot.

PARIS LAS VEGAS—THE WEDDING CHAPELS AT PARIS LAS VEGAS
3655 Las Vegas Boulevard South
877/650-5021; 702/946-4060
www.parislasvegas.com

Kitsch Factor: 2.5 & 5 Eiffel Tower	
Romance Quotient: 4	
Fresh Test: 5	
Comfy/Cozy Rating: 4	
The *One* **Way to Go:** *Mais oui! La Tour Eiffel, n'est-ce pas?*	
In a Nutshell: 100-guest Chapelle du Paradis (Paradise Chapel) and 25-guest Chapelle du Jardin (Garden Chapel); top-of-the-Eiffel Tower ceremony; two poolside options; musical accompaniment by pianist, acoustic guitarist, flautist, violinist, cellist, harpist, or, if your little heart desires, accordionist can be added to nearly all packages.	
Costs: $675 to $2,550, $8,200 for chapel ceremonies; $675, $1,695, and $1,995 poolside; $3,100 atop the Eiffel Tower.	
Yearly Weddings: 1,200	

Hours: 9 a.m. to 6 p.m. daily; closed Christmas and Thanksgiving.
Ceremonies: Non-religious, non-denominational Christian, Jewish.
Languages: Spanish and French; other languages pending availability of interpreters.
Bride's Room: Two, with restrooms, adjacent to the indoor chapels.
Groom's Room: No
Commitment: Yes
Location: South Strip.

Paris Las Vegas. The City of Light meets the City of Neon and the result is *très romantique*. Getting married here can bring you about as close as you can get—within a major hotel—to the Pink-and-Lace Palace look one expects of a Las Vegas chapel. Like the resort itself, which is rather ornate, festive, and fussed up just so, it works quite well.

The larger Chapelle du Paradis—for up to 100 guests—is adorned with gold-leaf on cream-white walls, crystal chandeliers, columns and draped alcoves, and a Paris-in-winter blue ceiling given over to cherubs and the heavens. Walk down this aisle and you can visualize Napoleon and Josephine seated in one of the wooden pews. The Chapelle du Jardin is done up in vivid murals offsetting dove-white pews with arched faux windows behind the altar. Suitable for 25, this facility has much more of the Vegas chapel look and feel than the grand Chapelle du Paradis.

"Poolside Petite" is a midweek package, which by Las Vegas' nuptial calendar means Monday through Thursday. Your ceremony takes place on the pool deck, though set back from the water, and depending on the time of day and month, you might be beneath the Eiffel Tower. The area is semi-private, with shrubs and flowers in raised beds and trees all about. The "Poolside at Paris" package moves you and your party of up to 20 guests poolside. Your ceremony will be held in front of one of the two cabanas included for the day. It's not particularly private, but if you've chosen this route, you probably already realized that.

But the *pièce de résistance*, if I can continue with my hackneyed French, is a morning or evening service—9:30 a.m. and dusk only—on the Eiffel Tower observation deck, 50 stories above the Las Vegas Strip. It's not cheap at $3,100, but what a way to go. The two of you, 12 guests, the guitarist, Bellagio down below on one side, Paris to the other, MGM Grand, Luxor, and Mandalay Bay to the south, Caesars Palace, Mirage, and TI to the north ... talk about memories. *Ooh la la!*

This is it, five-icon kitsch, and nearly a spot on the list of most quintessentially Sin City ways to get married. And the chapels? They're Vegas in a tasteful refined way, rating maybe a 2.5 on the Kitsch Scale.

PLANET HOLLYWOOD—PLANET HOLLYWOOD WEDDING CHAPEL
3667 Las Vegas Boulevard South
866/945-5933; 702/369-9053
www.aladdinweddingchapel.com

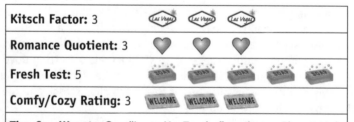

Kitsch Factor: 3				
Romance Quotient: 3				
Fresh Test: 5				
Comfy/Cozy Rating: 3				

The *One* Way to Go: "Love Me Tender" package. Planet Hollywood's far from the only place in town that can provide an Elvis impersonator, but this is the only hotel chapel that sits on the site where the King himself was married.

In a Nutshell: 50- and 12-seat chapels; traditional look yet neat and tidy; Elvis and Priscilla were married at the original Aladdin back in '67.

Costs: $399 to $2,699 (the popular "Elvis" package is a flat $999); renewal $379.
Yearly Weddings: 1,200
Hours: 8 a.m. to 8 p.m. Monday through Friday; till 10 p.m. or later (based on demand) Saturday and Sunday.
Ceremonies: Non-religious, non-denominational Christian, Jewish.
Languages: Spanish, Japanese, Chinese, German, French.
Bride's Room: Two, and they are small, so it's probably best to show up ready to go; restrooms are across the mezzanine.
Groom's Room: No (unless the other bride's room is not occupied by a waiting or departing bride).
Commitment: No
Location: South Strip.

If Planet Hollywood Wedding Chapel isn't ringing any bells, it's probably because the chapel and surrounding resort were until very recently known as the Aladdin. But, of course, that was not the same Aladdin that occupied this spot when Elvis took the plunge.

Planet Hollywood's two chapels are modern tidy renditions of the traditional Las Vegas wedding palace. The pews in the main chapel are gold-accented white, and faux ivy entwines columns framing the chapel's double doors; flesh tones, pinks, and mauve work well with the vivid colors of murals depicting idealized pastoral scenes and a pale-blue ceiling is dusted white with clouds. It's a Vegas chapel all the way, in the good sense of the phrase. This Archway of Love Chapel comfortably seats 50. A second 12-person chapel is not as ornate, and it has dark pews and the ubiquitous mural; the chapel feels tiny even for a group of that size.

Actually, the whole setting is somewhat compact. Office, reception, and wedding-planning functions take place in what's essentially the chapel foyer, and that's where you'll find your hideaway alcove (bride's room). And with people coming and going making wedding plans, it might feel somewhat like a beehive. On the flip side, the chapel has one of the best locations of any within a megaresort. You can get there without traipsing through the casino, the mezzanine level where it is located is open and spacious, and the resort's killer Elemis Spa—decked out in take-you-in Moroccan/Near East décor if the Planet Hollywood gurus don't muck up a good thing—is just down the corridor.

So you get a bit of "new" Las Vegas tossed in with the "old" and a chapel dappled in blue. Borrow some of the spirit of Elvis and the nuptial package is complete.

PLAZA—HERITAGE WEDDING CHAPEL
One Main Street
888/241-5000; 702/731-2400
www.heritagechapel.com

Kitsch Factor: 2	
Romance Quotient: 2	
Fresh Test: 2	
Comfy/Cozy Rating: 2	

The *One* Way to Go: "Veils & Vows" package ($569); hey, you get hitched and two nights in a petite suite for less than you'd pay for a quickie wedding at one of the Strip megaresorts.

In a Nutshell: Downtown's only casino-based chapel.

Costs: $189 to $899; $149 for a renewal.

Yearly Weddings: 800-900.

Hours: 9 a.m. to 5 p.m. Monday through Saturday; 1 p.m. to 4 p.m. Sunday.

Ceremonies: Non-religious, non-denominational, and Jewish.

Languages: Spanish, French, and German.

Bride's Room: No

Groom's Room: No	
Commitment: No	
Location: Downtown	

The Plaza has established a bit of a niche for itself by offering the only chapel in a downtown hotel-casino. Heritage Wedding Chapel is located on the hotel's second-floor landing near the famous Center Stage restaurant. The chapel seats 60, with space for an additional 40 in the foyer.

The foyer and chapel are carpeted in deep green, with mauve walls leading to white inside. The chapel is adorned with a white piano, several flower arrangements bracketing the altar, and a stained-glass window of green, gold, and white depicting lilies and intertwined ribbon. Ornamental circular white gates serve as the chapel doors. The chapel office is located in the foyer.

Like the Plaza, this is a rather straightforward what-you-see-is-what-you-get chapel that has a look and feel like many of the stand-alone chapels. If you desire a sense of isolation in your wedding, you might want to look elsewhere, because the chapel foyer serves as the crossing point from the first-floor casino to the third-floor bingo hall/convention area and is open to the third level.

RIO—THE WEDDING CHAPELS AT THE RIO
3700 W. Flamingo Road
888/746-5625; 702/777-7986
www.rioweddings.com

Kitsch Factor: 2	
Romance Quotient: 3.5	
Fresh Test: 5	
Comfy/Cozy Rating: 4	

The *One* Way to Go: Get the big chapel and throw open the curtains.
In a Nutshell: Gardenia, Roses, and Lily of the Valley chapels seating 50, 100, and 150, respectively; evening "beachside," 40th floor terrace, and golf club (Rio Secco) weddings; 10% discount to Total Reward members, Harrah's players club (Rio is owned by Harrah's).
Costs: $150 to $4,650; call for pool and golf club prices.
Yearly Weddings: 1,500
Hours: 10 a.m. to 6 p.m. Monday through Friday, till 9 p.m. Saturday; 11 a.m. to 6 p.m. Sunday.
Ceremonies: Non-religious, non-denominational Christian, Jewish.
Languages: Spanish
Bride's Room: Yes, with attached and detached restrooms; make-up, hair, and changing are A-okay.
Groom's Room: No
Commitment: Yes
Location: Center Strip (west of Interstate 15).

The Rio is the twin-towered red, blue, and purple resort about a half-mile west of Caesars on Flamingo. For more than 10 years, it has been a leading Sin City hotel-casino and decidedly one of the most popular, due to a long list of great restaurants, huge hotel rooms, nightlife, and a festive Mardi Gras theme.

The resort's three wedding chapels are tucked away on the third floor of the Masquerade Tower. Each is named after a flower, which figures subtly in the décor. Other than slight floral variations, the three share a similar aesthetic with green, olive, beige, and light-buff coloring, ivory brocade chair coverings, and the wall-to-wall floor-to-ceiling windows for which the Rio is justly famous. Flowing drapery keeps light and the world at bay, although the largest chapel is well set up to let the sunshine in. Being on the third level, the southward view is at about frond level of the palms that grace the front of the property. These facilities aren't chapels, per se, at least not in the pastel-mural-lace-gobs-of-pink sense. Rather, they're nicely decorated rooms in which wedding ceremonies are held. Gardenia seats 50, Roses 100, and Lily 150. Sound from the Rio's Masquerade Show in the Sky aerial parade can be heard in the reception area, but not inside the chapels.

Several alternatives to the chapels are offered too. "Barefoot on the Beach" takes you poolside, sandy beach and all, in the evening. Or try the outdoor terrace atop the Masquerade Tower with a fetching 270-degree view that takes in the entirety of the Strip and much more. Another option is the Rio Secco Golf Club, also owned by Harrah's. The course—one Las Vegas' finest—is in Henderson, about 20 minutes south of the Strip, and the setting is gorgeous with emerald fairways laced between desert arroyos, tumbledown rocks, and native vegetation.

RIVIERA—RIVIERA ROYALE WEDDING CHAPEL
2901 Las Vegas Boulevard South
800/242-7322; 702/794-9494
www.rivierahotel.com

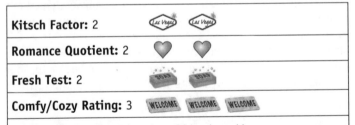

Kitsch Factor: 2	Las Vegas Las Vegas
Romance Quotient: 2	♥ ♥
Fresh Test: 2	BOAS BOAS
Comfy/Cozy Rating: 3	WELCOME WELCOME WELCOME

The *One* Way to Go: Take a lot of friends and have your ceremony up high with a view.

In a Nutshell: 50-person chapel; "fantasy" package featuring themed costumes—Elvis and showgirl, Superman and Superwoman, Rhett Butler and Scarlett O'Hara, and others; one of Las Vegas' historic hotel-casinos.

Costs: $179 to $975; $429 renewal.
Yearly Weddings: 1,200
Hours: 9 a.m. to 5 p.m. Sunday; 9 a.m. to 6 p.m. Monday; 8 a.m. to 8 p.m. Tuesday through Thursday; 9 a.m. to 8 p.m. Friday and Saturday; closing times may vary depending on traffic.
Ceremonies: Non-religious and non-denominational Christian.
Languages: English only.
Bride's Room: Yes, with restroom; come prepared, waiting only.
Groom's Room: Ditto
Commitment: Yes
Location: North Strip.

The Riviera's 50-person chapel is much like the hotel-casino that surrounds it—a reflection of classic Las Vegas, with a look and feel that resonates of another day and a historic style. Traditional colors of peach and burgundy are set against ivory and cream. A white baby-grand piano sits off to one side for the high-end packages that include a pianist instead of recorded music. Draped false windows on either side of the altar "look out" over purple mountains under a similarly hued sky. The chapel shows wear and tear, with some cracked floor tiles and scuffed pews, costing the Riviera a few notches in the fresh-test rating. Larger groups can book a top-floor ballroom that delivers a dynamite westward view; call for pricing.

SAM'S TOWN—MYSTIC FALLS PARK
5111 Boulder Highway
702/456-7777
www.samstown.com

Kitsch Factor: 5	
Romance Quotient: 4	
Fresh Test: 5	
Comfy/Cozy Rating: 4	
Depends on your nerves.	
The *One* Way to Go: Is the only way to go ... overlooking the atrium.	
In a Nutshell: Weddings are held on a second-floor balcony overlooking Sam's Town's indoor Mystic Falls Park. The terrace accommodates up to 100 guests.	
Costs: $350, $450, and $600.	
Yearly Weddings: 48—yep, 48—making this Las Vegas' best-kept wedding secret.	
Hours: There's no chapel office, per se, but ceremonies can be performed from 9 a.m. to 11:30 p.m.	
Ceremonies: Non-religious and non-denominational Christian; a rabbi can be provided.	
Languages: English only.	
Bride's Room: No, you need to show up ready to go, which won't be a problem if you're staying there.	
Groom's Room: Ditto. Hey, we're guys, how much prep space do we need?	
Commitment: No	
Location: Boulder Highway.	

Sam's Town keeps it simple—two wedding packages and three prices (basic midweek, basic weekend, upgraded any-day combo that includes some flowers and a suite for the night). Sam's also tosses in a perfectly Vegas *Neon Nuptial*-recognized setting: Mystic Falls Park. The "park" is an atrium rising 10 stories over more than a half-acre of trees, streams, and waterfalls, cobbled walkways, plank-and-split-log bridges, and animatronic mountain critters—raptors and other birds, plus wolves and a bear.

Weddings are performed on a second-floor deck overlooking the park, with seating for 100 folks. The deck is accessed via the casino floor, and although the separating wall is open on both ends, once the curtains are drawn, you'll forget all about spinning reels. The park itself is like something you'd expect at a top-flight amusement park. By day the sunlight pours through the glass ceiling and by night gazillions of twinkle lights blink hello. Four times each day, the Sunset Stampede rolls through with laser animation, dancing fountains, and a rousing orchestral soundtrack, but never during your wedding.

This is a great place to get hitched. It's public by virtue of people milling about in the park below and the casino just steps away, but if you're *that* shy, why marry in Las Vegas? The setting is fun, attractive, and romantic in a kitschy Sierra Nevada/Gold Rush theme-park kind of way. Some might find the Old West/mountain look, waterfalls, and nattering birds too campy or distracting. I think it's an arrow in the heart.

STRATOSPHERE—CHAPEL IN THE CLOUDS
2000 Las Vegas Boulevard South
800/789-9436; 702/383-4777
www.stratospherehotel.com

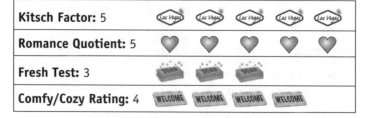

Kitsch Factor: 5	Las Vegas	Las Vegas	Las Vegas	Las Vegas	Las Vegas
Romance Quotient: 5	♥	♥	♥	♥	♥
Fresh Test: 3	SOAP	SOAP	SOAP		
Comfy/Cozy Rating: 4	WELCOME	WELCOME	WELCOME	WELCOME	

The *One* Way to Go: Does it really matter when you have such a view?

In a Nutshell: Terrace and Garden chapels on the 103rd floor of the Stratosphere Tower (seating 90 and 18, respectively); stand-up 10-guest ceremonies on the 108th floor observation deck; tower-topping thrill rides that have been the scene of more than a few weddings; outdoor patio at the base of the tower.

Costs: $199 to $2,799.

Yearly Weddings: 500

Hours: Ceremonies can be performed pretty much whenever you want to wed, except in the wee wee hours of the morn. The office is open 9 a.m. to 5 p.m. Sunday through Friday, and till 6 p.m. Saturday.

Ceremonies: Non-religious, non-denominational Christian and Jewish.

Languages: Spanish; other languages based on availability of interpreters.

Bride's Room: Yes, with a restroom; changing and final prep only.

Groom's Room: It's an equal-opportunity casino, so he gets a restroom too.

Commitment: Yes

Location: North Strip.

Chapel in the Clouds indeed. When you get married here, you do so more than 800 feet above ground, with valley's-edge views to the east from the 90-seat Terrace Chapel and to the west from the 18-seat Garden Chapel. Take the plunge at night and, phew, talk about your neon nuptial: There simply isn't a more romantic view in town.

Both chapels are colored off-white, with wood paneling, crown molding, sconces, and a mural backing the altar for a fairly elegant far-from-cherubic look and feel. And of course, those windows deliver the view that qualifies the Stratosphere for a Top-5 listing.

If your needs are less formal and your party smaller, you can say your vows on the tower's observation deck on the 108th floor. Or if you're feeling particularly daring and want your butterflies to flutter even more, three thrill rides on the rooftop—that's about 900 feet up—can be tied into a ceremony. (And although not the focus of this book, the Stratosphere's reception areas and the Top of the World restaurant offer sky-high dining and reception options as well.) For big groups or if your guy has acrophobia, a new patio outside, at the base of the tower, is suitable for a theater-style wedding with 125 guests.

This is perfect Vegas kitsch—an amazingly Cupid-, theme-, and Elvis-free kitsch—and high romance all rolled into one.

TEXAS STATION—THE WEDDING CHAPELS AT TEXAS STATION
2101 Texas Star Road
800/654-8804; 702/631-8268
www.texasstation.com

Kitsch Factor: 1	
Romance Quotient: 4	
Fresh Test: 5	
Comfy/Cozy Rating: 5	
The *One* Way to Go: Doesn't matter, 'cause you get the same gorgeous chapel.	
In a Nutshell: Two 100-seat chapels that can be combined into a single Texas-sized chapel; classy Southwestern styling; bowling, movies, and Kids Quest (where you can deposit the little ones if they get too rambunctious). A *Neon Nuptial* Best-Of.	
Costs: $225 to $1,600.	
Yearly Weddings: 150	

Hours: 9 a.m. to 7 p.m. daily.
Ceremonies: Non-religious, non-denominational Christian, Jewish.
Languages: English only; will work to find language-specific officiates, or you can bring in one of your choosing.
Bride's Room: Large and comfy with a restroom; changing allowed.
Groom's Room: Nearly identical.
Commitment: Yes
Location: Rancho Strip.

I absolutely love the feel of this chapel, as does my wife. Forget the oil derrick in front of the resort and the boot-and-spur look that holds sway in the casino. Texas Station's convention area, where the Jasmine and Magnolia chapels are located, is subtly ranch, yet a ranch without any pretext of the word "dude" in it. Think Scottsdale, not Dallas.

The identical chapels are decorated with Southwestern-style chandeliers hanging beneath high 15-foot ceilings and chestnut-hued wood accents and trim. There's a hint of light desert rose in the carpeting and the altar is a raised platform backed by draperies and a post-and-beam framed alcove within which sits a floral arrangement. Each chapel seats 100, and in a setup like Mandalay Bay's, the two can be combined into one, Amaryllis, for a Lone Star State-sized ceremony. Each of you gets a large well-appointed dressing area, leading to a wonderful anteroom in which your guests can assemble and mingle or perhaps enjoy sparkling wine service prior to your entry through double wood-and-glass doors. It is, in essence, a convention space, but it works, enough so that it made the best-of list.

Since it's owned by Station Casinos, one of the gaming corporations that caters to local residents, Texas Station also offers movie theaters, a bowling alley, and a supervised childcare center for the little ones if needed.

TI—THE WEDDING CHAPELS AT TREASURE ISLAND
3300 Las Vegas Boulevard South
888/818-0999; 702/894-7111
www.treasureisland.com

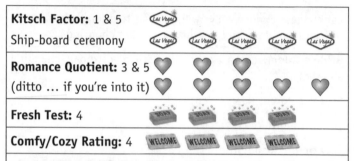

Kitsch Factor: 1 & 5 Ship-board ceremony	
Romance Quotient: 3 & 5 (ditto … if you're into it)	
Fresh Test: 4	
Comfy/Cozy Rating: 4	
The *One* Way to Go: The "Enchantment" wedding.	
In a Nutshell: 65-seat chapel; poolside ceremonies; "Enchantment" takes place on the Sirens' ship, *Song*, in the resort-fronting bay, and it's a neon nuptial *numero uno*.	
Costs: $499 to $2,999.	
Yearly Weddings: 2,000	
Hours: 10 a.m. to 7 p.m. Sunday through Thursday; 9 a.m. to 10 p.m. Friday and Saturday; phone information available from 8 a.m. to 6 p.m. daily; all hours subject to change.	
Ceremonies: Non-religious, non-denominational Christian and Jewish.	
Languages: Other languages available based on availability of trained personnel.	
Bride's Room: Two, with restrooms; having hair and make-up done is preferred.	
Groom's Room: No	
Commitment: Yes	
Location: Center Strip.	

TI, the resort formerly known as Treasure Island (although that name is still on the building), offers the ultimate neon nuptial—a ceremony on the *Song*, the ethereal white ship floating in Sirens' Cove, the faux harbor that sits but a few lengths of boardwalk from Las Vegas Boulevard. You, your guy, an officiate dressed up like a pirate, scalawags descending from the crow's nest to present your rings, guests arrayed along a Caribbean seaport wharf ... how could anything be more Vegas? In fact, no other ceremony or wedding site is, which is why this is #1. Any jokes here about walking the plank have more than a smattering of truth.

If you'd prefer an outdoor wedding spread with a little less symbolism and cheese, TI's Oasis package takes you out back near the pool, where you walk through a white trellis to a white altar in a small white gazebo, with tropical vegetation and swaying palms above as an accompaniment. Set back from the pool and separated by a fabric curtain, the Oasis setting is more private than the on-Strip Sirens' Cove, though Terrace Café diners and people in the resort's beautiful foyer will have a peek. This package, like Enchantment aboard the *Song*, is only available at 10:30 a.m. and 12:30 p.m., before the temperature, the atmosphere, and the sun worshippers get too overheated.

An indoor chapel seats 65 in a color scheme of gold and terracotta accented with green, with white pews and wood trim and the glow of shaded iron floor lamps. A second chapel is used for photographs and the chapel lobby offers extra seating and monitors for larger groups.

From the subdued warm chapel to palms and on to the lapping waves of Sirens' Cove, TI has the kitsch scale covered and an environment ranging from romantic to rousing.

TROPICANA—ISLAND WEDDING CHAPEL
3801 Las Vegas Boulevard South
800/325-5839; 702/798-3778
www.tropicanachapel.com

Kitsch Factor: 5	Las Vegas Las Vegas Las Vegas Las Vegas Las Vegas
Romance Quotient: 4	♥ ♥ ♥ ♥
Fresh Test: 3	SOAP SOAP SOAP
Comfy/Cozy Rating: 3	WELCOME WELCOME WELCOME
The *One* **Way to Go:** I like outdoor weddings and this is a great spot for an outdoor wedding, but the Island Chapel is "the bomb."	
In a Nutshell: You can get married in a garden, on a bridge, beside a waterfall, in a gazebo, in a Polynesian-style lodge, or off-site at Red Rock Canyon.	
Costs: $99 (Internet special) to $3,499; renewal $349.	
Yearly Weddings: 2,000	
Hours: 8 a.m. to midnight daily (office); weddings available around-the-clock.	
Ceremonies: Non-religious, non-denominational Christian, Jewish.	
Languages: Spanish, French, German, Chinese, and Japanese.	
Bride's Room: One in the chapel office next to the chapel; restroom in the hotel.	
Groom's Room: No	
Commitment: No	
Location: South Strip.	

Who knows what's going to happen to the Trop, so if you want one of Las Vegas' historic neon-nuptial experiences, strike now before the resort disappears ... if it does. Rumors have been circulating for several years that the historic Tropicana is going to be razed and rebuilt, seriously remodeled, slightly tweaked, or left as is. Whatever happens, hope the powers that be keep the Island Wedding Chapel.

Located in the center of this sprawling property, elevated above the meandering pool complex that was years ahead of its time, the Island Chapel is a taste of Polynesia brought to the corner of Tropicana and the Strip. The peaked-roof chapel—I think of it as a Polynesian lodge—has plank flooring and mat ceiling coverings, rotary fans beneath the open beams, and bamboo and a rock wall at the altar. It's Disney's crazy attraction without the talking tikis and spastic birds. Windows encircle the chapel that easily seats up to 100 in wooden pews. Ceremonies are also held at a gazebo that overlooks the pool, and the large "island" grounds support a bounty of water features and flora, all of which can be pressed into service for an outdoor wedding with a tropics-come-to-the-desert flair.

And don't miss a photo op with the skyline of Manhattan rising in the background; it's almost better than the total lack of pink, lace, or joyfully fat smiling little cherubs in the place.

THE VENETIAN
3355 Las Vegas Boulevard South
866/548-1807; 702/414-1000
www.venetianweddings.com

Kitsch Factor: 1 & 5	Las Vegas				
Gondola	Las Vegas	Las Vegas	Las Vegas	Las Vegas	Las Vegas
Romance Quotient: 5	♥	♥	♥	♥	♥
Fresh Test: 5	SOAP	SOAP	SOAP	SOAP	SOAP
Comfy/Cozy Rating: 4	WELCOME	WELCOME	WELCOME	WELCOME	

The *One* Way to Go: *Cerimonia Sul' Aqua* ... Ceremony on Water, performed in a gondola.

In a Nutshell: Three-part wedding chapel in Venezia tower; ceremonies overlooking the pool-and-garden courtyard, or indoors in a gondola or on a bridge of the Grand Canal.
Costs: $650 to $4,500.
Yearly Weddings: 1,700
Hours: Office open daily from 9 a.m. to 5 p.m.; ceremonies also performed after 5 p.m.
Ceremonies: Non-religious, non-denominational Christian, Jewish.
Languages: English only.
Bride's Room: Two bridal chambers for assembly/waiting, not dressing.
Groom's Room: Have him hang in the sports book.
Commitment: No
Location: Center Strip.

With St. Mark's Square, the Grand Canal, Camponile Tower, and the Doges' Palace, as noted later in this book, the Venetian just might have taken the concept of Las Vegas as Themeville to its greatest extreme. If you'd like a taste of this cultured camp in your wedding, your search should begin and end with Cerimonia Sul' Aqua, or the Ceremony on Water.

A signature neon nuptial, Cerimonia Sul' Aqua puts the two of you, one officiate, and one witness in a special white-and-gold gondola for a trip along the Grand Canal, a quarter-mile-long indoor waterway that, unlike the canal in the real Venice, runs clean and crystal clear; talk about a unique way to get down the aisle. As the canal wends it way through the resort's Grand Canal Shoppes, a shopping promenade dressed up in Venetian architectural finery, this is about as public a wedding as you'll find anywhere, allowing your family members to race ahead to snap the perfect photo of you lovebirds as you glide along; not only is this the Venetian's lowest-priced wedding, it is, not surprisingly, by far its most popular.

If the canal's the ticket, but you don't want to be out on the water, choose "Bridge Over the Square." As the name implies, your ceremony is on one of the bridges over the canal at St. Mark's Square, with seating for 10 and upright space for 40 more.

Traditionalists can opt for the Venezia tower's wedding chapel, a gorgeous salon that can accommodate groups of 50, 100, or 150 through the use of removable walls that, when in place, give the appearance of being the real McCoy. The chapel is located on the main level of Venezia, which is actually the 10th floor, as this newish tower was constructed atop the resort's parking garage. The chapel looks out over Venezia's courtyard pool and gardens, with Bouchon—a bistro owned by acclaimed Napa Valley restaurateur and chef Thomas Keller—on the far end. It's an inviting, even serene, setting and an altogether different experience than that along the canal.

HONEYMOON ...
IN VEGAS   5

GOOD BETS IN BEDS

Las Vegas offers more than 130,000 hotel rooms, about one for every marriage license issued annually; it's probably a good thing neon newlyweds don't all show up on the same night. Whatever type of accommodation you desire, you can find it in Sin City, and often for considerably less than you'd pay in other must-see vacation destinations around the world. Seemingly every national chain is represented, as are most of the top dogs in high-end hospitality, but given that this is your wedding and honeymoon, I'm going to skip right over the familiar names you see along the interstate and get right to where you want to be—places like Caesars Palace, Bellagio, Mandalay Bay, and the like. Along with the big guns in town, I suggest a few spots with which you might not be as familiar, although making their acquaintance should prove quite enjoyable. (And as this is the Excess Capital of the World, if you're looking for a little romantic getaway spot, Las Vegas' definition of a "boutique inn" isn't a place with a dozen rooms; try 600, even 3,000.)

Reviewed below are 12 hotels (at 10 resorts—there are actually three hotels within the confines of Mandalay Bay) that suit a neon nuptial as easily and naturally as Las Vegas wears glitz. The resorts all share attributes beyond Blazing 7s slot machines and whirling roulette wheels, as in: at least above-average accommodations, meaning bigger rooms and nicer amenities; appealing, even visually stunning, public spaces; a ton of things to do on site—from pools and lounges to restaurants and spas; great reputations and service to match; and an air and vibrancy that make you coo, "Ooh, we're here," and not want to leave.

Don't be put off if your favorite spot's not highlighted. This listing is by nature limiting and highly personal. I'm confident you won't go wrong staying at any of these resorts, as I'm confident you'll have an exciting and memorable wedding if you stay most anywhere else. It's actually a testament to the depth of what Las Vegas offers that a number of splashy and classy properties aren't outlined below, as in the case of a personal fave, TI. Also, no consideration is given to the quality of the gambling or complimentaries at each resort. (Las Vegas is famous for "comps," the ostensibly free rooms, food, beverages, shows, and more that casinos bestow upon those who put in time at the tables or machines.) Again, it's your honeymoon and I've approached where to stay solely with an eye toward fun, nice digs, romance, and having a great time; that there just happens to be a casino downstairs is a bonus.

The selected resorts are drawn from the many sides of Las Vegas: the Strip, Glitter Gulch, out in the suburbs, and at the valley's edge where you'll find two new breeds of resorts. One of the two is a so-called locals casino, the kind of place that appeals to area residents because it offers easy accessibility, varied and often moderately priced eateries, a reputation for more player-friendly gambling, and as often as not, movie theaters, bowling, and childcare centers. Yet the locals casino selected for this chapter also caters to an upscale, maybe even hip, overnight clientele. The other breed is a type of destination retreat that will have you wondering upon arrival if you got on the wrong plane and ended up in Palm Springs by mistake.

THE STRIP

From Mandalay Bay to TI and the new Wynn Las Vegas, this is it, the heart of the action, the hype, and the buzz concentrated along a two-plus-mile stretch of Las Vegas Boulevard South. This is where visionaries Benjamin "Bugsy" Siegel, Jay Sarno, and Steve Wynn defined over the decades the various images of what made Las Vegas "Vegas," setting the stage for the gambling and glamour getaway destination we see today.

Most of the world's largest hotels are bunched together here, as are the highest concentrations of, among other things, gamblers, celebrity chefs, Cirque du Soleil productions, awestruck tourists, and more architectural larceny than the law would seem to allow. Whereas Glitter Gulch might be the Las Vegas of history and legend, the Strip is the Sin City of imagination realized.

Viva Las Vegas, indeed.

This is the Las Vegas of pirates, roller coasters, and pyramids, casinos as big as four football fields, nightclubs that only get going hours after the curfew with which you were once saddled, $100-a-plate meals, and limos stacked up as if every night is Oscar night; in short, the land of superlatives. Honeymoon here and you will play, party, and be pampered.

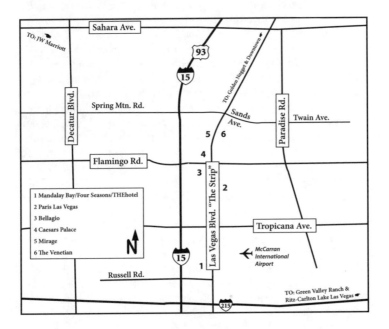

BELLAGIO

Bellagio sits back from the Strip behind an eight-acre lake, which laps at a Tuscan-styled village where you'll find some of America's most acclaimed restaurants ... and a beguiling spot for a wedding. A ballet of music, light, and 200-foot-tall fountains performs across the lake every afternoon and night. The lobby ceil-

GETTING INN

There are nearly as many ways to book a room in Las Vegas as there are surefire betting schemes "guaranteed" to make money. But at least when you book a room, you get a room. Outlined below are the most common ways to get in at an inn.

The mystical booking method is the infamous comp—the "free" or deeply discounted room that comes courtesy of the house based on your wagering history in the casino. If you have a relationship with a hotel-casino, then certainly check with the slot club or your host; for the majority of Las Vegas visitors, however, this is not an option.

The most typical way to book a room is directly with a hotel, either over the phone or through the Internet. Forget for the moment whatever aversion you have to paying rack rate. Room prices in Sin City are extremely volatile, so if Caesars Palace sounds exceedingly expensive when you call today, check back tomorrow, next week, or next month. (As a general rule of thumb, prices are highest far in advance and the days or weeks immediately preceding a particular arrival date. And obviously, prices will be higher on holidays, weekends, and during big conventions, concerts, and sporting events.) Furthermore, you usually can get a better room for less money in Las Vegas than in any other sought-after resort destination; those tables of felt and the spinning reels go a long way toward subsidizing all the Three, Four, and Five Diamond hotels along the Strip and spread out across the valley. Ask about AAA and military discounts, if applicable. A few places offer discounted rates for government employees.

If you aren't 'Net averse, consider booking online. Direct Web bookings often save you money over phone-in rates because hotels save on labor costs. And some have a low-price guarantee whereby they will beat any legitimate rate from a third party. (Speaking of the Internet, long before you head to Vegas, sign up on hotel-casino Web sites to receive e-offers; you'll be amazed at some of these deals, though the period in which to use them might be too restrictive.)

Peace of mind is the primary motive for booking directly with a hotel, and you can cancel up to 48 hours (typically) before arrival without penalty, affording you the opportunity to shop around for better offers in the meantime. And if you plan to gamble, a casino host might be able to absolve some or all of your room and related costs, but this will not be possible if you book through a third party.

If you're traveling with an entourage, consider booking through a hotel sales department. I have planned a number of Las Vegas get-togethers in this way, typically saving money and time. Most group sales departments require a minimum of 10 or 20 rooms and you might have to sign a contract guaranteeing to fill a certain number. The advantages here are better-than-rack rates, a sense of security knowing your friends and family can find a nice place to bunk, and you as the organizer might end up with a free, discounted, or upgraded room. It's not that intimidating; just make sure you have a good handle on the number of rooms you can reasonably fill and read everything before forking over a credit card for a hold or signing a contract.

Internet booking through a discounter—Expedia, Travelocity, etc.—is likely the best route to the lowest possible prices (excluding those hotels with meet-or-beat guarantees). The downsides are you're dealing with an absentee third-party, you will have more limitations on available hotels, and the cancellation or change provisions can be quite onerous. Again, don't be put off by any of this. Millions of rooms are booked this way and I'd say at least half my nights away from home are set up this way.

Another option is to try Travelaxe (http://www.travelaxe.com). Travelaxe isn't a discounter; rather, it searches most of the established online discounters, hunting for the best rates across properties that can be limited by name, price, or quality. The service is not infallible and on occasion it has returned too-good-to-be-true prices that indeed turned out that way when I've linked to the third-party site to book. In fact, as I'm writing this I'm running a Travelaxe search for an upcoming trip to Vegas. The initial search results returned a price of $56 per night for the Gold Coast, but when I linked to the reservation page, the lowest price available was $172 per night. Hmmm, that's a lot more than $56.

I know Travelaxe doesn't set or control third-party pricing, but it is frustrating when this problem comes up. And upon bringing this to the attention of Travelaxe, I've twice had my concerns met with what I considered a somewhat well-that's-the-way-it-is attitude. Nevertheless, I've been able to secure great rates using this service and I will continue to use Travelaxe for the valuable booking tool it can be.

As suggested above, there are other ways to find a place to stay in Las Vegas. For instance, if you're comfortable working with a travel agent or have had luck with a package provider, then have at it. The thing that matters most is that you get to Vegas with a room worthy of your wedding night awaiting you. Well, that and getting to the altar on time.

ing is planted with hundreds and hundreds of glass-impresario Dale Chihuly's hand-blown flowers and there's a conservatory that looks like a stationary Tournament of Roses Parade with an every-hue mantle of plants, trees, and flowers changing seasonally and for major holidays. Although you might expect the resort to be stuffy, gauche, and impersonal (or at least excessive), it's surprisingly warm, poised, and embracing. And that's why it's a *Neon Nuptials* top pick for accommodations—number one, in fact.

The resort is to Las Vegas visitors what San Juan Capistrano is to swallows, only these "birds" arrive day after day after day, year-round. They're drawn by the fountains, Chihuly, the botanical garden, a fine-art gallery with changing exhibitions, outstanding restaurants, and the casino—an effervescent airy space with room to roam.

Those who stay for the night (and many can with nearly 4,000 rooms and suites) will experience a AAA Five Diamond-rated resort with a room configuration that helped redefine the standard: nearly 600 square feet of space, electronically activated blinds, décor you wouldn't mind having at home, a soaking tub that actually accommodates a normal human body, and the cushiest bath mat ever to tickle a set of wriggling toes. The original hotel is comprised of three wings joined at a central tower; a second detached tower just opened. The most coveted rooms face the lake and are priced at a premium. It's not essential to look out over the fountains and beyond to Paris Las Vegas, but then again, how many honeymoons do you get?

A number of superb restaurants are arrayed lakeside, including Le Cirque, Picasso, Prime, and Todd English's Olives, while MICHAEL MINA (formerly Aqua) is adjacent to the conservatory. With several other big-name eateries, one of the best buffets in town, a café, and several quick-bite spots, Bellagio is a worthy contender for a top rating in the culinary arena.

Need more? Bellagio has seven bars and lounges, with one overlooking the fountains; a nightclub, Light; Via Bellagio, a shopping arcade lined with the likes of Prada and Chanel; a spa and salon; six pools fittingly cast within a Mediterranean-villa setting; and Shadow Creek Golf Club, a highly touted ultra-exclusive course available to guests of Bellagio and other MGM Mirage resorts.

Bellagio is also home to *O*—a production of the highly acclaimed French-Canadian Cirque du Soleil company—featuring athlete-artists (gymnasts, dancers, acrobats, high divers, contortionists, and synchronized swimmers), tellingly empathetic clowns, and a storyteller who knows more than perhaps the audience is led to believe. The heart of *O* is a 1.5-million-gallon pool that appears, disappears, and reappears almost imperceptibly throughout the show. Evocative of the French word for water, *eau* (pronounced like the English letter "O"), this story relates the universality of companionship and is played out within and above the pool. How fitting to find such an experience in belonging within a resort that's so inviting.

CAESARS PALACE

Of the few Las Vegas-defining originals left standing, Caesars Palace just might be the most iconic. Constructed in 1966 with 680 rooms, two restaurants, one pool, and cocktail-serving "goddesses," Caesars now tops out at 3,400 rooms, two-dozen eateries, four pools, and a kitsch rating that has never ebbed. Like the Roman Empire itself, Caesars expanded and evolved. A 4,000-seat showroom, the Colosseum, was added a few years back; new hotel towers pop up with regularity, each more luxurious than the one that came before; what's reputedly the most profitable shopping mall in existence—the Forum Shops—has undergone several expansions; and one of the pools went "European" (a.k.a. topless). Yet the fountain-adorned Italian-cypress-lined entry remains as a timeless reminder of the place that either created or shattered the mold, and perhaps both. Is it any wonder why Caesars is a Top-5 selection?

Everything about Caesars is grandiose, in a good way. You can get a room with a Jacuzzi tub just steps from the bed or catch a performance by Celine Dion or Elton John. There's a Roman temple in the middle of a swimming pool, statuary gods that move and speak, and a nightclub on a barge that imagination tells us carried Cleopatra down the Nile. Subtlety is decidedly not one of the ancient virtues replicated here.

And Caesars is just flat-out massive. Sure, MGM Grand has a larger casino, Luxor more rooms, and Planet Hollywood a more labyrinthine layout. But this resort stretches from Bellagio to the Mirage, or the same Strip frontage as five casinos on the other side of the street. Many of the recent additions and redesigns have made it easier to navigate the Palace and following is an oversimplified explanation of its layout: The Forum Shops are at one end, the original and two newest hotel towers and the pools are at the other, and in between unfold three casinos, two more hotel towers, various restaurants, lounges and nightclubs, a spa, race and sports

WHAT'S SO STANDARD ABOUT THIS ROOM?

One of the distinguishing marks of the hotels in this chapter is that their standard rooms aren't standard. There's no hard-and-fast rule, but a typical room in a typical hotel will have 250-300 square feet of living space, and within that you get a dresser, bed, straight-backed chair or two, place to put hangers, and utilitarian bathroom. It's not much, but the a-room-is-only-a-place-to-crash-and-shower set should find it sufficient.

Excluding the Golden Nugget, Mirage, and the older portions of Caesars Palace, the standard rooms in these neon notables run to just under 500 square feet at Green Valley Ranch to a 650-square-foot minimum at Venetian and 750 square feet and up at THEhotel at Mandalay Bay. You get high-speed Internet access; in-room safes, ironing boards, irons, and blow dryers; something other than Brand X toiletries; and a television remote that isn't bolted to the nightstand and affixed with an apocalyptic warning should you be tempted to take it home with you. Nearly all have bathrooms with separate showers and tubs (some with jets), many feature a water closet (toilet in its own room), and all have granite or marble on the floor and counter. Although standard rooms in the antiquarian (for Las Vegas) portions of Caesars and the Mirage lack some of the aforementioned characteristics, that these hotels are included alongside the new luxury palaces is testament to their style, revamped contemporary décor, great service, and the type of amenities throughout that make your stay a vacation.

Another Hotel 101 tip is that some of Las Vegas' all-suite hotels are not all-suite hotels. The way I look at it, a "room" consists of one room, a place where sleeping and hangout quarters share the same space. A "suite" has distinct bedroom and living spaces separated by a wall, and therefore are usually larger than rooms, by default. A two-bedroom suite has, you guessed it, two bedrooms and a living room. Mini-suites, a creation of the vivid imaginations of marketing people, are rooms pumped up with more square footage, perhaps an additional half-bath, and maybe a full-on living-room ensemble or a sleeping alcove. A Jacuzzi suite is a suite with a jetted tub (as a Jacuzzi room is a room with a jetted tub). Ironically, you need to look to some of Sin City's vintage hotel-casinos or motels to find a "honeymoon suite" decked out in lace and red velvet or some "romantic" theme.

Everything clear?

Ultimately, don't sweat it. THEhotel at Mandalay Bay is the only resort discussed here serving up a suite for a standard accommodation, which doesn't take anything away from the other properties, for each excels in its own way.

book, entertainment venues, and shops scattered here and there like Roman Legions garrisoning the far frontiers of the empire.

When it comes to bunking down for the night, I won't even try to explain your options, as the construction of five towers built over 39 years has resulted in a mind-boggling array of room and suite configurations and sizes (some three dozen or so floor plans in all). The Palace and soon-to-open Augustus Towers offer upgraded and enlarged accommodations across the board, and are priced accordingly. But it's also hard to argue with one of the older Roman Tower rooms with a jetted tub in the bedroom, frosted-glass walls in the loo, and a view straight down that famous fountain to the Strip and the Flamingo.

The aptly named Garden of the Gods sits at the foot of the Palace Tower. Here you'll find Caesars' four pools (including the top-optional Venus Pool), beautiful gardens, and several outdoor-wedding venues. And taking a cue from MGM Mirage, Caesars Entertainment, whose Vegas properties include Caesars, Bally's, the Flamingo, and Paris Las Vegas, has built for its biggest players a stunning break-open-the-piggybank golf course, Cascata, located in the foothills above Henderson.

As for continued trend setting, it was Caesars that launched the celebrity-chef/big-name-elsewhere restaurant craze that has consumed Las Vegas, and it all started with Wolfgang Puck's Spago in the Forum Shops (now complemented by Puck's Chinois). The tally for eateries both fine and casual includes outlets of New York's Palm Restaurant and Stage Deli, Planet Hollywood, the Cheesecake Factory, Bertolini's, eateries by Bobby Flay and Bradley Ogden, and in-house culinary gems like Empress Court, Nero's, 808, and Terrazza.

Along the one street in the world that would have you believe you've traveled in a matter of minutes from Arthurian England to Venice, with stops in between at Manhattan and Paris, Caesars still exudes Vegas like no other; the place is powerful, excessive, opulent, and kitschy, in a rich yet comforting kind of way.

Ancient Rome was built as much to intimidate as to awe. Fortunately for its subjects, Caesars Entertainment's modern-day empire only imparts the latter.

MANDALAY BAY
THEhotel AT MANDALAY BAY
FOUR SEASONS HOTEL LAS VEGAS

The first time you enter Mandalay Bay, it's hard to believe the resort was built by the same people who own Circus Circus and Excalibur. But if ever there were proof that evolution works, this is it. Mandalay Bay took the palm-and-vine idea from the Mirage (see below), fed it a dose of fertilizer, and for added measure tossed in a healthy dollop of influences from Burma and Angkor, the capital of ancient Cambodia, with its Travel Channel-grade temples and statuary. It's a tropical getaway for those who like their "jungle" experiences exotic, yet free of malaria and cannibals.

Mandalay Bay is unique in that there are three hotels on site— Mandalay Bay, the Four Seasons, and the newest arrival, THEhotel at Mandalay Bay (yes, *that's* the name and not a typo)—offering distinct looks and in-room experiences, yet sharing a number of getaway-enhancing amenities. As such, Mandalay Bay is a *Neon Nuptial* Top-5 accommodation.

Mandalay Bay proper is the big, gold-glassed, three-spoked, 3,200-room tower that dominates the Strip's southern horizon. Standard accommodations are on par with the competition, with cooling stone flooring and counters, twin closets, and 500 square feet within which to roam; the floor-to-ceiling window-wall in each room serves up almost unparalleled views. The in-room motif is softly tropical, but without the nearly enveloping lushness of the resort's public spaces.

The Four Seasons, a AAA Five-Diamond recipient, occupies floors 35 through 39 of the main tower. This 400-room hotel-within-a-hotel has its own entrance, valet, lobby, elevators, restaurants, spa (per Four Seasons tradition, guests receive free access for use of the facilities), and pool; a hushed more subtle feel than the happening and vibrant Mandalay Bay; standard accommodations that begin with a footprint similar to those in the surrounding hotel; and that special Four Seasons attention to customer care. Of the three, the Four Seasons is typically the highest priced, followed by THEhotel. Mandalay Bay, however, still comes in as one of Las Vegas' most posh hotels, as well as one of its most expensive.

The "L"-shaped tower out by the freeway is the all-suite THEhotel at Mandalay Bay. Where Mandalay Bay proper is tastefully Southeast Asian, THEhotel is sleek and modern with crisp clean lines, a color scheme that runs black and brown with alabaster offsets, and arguably the best-equipped standard accommodation in town—three TVs (including a 42-inch plasma number), wet bar, second (half) bathroom, and for honeymooners, a gorgeous marble-and-granite master bath with deep soaking tub, a glass-enclosed shower, and a handy push-button-activated do-not-disturb light. Like the Four Seasons, THEhotel offers its own spa, gym, lounge, and two eateries.

Since the three hotels share the same hunk of land, guests have access to the array of shared amenities that make "Mandalay Bay" justly famous.

Water is at the core of the resort's two star attractions, Mandalay Beach and Shark Reef. The first is an 11-acre oasis of water and palms that includes a 1.6-million-gallon wave pool with sandy beach, lazy river, several other pools that individually rival the entire pool complex of other hotels, a concert venue, and a nightclub. (The hotel's wedding chapels are adjacent to Mandalay Beach, though safely removed from the frenzy.)

Shark Reef is an aquarium, in the major-attraction sense of the word. In keeping with the resort's design theme, Shark Reef is evocative of temple ruins, through which you descend, passing from the realm of the terrestrial to the oceanic, from the world of reptiles to that of jellyfish, coral, fish, and sharks. The attraction culminates with two "inside-the-aquarium" rooms where the action takes place all around you.

Mandalay Bay sports an excellent array of restaurants, from one of the best coffee shops anywhere along the Strip and an overlooked buffet to eateries run by big culinary names including the "Two Hot Tamales" (Mary Sue Milliken and Susan Feniger), noted New York chef Charlie Palmer—who has a chop house on the Four Seasons side and Mandalay Bay's Aureole with its famous four-story wine tower rising up through the center of the restaurant—and Wolfgang Puck, whose name on a menu is nearly *de rigueur* for a major Las Vegas resort. Nightlife ranges from shopping at Mandalay Place, tipping a chilly martini at Red Square, and dancing behind rumjungle's wall of fire and water to catching a concert at the House of Blues or the Mandalay Bay Events Center.

A *Neon Nuptial* notable with three hotels, more than 4,000 rooms, a dozen-and-a-half or so eateries, multiple pools, three spas (the third is Spa Mandalay in the main complex), rolling waves, and circling sharks, there's so much to do you just might not notice the tram that links Mandalay Bay to Luxor and Excalibur ... and from there to the nearly limitless options of Sin City.

THE MIRAGE

The Strip's second classic icon, the Mirage, is widely credited with carrying Las Vegas from its casino-with-a-hotel past to its resort-with-a-casino present. Yes, plenty of Vegas hotels have been around longer and Caesars Palace—icon number one—married luxury to kitsch. Yet when it comes to the look, feel, and bearing of today's Las Vegas, the Mirage deserves the credit.

Until the opening of Bellagio, the Mirage was perhaps the one resort that most stood out in the minds of Las Vegas visitors and those longing to visit. This is, after all, the place with the volcano, indoor tropical rain forest, swimming-pool-sized aquarium backing the reception area, and the tigers and dolphins and ... well, that aroma, the pervading scent of vanilla, orchids, coconut, or whatever it is that tells your nose what every other sense organ has already figured out—this is *the* Mirage.

The Mirage's look is branded as contemporary Polynesian, featuring Asian-inspired flora, artwork, and architectural treatments inside and out that hint at the era of European Colonial rule. Some resorts scream "wow" and others exude a calming "ooh." The Mirage simply embraces you. It's the kind of place where once inside, it's only with great reluctance that you leave. And that goes for overnight guests or those just passing through for a look-see.

The hotel's 3,000-plus rooms and suites were remodeled several

I DON'T CARE HOW SAUCY—ACTUALLY SILLY— THEY MADE THE PIRATE BATTLE ...

Let me say it right up front, there are a lot better places to take your kids than Sin City. Anaheim comes to mind. Orlando. San Diego. Maybe even Saskatoon. Vegas, despite previous attempts at making it a family destination, remains largely an adult mecca.

But kids aren't verboten. They won't be held at McCarran International or the state border and there are surprisingly many kid-perfect things to do in and around town. So if you or your guests have rugrats underfoot, you might want to consider staying at a place that has built-in daycare and babysitting services.

Many of the locals' hotel-casinos and the high-end resorts offer a place in-house to deposit the little bundles of joy—other properties might be able to provide a listing of certified sitters—though all have some combination of age restrictions and limitations on how long the kids can stick around.

years ago, with marble in the entries and bathrooms and tasteful botanical prints and colors that run toward the soft end of yellow or cedar, which is a distinct improvement over an earlier look that was too green and tropical. The Mirage's rooms aren't huge by current Las Vegas practice—370 square feet for starters—and the bathrooms are markedly average—small combo tub/shower—in light of what has been constructed since the hotel rose from the desert in 1989. Yet like the rest of the resort, the accommodations render an inviting feel.

Come meal time, the top of the scale was occupied by Chef Alessandro Stratta's AAA Five Diamond-winning Renoir, which closed at the end of October 2004; at press time, there was still no indication as to what would replace it. Low-carb fans need look no farther than Samba Brazilian Steakhouse, with a range of meats carved tableside from skewers in *rodizio* fashion. Moongate serves up high-end Chinese in a courtyard setting and Mikado delivers *teppan-yaki*, sushi, and à la carte Japanese fare. Kokomo's is surf and turf set within the atrium rain forest, and the quietly excellent Onda—one of 10 eateries highlighted in the next chapter—features Italian/New American fusion. For a meal with less fanfare, try the café (with noodle shop), California Pizza Kitchen, redesigned buffet, or the casual poolside eatery that's open during the warmer months.

The Mirage's pool is shrouded in the resort's hallmark tropical

... KIDS ARE STILL WELCOME IN VEGAS

The Coast and Station brands lead the way with three facilities each. The Orleans, Gold Coast, and Suncoast offer daycare facilities for kids at least 2 or 2-½ (must be potty trained). The Palms has a similar facility with a minimum-age requirement of 3 (potty training also required). Boulder Station, Sunset Station, and Texas Station take 'em as young as six weeks, though you'll need a reservation before dropping off anyone under 30 months of age. The two Lake Las Vegas resorts—the Hyatt Regency and Ritz-Carlton—offer Camp Hyatt (minimum age of 3) and RitzKids (5-year-old minimum). These are interactive, guided-activity programs and participants must be potty trained. The upper age limit for most of these childcare providers is 12. The Four Seasons has a private in-room nanny service catering to children of all ages.

foliage. With swim-through waterfalls, islands and grottos, waterslides, a quarter-mile of "shoreline," and three Jacuzzis, it's in demand, so you have to arrive pretty early to snag a couple of the sailcloth-clad lounge chairs. Just beyond the pool sits the Atlantic bottlenose-dolphin habitat and tree-canopied enclosures for some of Siegfried & Roy's critters. Back inside you'll find an indoor enclosure where a tiger or two are usually on display, Spa Mirage and Salon Mirage, and a shopping promenade. Add entertainment by master impressionist Danny Gans to the list of fun things to do.

About the only thing you can't do at the Mirage is get married, as there's no chapel, though I'd venture to say that an enterprising couple could arrange for a minister to pop on by for a quick round of I dos, with the volcano going off in the background.

The volcano, Las Vegas' tribute to Pele, the Hawaiian goddess of fire, has been performing nightly for more than 15 years, not long when it comes to geological time, but nearly forever in Sin City. The volcano extravaganza is corny, the flames and "lava" won't fool anyone, and the entire spectacle long ago lost the title of best free show in town. Who cares? The volcano—in fact the entire three-acre palm-adorned Mirage-fronting lagoon where it sits—is both emblematic and the most visible sign that a casino can be much much more than just a casino, and Las Vegas can be any place in the world.

PARIS LAS VEGAS

Welcome to the City of Light, reproduced in fit-it-between-Bally's-and-Planet Hollywood scale, and complete with renditions of Monsieur Eiffel's tower and the Louvre, crêpes on the run, and way too many types of bubbly to properly sample in a few days.

Vive la France! ... in Nevada.

In addition to the aforementioned landmarks, which coincidentally house two of the establishment's many fine eateries (Mon Ami Gabi and the Eiffel Tower restaurant), the hotel itself is patterned after Paris' City Hall, the Hôtel de Ville, and there's a scaled-down Arc de Triomphe rising over the driveway. Three legs of the tower pierce a casino ceiling of light blue dusted with white springtime-by-the-Seine clouds, while street signs, ironwork, and gleefully Parisian façades blend well with hospitality and casino staffers offering up a heartfelt *salut, merci,* or *bonne chance.* From the casino, Le Boulevard, a cobblestone *rue,* leads to the hotel elevator, lobby, convention area, parking garage, and sister-property Bally's, while passing more eateries (including a buffet rivaling the Strip's best), shops, Napoleon's Champagne Bar—one of my favorite places in all of Las Vegas for bubbly, chocolate-dipped fruits, and good jazz—and on most days, performance art by some extremely talented mimes and human statues. (If jazz and bubbly aren't your thing, try Risqué, Paris' version of the late-night ultralounge, complete with Strip-view balconies.)

This is the newest from-scratch resort by the good folks at Caesars Entertainment, so expect better-than-usual hotel amenities; baths with separate shower and tub, plenty of marble, and linen hand towels; crown molding (okay, it probably really doesn't matter, but it *is* a nice touch); and French fabrics. It all comes together nicely without any excessive frill. A $35-per-day upgrade allows access to Le Rendezvous, a 31st floor "members-only"-like lounge that offers a comfortable spot to grab your morning coffee, croissant, paper, and other light foods and refreshments throughout the day, and partake of a killer view. Like every other resort, various mini and full suites are available, but whatever style of accommodation you choose, push to get a room looking out over the tower and Bellagio.

One spot where Paris doesn't get a ton of credit, although I think it should, is at the pool atop the casino roof. This is a pool for sunning, swimming, and relaxing, so while there are no waves, sand, or rapids, you also won't find as many little ones running around. The seasonal café serves up fare that approaches cuisine. You can run quickly and easily back and forth to the spa, which is operated by the acclaimed Mandara people—spa purveyors, not some Stone Age tribe. (Heck, if you're really impatient, the chapels are just a few steps past the spa.) The site is framed in well-kept gardens and is guaranteed to be the *only* place in the world where you can seek shelter from the searing Mojave Desert sun in the shadow of the Eiffel Tower.

This Top-5 resort is frolicsome—it's playful, spirited, fun, romantic. Paris Las Vegas with your loved one is all about giggling, having lattés and croissants laced with dark chocolate, the clink of Champagne flutes ... kissing.

C'est magnifique!

THE VENETIAN

Fans of the Big Apple or the French capital may have a good argument, but for my money, the Venetian is the most over-the-top edifice, inside and out, in Sin City. Nothing about this resort is subtle, nothing. There's a quarter-mile-long indoor canal on the second floor where you can take a gondola ride complete with singing gondolier—*the* spot for a wedding Venice-style. You can stroll St. Mark's Square deciding between sushi, Southwestern, or Sicilian for dinner. The exterior is done up like the Doges' Palace, frescoes and inlaid marble adorn huge expanses of ceiling and floor, and there's a faux Rialto Bridge with moving sidewalks. A 3,000-room hotel was followed by a second 1,000-room tower; a related resort, set to be the tallest in Las Vegas, is going up next door. Super chef Emeril Lagasse is in the house serving up steak and the like with a N'awlins twist and the spa sports a multi-story rock-climbing wall. The Guggenheim Hermitage Museum presents world-class art and Madame Tussaud's wax museum brings in culture of the pop kind. The Venetian is flamboyance perfected, the Liberace of hotel-casino resorts.

For a time, the Venetian offered the largest standard rooms in town, which start at 650 square feet. They remain about as big as they come, and nearly unequalled in appointments, with a step-down living area (in most rooms) containing a full-size couch, upholstered chairs, workspace, and dining table; crown molding and baseboards; a canopy draping the head of the bed; and a separate lighted vanity in a bathroom rich in Italian marble and the usual amenities of an upscale Las Vegas hotel. The newer Venezia tower offers similar accommodations within a setting removed from the main portion of the resort and casino. It has its own upper-floor reception area and lobby, courtyard pool, and a concierge-level upgrade (at about $100 extra per night) for a Strip-side room on one of the top five floors, private access and check-in, morning coffee service and a continental breakfast, evening cocktails and appetizers, and unpacking and turn-down service.

Despite the renown garnered by the accommodations, it's the architectural treatments and all the goodies stuffed inside that make the Venetian sing. The heart of this Italy-in-the-desert is the Grand Canal Shoppes, a Venetian-themed mall where period performers sing and mime, façades are richly colored and adorned with colonnades, balusters and balconies frame boutiques and restaurants, and gondoliers ply a canal criss-crossed with high-arching footbridges. (Gondola rides are also available on the outdoor waterway fronting the Venetian.) If you want warm-you-all-over camp with your cannoli, this is the place.

A number of the resort's many outstanding restaurants are located along the canal, and they run the gamut from pan-Asian at

Tsunami Grill and Italian at Zefferino and Canaletto to New World (American) at Postrio and Mexican/Southwestern at Taquería Cañonita, which serves up an outstanding sangría. One floor below, just off the casino sits one of Las Vegas' best eateries, Delmonico (by the aforementioned Emeril Lagasse), and a personal favorite, Pinot Brasserie, a vibrant spot serving up French-California fusion and no corkage fee if you decide to bring your own wine. And this is only the tip of the dining iceberg.

Leading from the casino to the main lobby is the Galleria, with a look as close to a European palace as you'll find in Sin City. A good hunk of the Venetian's acres of eye-pleasing frescoes, gilding, and inlaid flooring play out here—beware the latter's Escher-like synapse-teasing power. Even if you aren't staying at the hotel, you need to stroll through, camera in hand; it's that beautiful.

The casino rooftop is given over to an Italian garden splashed aqua with the Venetian's many pools, and on the far side, Canyon Ranch SpaClub. The pool complex is all about swimming, tanning, and relaxing—there are no crashing waterfalls, inner-tube rides, or waves. And a similarly purposeful quality carries over to Canyon Ranch, operated by one of the nation's preeminent spa purveyors. Canyon Ranch stresses holism, so a day at the spa might include a few rounds with a Stairmaster and an ascent of the rock wall, relaxing with steam, sauna, and a treatment, and dining sensibly at the adjoining café, where nouvelle gourmet low-fat-and-carb cuisine comes together. Compared to the resort—a place where a replica of the Camponile Tower is complementary, not excessive—Canyon Ranch is subtle, restrained.

Venice brought together the best in Italian art, architecture, and culture. The Venetian brings together the best in what makes a getaway vacation, or a honeymoon, memorable.

AROUND THE VALLEY—HENDERSON

For years, all the activity in Las Vegas centered on the Strip or downtown, where real gamblers went to really gamble. Sure, there were hotel rooms, food at both ends of the spectrum, big-name performers, and as often as not a pool, perhaps a spa, and in a handful of cases, a golf course; the accoutrements of resort living were present. Yet flirting with Lady Luck was the *raison d'être*.

How things change.

A LOT OF GREEN IN THE DESERT

Money greases Las Vegas like it lubricates no other place in the world. Pretty much everywhere you turn someone is going to be doing something for you, and you in turn need to do something for them: tip, or in gambling parlance, toke.

The list of people who legitimately have a reason to hold a palm open could run to dozens of entries. Rather than bore you, I'm just listing those with whom you are most likely to interact. I've included some thoughts on how to tip and suggestions regarding an appropriate amount.

As tipping is highly personal, remember that these numbers are not carved in stone. And a gratuity is not a service worker's entitlement; it is a reward for providing service, so keep that in mind if Attila the Hun's slinging your drinks. By the same token, if someone goes the extra yard, don't feel constrained in how to respond.

I you want more info than any normal person should likely possess, check out www.tipping.org.

Bellmen: *These are the folks who schlep your bags from the car/ taxi/limo into the hotel and ultimately to your room (and the reverse as well). Standard practice is $1 per bag with a $5 minimum. You should tip on the back end; in other words, when your stuff gets to the room on the way in and at the car/taxi/limo on the way out. A good bellhop will show you around your room, highlighting the salient features—light switch, bed, john—tell you about the resort or a hot restaurant, and often offer to get anything you might be missing. If he or she provides a particularly good piece of information or hauls in some ice, up the ante a little. Use the same tipping rules for skycap services at the airport.*

Valets: *Short of "free" drinks while gambling, valet service is in my book the best perk in Vegas. It is almost always offered without charge (tonier places like the Ritz-Carlton levy a daily fee), and when you drop off your rig, you're invariably smack dab at the heart of the hotel-casino, and not out in a several-acre, several-story, self-park facility beyond the delivery bays. People tipped a buck when cars had 8-tracks, so make it at least two. This is another back-loaded transaction; i.e., you should tip when you pick up your car. If you plan to run in/out in a hurry, produce a five- or 10-spot up front and ask the attendant to keep your car close by. Finally, some valets are notoriously slow—MGM Grand comes to mind. Although I can't guarantee the results, you might be able to move a bit closer to the head of the class if you fold up a* *bill that will get noticed (that means George stays in your pocket) and present it with your claim ticket.*

Housekeeping*: When you think about it, who is more essential in assuring you have a nice time away from home than the person who keeps your room in ship-shape condition? Sure, you hope the valet doesn't dent a fender and the busboy's hands are clean. But I'm talking sheets here, and towels, and running around in your bare feet, and having enough bottles of shampoo, conditioner, lotion, and mouthwash that you can go home with some for presents. I think $4-$5 per day (paid daily because work schedules change) is fair, particularly if you ask for extra towels and goodies. I also leave the gratuity with a note of thanks, since some hotels are wary about employees picking up anything of value from a room.*

Drink servers*: Except for the tightwads at Mandalay Resort Group who have cut way back on the practice, being served drinks while you play is just part-and-parcel of the Las Vegas experience. One dollar per drink per round works for me, although some people claim—and they aren't necessarily wrong—that a buck between two people playing side-by-side is just compensation.*

Bartenders*: I'm of the buck-a-drink persuasion. If the tender is indifferent and I'm playing with someone else, I leave $1 per round. Now if you saunter up to a bar and order three mai tais, one blended margarita and one on the rocks, and several beers, go with the old 15%-20% of the tab rule.*

Wait staff*: Please recall my entitlement comment above: 15%-20% of a meal tab is not the minimum required gratuity. Please repeat that to yourself several times and take it to heart. Call me a curmudgeon, but apathy and ensuring that my plate arrives at my table with my food on it doesn't qualify Susie Server or Wally Waiter for a predetermined cut. I will leave something (and I'm not talking a penny, but it won't be $12 on a $60 check either) and explain to the manager why the tip was what it was. And despite what some food-service acquaintances of mine contend, you do not have to tip on the added tax. On the other end of the spectrum, 20% is not a glass ceiling.*

Buffet*: I don't care that you served yourself, it cost $3.95, and you both got in on a two-for-one coupon, leave a buck or two per person.*

Taxi/Limo: *The 15% rule works for a cabbie. However, if it's a short hop, fork over at least a buck. Twenty dollars is adequate for a burly guy in a tux driving you around in a sedan on steroids. But if he's particularly good about getting doors, smiling, and addressing you like a high roller, make it $30 or $40.*

Minister: *This one chaps my hide. You spend some sum of money on a "complete wedding package," yet you might have to toke the person who provides the service for which you've paid? Weird. (A Superior Court judge presided over our wedding, and Terri and I reciprocated with a donation to a charity of his choosing. So, my beef is not about the money; it's about hidden charges.) When you sign your contract, make sure you know whether the standard minister "fee" of $50 is already rolled into the cost. (The same thing goes with spa treatments and room service; in some cases, the gratuity is included in the charge.)*

Like Rats From a Sinking Ship ... the Casino Handpay: *What do you do if you hit a jackpot that's too big for a machine to pay out? You sit around and wait for several people you've likely never seen before to arrive with your cash. And if your payout is a nice round number like $1,000, you'll get something like nine $100 bills, and five $20 bills. Why? Because the payout retinue is expecting a tip. One convention holds that you should tip up to 4%, or $40 on that $1,000 win. But wait, that would be $400 on a $10,000 win; money's not so heavy that it's significantly more taxing to bring to you a windfall with an extra zero at the end. One person standing in the casino equivalent of the welfare line might actually be a change person who has helped you out along the way, so a tip seems fair and appropriate; I'm inclined to tip as the service is rendered. Now the second and/or third person in the payout party did what for you? That's right, nada. Let your conscience and comfort level be your guide, and if that means a $5 bill here or a fistful of $100 bills there, so be it.*

Dealers: *Ardent, knowledgeable gamblers aren't inclined to tip dealers as tokes take away from whatever edge they might have gained in a game that likely leans in the favor of the house. But if you're playing for fun, the dealer's something other than a robot, or you just think it's good karma, go ahead and tip, or make a side bet for the dealer. Practices and etiquette differ from game to game, so if you don't know how to make the side-bet play, just ask. Should you use one of those silver tokens or a green chip? That's wholly up to you.*

Today, people actually go to Las Vegas to play without touching green felt or a one-armed bandit. Sin City has become a stay-and-play destination, which is just right for you and your guy (or gal). Perhaps nowhere is this phenomenon more evident than on the edges of the valley, away from Glitter Gulch and Las Vegas Boulevard. From Henderson to Summerlin, some of the biggest names in the resort biz have set up shop with world-class hotels offering luxury, comfort, and relaxation as the first orders of business.

This is a different type of Vegas experience—toned down, more directed toward leisure (and no, it's not boring, but instead somewhat unique when it comes to Las Vegas)—in places where you can check in and get to your room without wandering endlessly through a casino, though one isn't far away. And with the exception of one of the three resorts listed here (Green Valley Ranch Station), you're largely left to your own devices for nighttime entertainment, which isn't such a bad thing on your honeymoon.

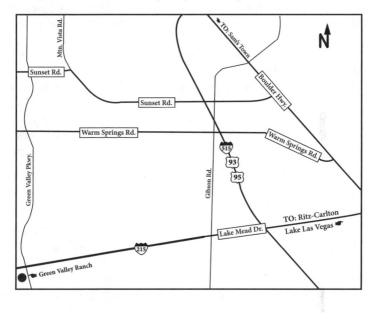

GREEN VALLEY RANCH

Down comforters and turndown service, bustling nightclub, buffet and 10-screen cineplex—is this a boutique hotel, a hip and happening place, or a haven for local retirees? Yes ... across the board. Situated amidst the middle-class suburban neatness of

Henderson some 15 minutes from the Strip, Green Valley Ranch is a mad experiment gone wholly right.

Here, as nowhere else in town, you can find most of the attributes that make the many types of hotel-casinos prosper: diverse restaurants including BullShrimp (founded though recently sold by local culinary legend Gustav Mauler), Il Fornaio, China Spice, sushi, and an Irish pub, to name a few; a great buffet; player-friendly gaming in an attractive setting; a theater and food court geared to give locals their celluloid-and-fries fix; high-end accommodations, spa, tennis, and nearby golf; an outstanding pool; and a stylish place to prowl when the sun goes down. Furthermore, the resort's all-of-Las Vegas views, at least from the north side of the property, could be the best in town.

Green Valley Ranch's nearly 500-square-foot standard rooms offer mountain or pool/Strip views, robes, coffee pots, and a wet bar; the morning newspaper, twice-daily housekeeping, and the evening turndown service you'd expect of a small inn (though this place has nearly 500 rooms); soaking tubs and marble in the bath; and furnishings and décor in step with the Tuscan style of the larger resort—sun-warm colors offsetting earth tones, stacked-stone pillars, leather and textile, wrought-iron fixtures, and wood beams working in concert for some aesthetic magic. As befits this new generation of resort, the hotel is over *here* and the casino over *there*. So if you want to keep your relaxation and recreation separate, you can. Yet the cling-clang of the casino remains only steps away, which is a good thing come mealtime, as that's where you'll find all the eats, in addition to a fun gotta-try watering hole called the Drop Bar.

The resort's backyard is simply and plainly cool, and it begins with the infinity-edge pool with a sandy beach at one end. Arrayed around the pool are funky poster-bed-like cabanas, an amphitheater for concerts, Italian-inspired gardens, a working vineyard—a popular spot for weddings, though packages here all require a reception—and the newly revamped Spa at Green Valley Ranch, which offers the full spectrum of therapies and a number of treatment rooms capped by glass ceilings rippling with pools of water. Now that's soothing and chic. The pool complex is given over during the spaghetti-straps-in-the-evening months to Whiskey Beach, the outdoor playpen for the resort's famous Whiskey Bar.

Green Valley Ranch is a bit like the resort version of a vinegar-and-oil dressing, a compilation of ingredients that on appearance don't seem to mix easily. Yet in this case, no agitation is required to make it tasty.

RITZ-CARLTON LAKE LAS VEGAS

The Ritz-Carlton is a gorgeous *palazzo* aside the private 320-acre Lake Las Vegas, the centerpiece of the eponymous resort and high-end residential development in Henderson 17 miles southeasterly of the Strip. The hotel anchors the west end of the lake and shares the water's edge with MonteLago Village, a warren of bricked walkways lined with shops, galleries, and townhomes in clustered stacked buildings vividly cast in mustard, burnt orange, deep moss, and cinnamon—a color palette similar to the Ritz-Carlton's—all capped in red tile. Alongside lies Casino MonteLago, a compact and elegant gambling house dressed up in a warm Tuscan-winery look. (The beautiful Moroccan-themed Hyatt Regency occupies the northeastern shore of the lake.)

The resort likely reigns as Las Vegas' best getaway-from-it-all destination. As a spot for a neon honeymoon, it fought long and hard with Bellagio for the top ranking in this book, ultimately slipping behind by just the thinnest of margins, mainly due to the multitude of dining and entertainment options within and surrounding Bellagio.

A portion of the hotel spans the lake in a rendition of Florence's Pontevecchio Bridge and is home to the Ritz-Carlton's signature Club Level accommodations. This $100-per-day upgrade offers a view of the lake and mountain, access to a personal concierge, a private lounge with four daily food *presentations*—they're not cheese and crackers—and full beverage service; it's well worth the expense. Whichever of the 349 accommodations you draw, however, all are Five Diamond Ritz-Carlton grade, meaning thick firm mattresses, crisp soft linens and beautiful bedding, perfect pillows, and the kind of toiletries you hide in your luggage—all wrapped up within at least 490 square feet of true *living* space. And, of course, impeccable service pervades the establishment from "hello" and "good evening" said with warmth and a true smile to bell, valet, and concierge staff who know your name the second time they see you.

The resort has but a handful of eateries—in marked contrast to the megaresorts on the Strip. Yet foodies need look only one place for taste-bud enlightenment, Medici Café and Terrace. Following casual breakfast and lunch service (or the weekend brunch), Medici is transformed into one of Las Vegas' must-experience restaurants. The fare is pan-Mediterranean and the ticket is the ever-changeable six-course tasting menu, with paired wines if desired. Mmmmmmm.

The Ritz-Carlton offers two pools, one a sand-fringed lagoon with water spilling in and through to Lake Las Vegas. The "action" here is subtle, subdued, and elegant yet not pretentious, so you won't find the hip-hop-and-a-margarita crowd of the Hard Rock or Mandalay Bay, or hordes of splashing munchkins. One side of the pool gives way to a stepped-down grassy terrace, which is one of several spots for a wedding (another favorite is the Florentine Garden in the lee of the hotel). Mere steps in the other direction resides Spa Vita di Lago. The spa includes a full-on fitness center, salon, boutique, and café, as well as a courtyard for relaxed contemplation. There's no hype to the spa. The lines and look are uncluttered and straightforward with an emphasis on functionality. The air is relaxed yet focused, the requisite amenities are offered, and services take a back seat to no one; it is a Ritz-Carlton, after all.

If you want to risk losing yourself or your guy to the golfing gods, Lake Las Vegas features 36 holes of adrenaline-inducing golf by two of the greatest designers in the game, Jack Nicklaus and Tom Weiskopf. Still desire more things to do in the great outdoors? Consider renting a sailboat, kayak, or bike, or sign up for a guided excursion to hike the rugged regal desert hills or view the heavens on a stargazers walk.

But whatever you do at the Ritz-Carlton, you must stroll the village, lake edge, and the exquisite gardens ... in the evening ... hand in hand.

AROUND THE VALLEY—NORTHWEST

JW MARRIOTT LAS VEGAS RESORT

If the JW Marriott Resort has a familiar quality to it, don't be surprised. White walls and red tile, lush grounds beyond a warm lobby, golf at the back door, pampering spa, fine eats, petite yet stunning casino—it's all so reminiscent of the late great Desert Inn.

The JW Marriott's design and look are a memorable and tasteful Mediterranean with a bit of Spanish Revival. Water is central to the aesthetic, as man-made lakes and meandering stone-lined streams abound, and the foliage is dense, with soaring palms and draping peppers framing ambling paths and green, green lawns. Most weddings are held outside on one of the lawns with a faraway view to

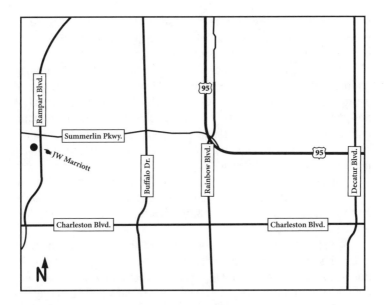

the purple-red-gray Spring Mountains. It's a small hotel by Las Vegas standards—541 rooms and suites divided between the six-story Palm and Spa towers—but its rooms are not. Regular accommodations feature nearly 600 square feet of elbow room, walk-in closets, French doors, firm beds triple sheeted with appropriately high-thread-count sheets, and the type of comfortable well-crafted furniture upon which you could sit for hours and read. The bathrooms are dynamite with dual vanities, water closet, a deep jetted soaking tub suitable for two, separate shower with a drenching-rain showerhead in the ceiling, marble everywhere, and Garden Botanika toiletries.

Outward-facing rooms in the Spa Tower take in the adjoining Angel Park Golf Club, the Suncoast resort, and, at one end of the tower, faraway views of downtown and the Strip. Palm Tower rooms with a westward orientation treat you to another golf course, seven-figure homes, and Red Rock Canyon and the Spring Mountains; get up early one morning and take in the rainbow of colors the sun conjures up. Interior views from both towers are of the lush grounds.

In short, it's the best standard room/bathroom combo in a town renowned for great accommodations.

The fun-in-the-sun crowd can rent a cabana and bask away the day by the pool, which is huge and lushly landscaped, and features a swim-through waterfall. If a bit more activity is in order, the resort sits amid some of the best golf courses in Las Vegas and it's only minutes to Red Rock Canyon, where hiking, mountain biking, and rock scrambling are the orders of business.

The JW Marriott's Aquae Sulis Spa is named after the Roman goddess of water, whose vestige shows in the amenities—coed whirlpool, steam, and sauna; sex-segregated "ritual rooms" with hot and cold plunges, inundating waterfall showers, warm float pool, and additional steam and sauna areas; and a for-spa-patrons-only swimming pool with built-in hydrotherapy alcoves. The full complement of body, facial, and massage therapies is offered and for the truly inspired, there's a state-of-the-art fitness center—with huge windows that look out to the hydrotherapy pool—offering health and wellness programs. In my book, figuratively and literally, it's the best spa in town.

Rampart Casino anchors one corner of the resort and, like the hotel, it's small and classy, with a black-and-gold palm-frond-silhouetted dome over the table area and slots and video poker machines radiating out into the circular room. Addison's Lounge and a wood-and-leather-accented sports book complete the effect, and just down the promenade you'll find a cigar bar and an ultralounge. On the culinary side, the resort offers Master Chef Gustav Mauler's imaginative Italian fair at Spiedini, J.C. Wooloughan Irish pub, and Ceres, a warm open eatery backed by trees and streams, and in the casino you'll find a café, buffet, and the high-end Carmel Room.

Lounging by the spa pool—post-treatment—my mind's eye always wanders off to the Spring Mountains that rise above the desert-fringed green fairways and the ember-glow geology of Red Rock Canyon. Yet the slot canyons of Las Vegas Boulevard are only 20 minutes away. That's a comfort, in several ways.

DOWNTOWN

This is where Las Vegas began—Fremont Street, Glitter Gulch ... downtown. Anachronism to some, true Vegas to others, there's no denying that the pulse of Sin City as first, foremost, and forever a gambling mecca still beats along a several-block stretch of neon-draped asphalt turned over to a pedestrian mall.

The hotel-casinos are smaller and more densely packed in this area. With an exception or two, there's some commonality to the accommodations and eateries, less fuss in the air, and fewer frills in the house; the sharks here work the casinos and the coasters sit beneath stiff drinks. A bit seedy, unconventionally trendy, most of the downtown joints are time worn in an honored sense. You come for lower stakes and better odds, solid value-priced dining, double-digit-priced hotel rooms, and the ability to amble by three, four, or five establishments in the same amount of time it would take to get from your room to the spa or casino at many of the Strip's megaresorts.

Downtown's not for everyone. But for those who like it, it's just right.

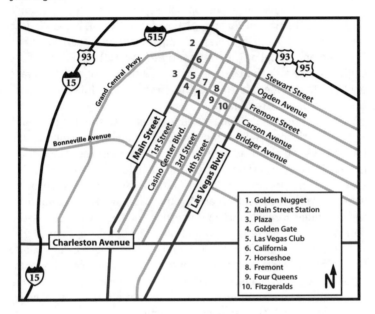

1. Golden Nugget
2. Main Street Station
3. Plaza
4. Golden Gate
5. Las Vegas Club
6. California
7. Horseshoe
8. Fremont
9. Four Queens
10. Fitzgeralds

GOLDEN NUGGET

Perhaps the best way to experience both old school and ritzy Las Vegas is to book a stay at the Golden Nugget, downtown's signature resort and a worthy competitor to the larger show palaces on the Strip.

The Nugget is a fitting fusion of old and new with 1,900 good-sized (370 square feet) comfortable attractive rooms, resort amenities, a production-style theater, and a lively airy casino decked out in gold and white-leather seating. On the classic side of the ledger you'll find a compact casino that's easy to navigate, restaurants and hotel towers that are steps and not miles apart, and a throwback-chic atmosphere.

Most of the credit goes to Steve Wynn, the man who transformed this one-time bingo parlor into a showpiece before going on to greater fame building the Mirage, TI, Bellagio, and the new Wynn Las Vegas. Golden Nugget is now owned by Tim Poster and Tom Breitling, young millionaire entrepreneurs who have vowed to put a bit more hip in the establishment and better games in the casino while maintaining the Golden Nugget's reputation as downtown's most highly rated hotel.

Though downtown is boutonnière-deep in chapels, you won't find one at the Golden Nugget, although the license bureau is just steps away. You *will* find casual and fine dining—Carson Street Café, Stefano's (Italian), Lillie Langtry's (Chinese), and ZAX, where contemporary fare and evening music blend—a gym and courtyard pool (by far the best in this part of town), and a full-service spa, the only along Glitter Gulch.

Some of the Golden Nugget's allure is its place along the Fremont Street Experience—a light-and-sound extravaganza played out on a four-block-long overhead canopy that's a cross between the world's largest Erector Set, brightest Lite Brite, and loudest boom box. This section of the street is the Glitter Gulch of fame and now closed to vehicular traffic, so you can amble along as you please, going from the no-longer-Binion's-owned Horseshoe and the Golden Gate—the oldest standing hotel in town and home of the justly famous 99¢ shrimp cocktail—to the Plaza, Fremont, or Four Queens. Performers, bands, and musicians appear during holidays and special events. It's a kinda glitzy, somewhat gritty, urban American street fair done up in endless strands of neon and millions of lights and flanked by some of the most historic names in gambling.

And tucked away in the middle lies the Golden Nugget, the crown jewel of downtown and a resort in every sense of the word.

MORE HONEYMOON ... IN VEGAS 6

EATS AND TREATS

A crazy thing happened on the way to the 21st century—Las Vegas turned into a full-on getaway spot. Of course there were, back in the day, spas and great entertainment and good food and golf and, well, pretty much everything that makes a resort environment a place you really want to find yourself. And today's casinos still pull in gazillions of dollars. But not that long ago, Las Vegas was *all* about gambling—the tables, slots, and tempting Lady Luck—and the other goodies were diversions begrudgingly thrown in because most people just couldn't play 24/7 at a crap table, much to the casino owners' chagrin.

Whenever the transformation took place—and indeed it evolved over time, although the 1989 opening of the Mirage was probably the greatest contributor—the result is clear: Sin City became a top-notch vacation destination with all the trappings.

Las Vegas entertainment is world class, the food is hot and happening, shopping is on par with Rodeo Drive, and the golf courses are tour-proven. You can visit a different spa every day for weeks on end without a repeat, hike a wilderness trail 30 minutes from the Strip's neon sear, or pilot a jet ski on a desert lake that's larger than many states. You can drop a mortgage payment over dinner and a show or fill every waking hour with the most bang-for-the-buck offered anywhere on the face of the planet.

This chapter takes you through the sights, sounds, and tastes of Sin City that would meld perfectly into a neon nuptial or, for that matter, any Las Vegas getaway with the one you love. It's about food and entertainment, pampering and play. The field of review is not exhaustive—tons more restaurants, shows, and even entire forms of diversion or recreation exist in Las Vegas than appear here. And I've tried to avoid too-often-hollow superlatives like "the best," though each entry does easily hold its own. Because this book is a wedding primer, this chapter largely focuses on pursuits that pair well with *amoré*, be they frolicsome, romantic, or both.

Every one of the suggestions herein is a first-hand account of something I've tasted, touched, or experienced, along with my wife in all but a few cases (the majority of those involve golf). These are things that we've enjoyed—and often continue to enjoy on our many trips to Las Vegas—and are confident that you will too.

A QUICK COURSE IN MULTI-COURSES

Most of Las Vegas' better eateries offer either multi-course tasting menus or fixed-price (a.k.a. prix fixe in hautespeak) dinners. What does it all mean? Typically, a lot of food for the former and a few bucks saved for the latter.

A tasting menu is just what the name implies—a selection of dishes to taste or sample. No, the waiter doesn't remove your plate after the first bite. Rather, each course features a smaller portion than you'd get if you ordered it à la carte, whether an appetizer, salad, entrée, or dessert. The idea is to let you taste across the menu, often with several appetizers or starters and several main dishes, for a total of six, seven, or however many courses the house offers. It's a great way for chefs to show off their skills and for diners to experience a greater expanse of the menu than otherwise would be practical, physically possible, or affordable. Tasting menus are offered with optional wine pairings—vintners, varietals, and vintages selected by the sommelier (or chef) to accent and enhance each course. When you opt for a tasting menu, keep in mind that typically everyone at the table will need to do the same. It's an outstanding way to have a true evening out of eating, sipping wine, and conversing—a veritable dining experience. A tasting menu is often denoted as a "degustation menu" (a term I don't use, because I think it sounds disgusting, like regurgi ... oh, never mind).

A fixed-price offering has three, four, or five courses, with several options within each course. Portions are their normal size and you typically save a few bucks going with the package deal.

RESTAURANTS

Modern Las Vegas' culinary sophistication rivals any gastronomic hotbed in America not otherwise known as New York City. The city sports multiple outlets owned or run by James Beard Award winners and chefs as well-known for their presence on television as for their talents in the kitchen. Several local giants—home-grown in the sense that they long ago arrived in Vegas—don't take a back seat to anyone. An unassuming little storefront restaurant garners national acclaim.

Like Gotham, if you want it on a plate, you can get it in Las Vegas, and often into the wee hours.

Sin City is also home, as of 2004, to more than 20% of the master sommeliers in the U.S. (and 10+% of the world's total) and eight of the world's 10 female master sommeliers. The desert is hot, and so is its wine culture.

The buffet is not dead in Las Vegas, although in most cases, the "groaning board" has grown up a bit. The food is a more vibrant mix of international fare—Italian, Chinese, Mexican, Japanese—along with good old meat and potatoes, and much of it is prepared right before your eyes in live-action cooking stations. A lot of it is surprisingly tasty too.

The leaders for quality value-priced all-you-can-eat meals are the casinos scattered about town that cater to local residents. Some of the best of these buffets are at Green Valley Ranch and Sunset Station in Henderson, and the Orleans about a mile west of the freeway on Tropicana. Of greater interest to foodies is what's going on at Paris Las Vegas, Bellagio, and Mirage, where the buffet tradition has been taken to new heights, with offerings that more closely approximate "cuisine" and exotica, from salmon in parchment to rack of lamb. Their $20- and even $30-plus dinner prices mark the evolution as well.

But this isn't a tribute to buffets.

The 10 restaurants that follow are sure-fire winners. As I wrote above, I won't be so bold as to categorize one as "best this" and another as "best that." They're all, however, great places to eat and, as often as not, just flat-out fun or coyly memorable places.

Think of the restaurants as 10 spots where my wife Terri and I really *really* like to eat, and places we really *really* like to be while eating. Some offer cuisine that's as world beating as the prices are checkbook bashing. Others serve it up just right and reasonably priced. If there's a commonality, it's that all represent dining value—the food is outstanding in relation to the price and the dining experience. Simply being expensive isn't enough and simply being cheap doesn't help either.

Again, this is not an exhaustive listing or an attempt to corral every top eatery in Las Vegas. A large number of famous and not-so-famous restaurants just as easily could have made the list. Think of this as a snapshot of the most rapidly improving and expanding culinary climate in America or, better yet, a quick note jotted down for a lifelong friend and a first-time visitor who asks, "I have ten nights in Vegas and I want ten won't-fail-me dinner bets. What do you recommend?"

This is a friend's reply ... straight from the stomach. And please note that prices relate to dinner-menu items and are subject to change.

ANDRÉ'S FRENCH RESTAURANT
Downtown—401 South 6th Street
702/385-5016
www.andresfrenchrest.com

Appetizers/Starters: $9 to $25, market price for caviar.
Main Courses: $25 to $42, market price for lobster and fish.
Tasting Menu: $85 and $135 with paired wines (six courses plus a sorbet *entr'acte*); $125+ for regularly scheduled food/wine collaborations with the local wine society.

Chef and restaurateur André Rochat isn't a native Las Vegan—he's from the Savoie region of France. But he's been in town more than 30 years, plying his craft when many of the later-arriving big guns were still dicing onions on a prep line (or in culinary school, junior high, or, hell, even in diapers), so he passes for homegrown ... and a true culinary institution.

His restaurant occupies a converted residence downtown with a relaxed comfortable look that varies across several dining rooms. Outdoor seating is available most of the year. The fare is wholly French and changes seasonally. Likely appetizer selections include an heirloom tomato Napoleon, several variations of foie gras, and traditionally prepared escargots. Vichyssoise and French onion soup can precede a salad course, and the main courses run through several fish options, duck, rabbit, lamb, and beef, all napped in those wonderful sauces that so define this cuisine. And, of course, a cheese course is available.

A second André's is in the Monte Carlo. Another Rochat eatery, Alizé, sits atop the Palms. And his Mistral graces the Las Vegas Hilton.

CHARLIE PALMER STEAK
Four Seasons Hotel
702/632-5120
www.charliepalmersteaklv.com

Appetizers/Starters: $10 to $25.
Main Courses: $17 to $35.

Las Vegas has steakhouses, *good* steakhouses, like the surrounding desert has yucca. Almost every hotel-casino has a "steak place" and standalone steak joints abound; most are quite accomplished at searing beef and some are truly outstanding at the practice. So choosing a "best" is tough, and probably foolhardy, given competition from the likes of Emeril Lagasse's Delmonico, Prime at Bellagio, and across-the-nation favorites like Ruth's Chris, Morton's, and Smith & Wollensky. Equally worthy of acclaim, although not as well known, is Charlie Palmer Steak at the Four Seasons Hotel.

A sister establishment to the justly famous Aureole at Mandalay Bay, Charlie Palmer Steak is, no surprise, all about turf (and surf). The dry-aged, certified, black Angus beef is prepared to perfection. Like only a handful of places can do—be honest, you know a lot of proclaimed steakhouses that struggle with doneness—when you order a rare New York strip or 38-ounce ribeye for two, no one in the kitchen presumes that you don't know what you really want and then takes it upon himself to apply a little extra time on the flame. At Charlie Palmer, the USDA Prime cuts are treated like the artwork they are.

The dining atmosphere is commensurate to the food. The main dining area is colored like a light roux or perhaps a dark honeycomb, with mahogany paneling and a style that hints at Spanish Revival. The atmosphere is classy and low key, as is the impeccable service. A second dining area, actually the one you first enter, is more clubby, but without the dark brooding English manor look preferred by so many purveyors of steak; cigar smoking is allowed in this room. The wine list touches all the bases, yet doesn't overwhelm with a huge selection that exists solely for the sake of being a huge selection, and the sommelier makes suggestions, if desired, without pretense or any attempt to upsell.

Charlie Palmer is one of the most acclaimed chefs in America and his signature steakhouse in Sin City deserves to be talked up with his other great eateries.

STEAK ...

Beef is the most popular item ordered at restaurants throughout the nation, nearly beating out chicken, seafood, and pork combined, according to beef-industry statistics. And consumption is on the rise. Despite this popularity, it can get confusing.

"Beef" is a broad category, taking in hamburgers, pot roasts, French dip sandwiches, London broils, and loin steaks. Technically all are, or were, "steak," which is something to keep in mind the next time a tuxedoed server pushes you toward the to-die-for $46 strip steak in beurre blanc. And a steak can also be a hunk of salmon or tuna. Hmmm, confusing indeed. But it really needn't be, as I learned after talking to a few experts.

"Steak doesn't mean anything other than a slab of meat," says Bob Butler, meat specialist at the University of Nevada-Reno's College of Agriculture. "The steak that consumers think of as 'steak' is the middle meat, the rib and loin" of beef cattle.

Now we're getting somewhere.

The short-loin portion of cattle—on the rump-end of the ribs— produces three of the five steakhouse standards: tenderloin (filet mignon); the top-loin or strip-loin steak, which is known by names as varied as New York, Kansas City, shell, strip, or club; and the double-sided "T" steaks, the porterhouse and T-bone, both combining tenderloin and the strip. For the record, the difference between the two "T" steaks is that the USDA requires the porterhouse to have a tenderloin portion at least one and a quarter inches in diameter; the T-bone can go down to a half-inch.

Behind the short loin is the sirloin, producing top sirloin, perhaps the most popular cut overall. (A specialty cut, the culotte or baseball steak, is also carved from this area.) The ribeye rounds out the menu,

COMMANDER'S PALACE
Desert Passage Mall at Planet Hollywood
702/892-8272
www.commanderspalace.com/las_vegas

Appetizers/Starters: $8 to $17.
Main Courses: $25 to $40.
Fixed-Price Dinner: $35 (three courses).
Tasting Menu: $85, plus $45 for paired wines (seven courses).

The food of the Big Easy in a Spice Road-themed shopping mall:
Where else could it be but Vegas? Commander's Palace, brought to

... 101

and it's the only one of the Big Five (tenderloin, top or strip loin, porterhouse and T-bone, top sirloin, and ribeye)—counting the two "T" cuts as one—coming from the rib section of cattle.

"Tenderloin is the eat-out crowds' favorite," says Rachel Buzzetti, the Nevada Beef Council's executive director, "followed by the New York/strip loin, top sirloin, ribeye, and porterhouse/T-bone, and steak aficionados tend to be rather cut-loyal." Buzzetti, a cattleman's daughter and a rancher in her own right, will go for a ribeye "every time," for instance.

The top three beef grades, tags applied by federal inspectors and talked up by restaurateurs, are "Prime," "Choice," and "Select." USDA Prime Grade meat is typically from younger well-fed cattle. It's the best marbled and, consequently, the juiciest, most tender and flavorful beef; it's what you'll find at the best eateries and it's priced to match. Prime makes up a fraction—just 2%-3%—of the market and a good portion of that is exported, so diners should be aware that the standing roast they're eating may indeed be a prime rib, but it's probably not Prime Grade prime rib.

More than 40% of graded meat checks in at Choice. Choice is what you'll find at better steakhouses and higher-end meat counters. Select is the leanest meat. You'll likely encounter this grade at more run-of-the-mill restaurants.

As with cut, steak grade is a matter of personal preference and judgments based on "best" are mere talking points; a strip-steak lover might be as likely to avoid a ribeye as a Select Grade fan would the better Prime cuts. The thing to remember is that the world's a big place and a steer's a big animal—in both, all meat eaters can find a slab of beef to please the palate.

the Mojave Desert by the Brennan family of New Orleans culinary fame (and the reputed inventors of Bananas Foster), presents big bold Cajun/Creole food in a big, comfortable, yet sophisticated way. The food of southern Louisiana reflects one of the truest and most vivid expressions of fusion cuisine to be found anywhere in the world, with influences from Spain, Africa, France, Canada, the Caribbean, and pre-European America. And just as the cuisine has been built up across cultures and generations, so too does the food show an immense complexity, a layering of textures and tastes.

Many of the dishes—shrimp rémoulade, turtle soup, Louisiana blue-crab cakes, gumbo, blackened anything—are the stuff of legend, and at one time or another you can find 'em all at Commander's. And if you're debating between the arugula salad or alligator *cordon bleu* for a starter or redfish on a crawfish-tasso cream sauce or the pork trio entrées, consider the tasting menu, a nearly unprecedented gastronomic event.

The service at Commander's is impeccably Southern, which means attentive, seamless, and hospitable. The servers and management understand the cuisine and can field just about any question, which makes sense after you hear the accent of a few of them.

And whatever you do, get the Bananas Foster, made tableside.

EMERIL'S NEW ORLEANS FISH HOUSE
MGM Grand
702/891-7374
www.emerils.com/restaurants/fishhouse

Appetizers/Starters: $7 to 18.
Main Courses: $19 to $36, and $28/pound for lobster.
Tasting Menu: $65, variable price wine pairings available (six courses).

I'm not trying to establish a N'awlins theme here, really. It's just that when two great eateries, each with great Big Easy pedigrees, sit in such close proximity, how do you choose between them? I decided not to.

Like the "Bam"-happy guy with his name out front, this is a lively place to dine. And like it says out front, it's all about fish,

fish, fish ... and shellfish. There's always gumbo in the pot, oysters at the seafood bar, great chowder, and Emeril's signature barbecue shrimp, but the entrées change with the tides, rather literally. Like Commander's Palace, the best way to go is with the six-course tasting menu, so you won't have to decide between, say, the pan-fried sole set upon a fresh tomato and jumbo lump-crabmeat risotto with fried capers and parsley-lemon butter sauce or the pepper-seared yellowfin with sweet-potato dumplings, braised leeks, house-cured bacon, and a Pinot Noir reduction. The more terrestrially inclined may want to take a bite out of a cedar-plank grilled steak with smashed potatoes and homemade Worcestershire sauce (that's right out of Emeril's *Louisiana Real and Rustic*, for the cookbook fans in the audience). Good *boeuf*, indeed, but if steak's your primary target, focus your aim a bit more northerly to Delmonico at the Venetian.

Fish, fusion, flair. What else would you expect of the Food Network's Emeril Lagasse, the Portuguese guy from New England who's become one of the Crescent City's—and the country's—most acclaimed chefs?

EMPRESS COURT
Caesars Palace
877/346-4642
www.caesars.com/Caesars/LasVegas/Dining

Appetizers/Starters: $9 to $22.
Main Courses: $15 to $35, market price for lobster and some other items.
Fixed-Price Menus: $40 and $55.

If you've never thought of "Chinese food" in conjunction with "fine dining," your thought processes are about to change. At Caesars Palace's Empress Court, Hong Kong-trained chefs create authentic Cantonese-style food alongside some items that might look more familiar to the sweet-and-sour-pork brigade (although I can guarantee there's nothing gelatinous or pink about Empress' pineapple pork).

On the gourmet side of the ledger sits shark fin (widely touted as an aphrodisiac ... how apropos for newlyweds), abalone, various lobster and bird's-nest renditions, and the mandatory Peking duck. If these items are too rich—in exotica, flavor, or price —the seaweed-roll appetizers and various soups, moo shu, braised black mushrooms with seasonal greens, pan-fried noodles, and chicken with curry sauce—heck, practically the whole menu—will sit just right with any lover of great food. Several all-inclusive dinner menus are available too and they won't be anything like the takeout from Tony's Palace of the Gilded Dragon down the block. Empress also presents a small but extremely representative wine list, but nothing goes with this fare quite like a bottle of Champagne or sparkling wine, a spicy Gewurtztraminer, or a floral Riesling.

The restaurant's aesthetic is likewise a knockout. It's located toward the back of Caesars Palace near the Palace Tower. Access is by elevator to a second-floor perch overlooking the Garden of the Gods, the resort's pool and garden complex. The interior is open and airy, with clean lines, plants, ample spacing between tables, and big big windows. If you have the chance to dine while late afternoon transitions to evening, the room's ivory hue takes on a warm amber glow. And this is the type of restaurant where you'll dine over a sufficient enough sweep of time to take it in.

LOTUS OF SIAM
953 East Sahara Avenue, Suite A-5
702/735-3033
No Web site

Appetizers/Starters: Most under $10.
Main Courses: Most under $10.

Thai food done right is nearly without peer—carefully balanced heat, complexity, and the sensory rush of a spice-merchant's cornucopia of seasonings. And Lotus of Siam does Thai right.

The menu features the coconut-milk-infused dishes of Bangkok and southern Thailand and the mild curries of the north that arrived via Burma and India. Yet the distinguishing mark is northeastern or Issan-style fare with its Laotian influences—lime juice, fish sauce, papaya, an abundance of fresh chiles and herbs, varied meats (such as freshwater fish and crustaceans, beef, and chicken), and glutinous rice, which the north favors over the less sticky jasmine variety of the south.

Two standout Issan appetizers are *nua dad deaw*, Issan beef jerky, and *nam kao tod*, a yin-yang mixture of sour sausage, scallion, fresh chile, ginger, peanuts, crispy rice, and lime juice. For entrées consider *koi soy*, a Thai spin on steak tartare in which lime juice, fresh herbs, and chiles figure prominently. Or try *hoh mok*, sliced cabbage, egg, and curry paste cooked in a bowl with fish or chicken.

Lotus has an encyclopedic list of German wines, which, with low alcohol and high sugars, offer a good counterpoint to the heat of Thai cuisine (and Lotus can crank it up as high as you want)—as does a glass of milk. This unassuming restaurant has garnered national culinary acclaim—it's *that* good, which is why it's here among restaurants with a whole lot more visual cachet and ambience. It's located about one mile east of the Strip, in a huge box of an older shopping center that looks like the UN of dining (Vietnamese, Thai, Japanese, Mexican ... you get the picture). Go for dinner; or if you choose lunch, skip the good but heavily Chinese-oriented buffet.

MEDICI CAFÉ AND TERRACE
Ritz-Carlton Lake Las Vegas
702/567-4700
www.ritzcarlton.com/resorts/lake_las_vegas

Appetizers/Starters: $9 to $17.
Main Courses: $32 to $40.
Tasting Menu: $130 for six courses with four wines ($90 vino-free).

When it comes to dinner at the Ritz-Carlton's Medici, the winning hand is the chef's "Market Menu," a multi-course dinner—with optional paired wines—that to this day represents something up near the very very best of my Las Vegas dining experiences. The menu changes with the whims of the chef, and if there's something he's come up with that doesn't match your tastes or dietary needs, just let 'em know ... it's a Ritz. One magical evening my wife and I were treated to: marinated tomato salad with goat cheese, pecorino, shallots, and Jerez vinegar; Maine crab cakes with tartar sauce (don't even let your mind go *that* direction—you know, the speckled-green and white guck you get from fast-food joints) and frisée; roasted bay scallops with corn fricassee and herb salad; truffle pasta with parmesan crema; meat duo of shredded oxtail and New York strip with pomme purée and caramelized onions; passionfruit with lychee ice cream, espresso bean tiramisu, and caramel chocolate dome. Gluttony is decidedly not a sin in Sin City.

KOSHER GRITS

No, it's not Mississippi matzoh meal; it's the kosher food outlets of Las Vegas, as assembled by the Jewish Federation of Las Vegas. The list includes several restaurants, including one that serves Chinese food, two caterers, two hotels with kosher kitchens, perhaps the best bakery in town, and one wholly kosher market; supermarkets that offer kosher meats and other items are not listed. Additionally, the Venetian offers kosher meals on a limited basis for in-room dining and a kosher kitchen can be arranged for banquets and conventions.

Adar Kosher Pizza (restaurant)
318 W. Sahara Avenue
702/385-0006

Four Seasons (kitchen on site)
3960 Las Vegas Boulevard South
702/632-5000
www.fourseasons.com/lasvegas

Freed's Bakery (bakery)
4780 S. Eastern Avenue
702/456-7762
www.freedsbakery.com

Galia Bar-Zvi (catering)
(702) 248-6303

Haifa (restaurant)
855 E. Twain Avenue
702/791-1956

Las Vegas Kosher Mart
(market)
4794 S. Eastern Avenue
702/450-0099

Rio (kitchen on site)
3700 W. Flamingo Road
702/777-7777
www.harrahs.com/our_casinos/
rlv/location_home.html

Shalom Hunan (restaurant)
4850 W. Flamingo Road
702/871-3262

Shoshana Segelstein
(catering)
702/348-8778

Medici offers an à la carte menu with selections ranging from lobster ravioli and spring rabbit strudel to pan-roasted monkfish in a coconut-curry broth or veal chop on polenta with wild mushrooms. It's the same fusion/pan-Mediterranean fare as appears on the tasting menu and every bit as outstanding. Medici also serves breakfast, lunch, and a weekend brunch.

The restaurant is casually elegant and it's one of those Las Vegas eateries where you won't be in the minority dressing a bit closer to the nines. The room has high ceilings with artwork-adorned walls, fresh flowers for color, and beautifully upholstered armchairs to cradle you during your culinary journey. An exhibition kitchen, attentive and engaging servers, and a view overlooking the resort's Florentine Garden stifle any sense of stuffiness. In late 2003, *Esquire* magazine named Medici one of the country's best new restaurants; the accolade was, and still is, deserved.

MON AMI GABI
Paris Las Vegas
702/944-4224
www.monamigabilasvegas.com

Appetizers/Starters: $8 to $16.
Main Courses: $17 to $30.

Never mind that it's a small chain with outlets in Illinois and Maryland. None of those have a half-scale Eiffel Tower soaring overhead or seating along the Strip with a view of Bellagio. And the food's outstanding. So it stays.

Mon Ami Gabi is a French steakhouse built into the corner of this wonderfully faux City of Light. The restaurant is a series of warmly decorated dining rooms and alcoves both small and large, with tile flooring, dark paneling, tapestries, and stained glass, and toward the back, a girder-and-glass solarium that gives way to Strip-side sidewalk seating. Outdoor seating is on a first-come first-served basis, and while the *al fresco* quality is novel, it can be noisy and fumy, so you just might want to opt for an indoor table with a view of the fountains across the way.

This restaurant's focus is steaks, fish, and *pommes frites*—real, wonderful, crispy, non-greasy French fries (which, incidentally, were invented by French-speaking Belgians). Steaks run through several cuts and grades, including USDA Prime New York, and several wholly French toppings—maitre d'hotel butter, brandy peppercorn sauce, shallot *bourguignonne*—and all come with the spuds, which are available as a side dish too. Sea bass, trout, salmon, and particularly skate (related to the sea ray) highlight the bounty of the ocean (and stream), and there's always a daily special or two. Bistro fans can order up a classic cassoulet and, whatever else you get, make sure you start with the frisée salad with chicory, hunks of bacon, and blue cheese. Oh, the individual-sized baguettes come out in paper bags. How quaint. Round out your meal with a selection from the ample wine list or, if you want to bounce around a bit, a few selections from the seemingly several-dozen by-the-glass offerings on the jaunty little wine cart.

Aside from great food at reasonable prices and comfortable capable service, dining at Mon Ami Gabi is really about one word: fun.

ONDA
The Mirage
702/791-7223
www.themirage.com

Appetizers/Starters: $8 to $14, market price for the seafood platter.
Main Courses: $19 to $39, market price for lobster.

Although Onda could be one of the least talked-about Italian restaurants in a town abounding with Italian restaurants, it certainly ranks at or near the head of the class. I don't make that distinction lightly; there *are* a lot of great Italian places to choose from in Vegas. Onda's fare is rustic Italian with flair, and even though it's branded as Italian/new-American fusion, don't let that affect your image of the classic Italian chow it serves (with a light hand on the sauce), gourmet-room-grade service, and no checkerboard cloths on the tables.

So how traditional is Onda? This traditional: caprese salad, *pasta e fagioli*, beef carpaccio, and a true antipasti platter up front; spaghettini carbonara, lobster fra diavolo, and linguini with red or white clam sauce as a pasta course; chicken saltimbocca, veal picatta, and orange roughy cioppino from among the *carne* and *pesce* offerings; and on-the-menu specials ranging from melt-in-your-mouth osso bucco to gorgonzola and portabello-crusted filet. Keep an eye out for daily specials too; I once had an unbelievable hunter's-style chicken (cacciatore) that was prepared in somewhat of a deconstructed manner, much less like the stew typically served under that name.

Tucked away in a corner of the Mirage, set behind a comfortable lounge, Onda is worth seeking out.

PINOT BRASSERIE
Venetian
702/414-8888
www.patinagroup.com

Appetizers/Starters: $9 to $14, and market price for foie gras.
Main Courses: $20 to $36, $68 for Chateaubriand for two.
Tasting menu: $65 and $90 with paired wines (six courses).

Pinot Brasserie is a convivial spot that combines the good food, good cheer, and good drinks of that prototypical City of Light-style of eatery, the brasserie, with a splash of Golden State culinary fusion, which means a little bit of this mixed with a little bit of that, so long as it's all fresh. And the union makes sense, since it's part of the Los Angeles-based Patina Group of restaurants founded by noted German but French-trained chef Joachim Splichal.

This standout eatery sits along restaurant row at the Venetian, just past Valentino's and before Royal Star. In some sense, and I think unfortunately, it seems overlooked within the pantheon of great restaurants that make this resort one of the top culinary outposts in Las Vegas (perhaps Americans don't realize that a brasserie is a restaurant/bar and not a ladies' undergarment boutique).

In a nutshell, Pinot serves bistro food, which is French comfort food where the pretension of "proper" French techniques takes a back seat to food that's fresh and simple, yet imaginative and tasty. Standout entrées have included a butternut-squash gnocchi with arugula, onions, blue cheese, and balsamic butter; free-range New Zealand ribeye served (perfectly rare, if that's your thing) alongside mashed spuds and draped in a porcini sauce; sea scallops over garlic-chive risotto; and a truly outstanding dish of braised short ribs and root vegetables with a mushroom spring roll (talk about fusion).

The restaurant's décor is wholly Parisian bistro, with dark wood, brass fixtures, red-leather booths, and artwork and decorative pieces straight from France. "Outdoor" dining is located along the Venetian's restaurant promenade and two salons are available for private groups. The main dining area opens under a voluminous ceiling with white-draped tables cozily bunched together for a dining experience straight from the Left Bank, yet no one will look cross if you don't speak a word of the mother tongue. There's also an oyster bar (more aphrodisiacs for you newlyweds). Pinot is a lively dining experience, so unless you catch a more intimate table when one of the salons is open to general dining, your whispered conversation might go for naught. The service staff is efficient, professional, and friendly.

Pinot Brasserie offers up great food in a festive environment and is certainly a Sin City eatery not to be missed. And if that's not enough, you aren't hit with a corkage fee when you bring your own wine. *Ooh la la.*

ENTERTAINMENT

If you think Las Vegas has a lot of restaurants, hotels, and wedding chapels, wait until you try to figure out what to do for entertainment (other than the obvious honeymoon and wheeee-I'm-in-gambling-mecca stuff): headliners, extravagant long-standing production shows, smaller revues, classic Vegas showgirl shows, tribute bands, knockoff artists, Mr. Vegas icon Wayne Newton, legendary performers like Celine Dion and Elton John who have taken on some form of residency, a who's who of superstars coming through on tour, boxing matches, great free stuff, some silly stuff, even Broadway productions with the music of ABBA and Queen. Then there's the night scene, where bars are competing with nightclubs competing with dance clubs competing with lounges competing with ultralounges competing with ... hey, what exactly is an "ultralounge"?

Like the rest of this book, highlighted below are ways to find some of the best entertainment in a city full of the best entertainment. It's a winning list and intentionally far from exhaustive.

FREE STUFF WORTH SEEING

In the land where cash rules and big cash really rules, a surprising number of things to see and do in Sin City are interesting, worthwhile, and, get this, free. Yes, gratis. And not the type of "free" in which the casino "gives" you a room and two buffet passes in exchange for the paycheck left behind in a slot machine.

BIG SIGHTS AT BELLAGIO

When the Fountains of Bellagio come to life, 1,000 water cannons dance along a quarter-mile front, bathed in light and choreographed to show tunes, the classics, or the Chairman of the Board. My wife and I have seen it scores of times, and one particular experience stands out. It was shortly before Christmas, late at night. The music was Placido Domingo's rendition of "O Holy Night." We were atop the faux Eiffel Tower just across the street. It got to us ... honestly. Yuletide season or not, shows rotate every 15 to 30 minutes depending on the time of day, beginning at noon on weekends and 3 p.m. during the week.

Before, after, or between shows, take in *Fiori di Como*, a rainbow-hued sculpture on the ceiling of the hotel lobby comprised of 2,000 glass flowers hand-blown by artist Dale Chihuly. The lobby is only paces away from the Bellagio Conservatory & Botanical Garden, a living breathing tribute to the magic of horticulture that changes with the seasons and holidays. It's an experience that ignites the senses.

BRING UP THE LIGHTS

Nightfall is Las Vegas' cotillion; make sure to see the Strip after the sun falls and the neon rises. If you don't have a Strip-facing room, resist the temptation to drive—and its accompanying hassle—and walk instead. Night's also a particularly good time to make your way to the area north of TI and the Venetian. This is where

A SPARKLE IN HIS EYE

Low-cost bubbly likely has caused more, well, adverse reactions—come on, you know what I'm talking about—than Señor José, a bag of limes, and a shaker of salt. Even if your experience hasn't been quite that bad, you still may not have gotten much past Monsieur André and a glass shaped like an undersized birdbath, an encounter that certainly left you as flat as the wine 30 minutes after the plastic "cork" was popped.

That's too bad.

A product of happenstance—legend says that French monks discovered in the late 17th century that otherwise mundane inert wine left bottled in caves over the winter would effervesce and take on an entirely new quality—Champagne is the king, queen, and regent of beverages. Yet unlike nobility, Champagne (and sparkling wine) need not be unapproachable to the likes of us.

Gabriele Babini knows a thing or two about celebrating and entertaining. He has overseen acclaimed restaurants and their wine selections all over the world; he's certified as a chef and a mixologist; his hotel-management degree came with honors; his family is in the hospitality business and owns a winery in Italy; and he's reportedly the youngest-ever recipient of the *Associazione Italiana Sommeliers'* highest accreditation for wine mastery, the "Taste Vin d'Or." In short, he's a sommelier, someone trained to the nth degree in the mystique and math of wine and its interaction with food. Mmmmm, sounds good. Babini's presently the food and beverage guru at the Ritz-Carlton Lake Las Vegas and he shares with us some of his insight on all things bubbly.

First things first, what is Champagne and what is sparkling wine?

Poetically, Champagne is a dream in a glass, a sign of class, beauty, and elegance. It is also a sparkling wine made only in the northern region of France called Champagne. It is a wine made from red grapes and Chardonnay, and it re-ferments and ages in the bottle, sometimes for many years. Sparkling wine is a wine that has fermented in a vat with added carbon dioxide or sugar, or a wine that has been made in the same style of Champagne, but in another region of the world, including anywhere in France outside Champagne.

Why is sparkling wine (including Champagne) so singularly associated with celebrations?

When it was first discovered that most bottles of Champagne would pop, guests were reminded of the military salute achieved with the firing of guns during royal celebrations. The product was also sweet and bubbly, making it so much more attractive than the flat and sometimes vinegary wines that were commonplace. Royals and wealthy people everywhere also favored Champagne since its creation and marketing was a big deal even in the 1700s!

Yet sparkling wine is appropriate for more than toasts and New Year's Eve, correct? How do you go about pairing bubbly and food?

Champagne is the only wine that is classically paired with the entire meal. If you order Champagne (the French one) in any restaurant, you'll always be regarded as an expert and a guest of good taste. The classic dry versions, however, tend to be a bit too dry for desserts, so coffee or sweet wines, including those that sparkle, should be drunk instead.

It goes without saying that everyone knows of Champagne, but what other parts of the world produce commendable sparkling wines? Any up-and-comers to look for?

Italy produces some of the finest "bubbly"; however, the limited production does not allow the export of the best products. The best value is still found in Spanish Cava (sparkling wine), and California also produces some of the finest sparkling wines. In the near future, Asia and South America will produce exciting ones.

Is there a renaissance going on with sparking rosé? How is the tint achieved?

It may be a bit too much calling it a renaissance, but there is a segment of the market that seems to enjoy that pink shade. The color is usually achieved by letting some of the skins macerate to release some of their pigments to the future wine. [Macerate, in this case, means the grape skins soak in the juice for a period of time.]

Sparkling reds appear to be showing up in greater frequency—and particularly from Australia. Is there a "movement" going on?

Australia and Southern California are trying to market some good, light, and easy-to-drink red sparkling wines; I think they are "summery." Traditionally Italian Lambrusco (sparkling wine) and French red sparkling wines of good quality would be the other options.

What are the terms used to denote the varying degrees of sweetness/ dryness in sparkling wines?

One can go from "brut" (the driest) and "extra dry" (still quite dry) to "sec" (almost sweet) and the decidedly sweet "demi-sec," with every shade in between.

What do the bubbles tell us about the wine?

The finer, tinier, longer-lasting, and more persistent the bubbles, the finer the wine. The bubbles carry the secret flavors and nuances of the wine to your olfactory senses.

At what temperature should sparkling wine be served and what type of glassware should be used?

Always very well chilled. The classic "flute" is the perfect glass to convey the subtle flavors to the nose and facilitate the bubbles' rise from the bottom of the glass to the top.

Is there a typical mix of grapes used in the sparkling wines from the major producing regions around the world?

Red grapes Pinot Noir and Pinot Meunier, and Chardonnay (white).

What is your personal favorite at the following price points: up to $25/bottle; $50 to $75; $100-plus?

In the least expensive category, I suggest a Prosecco from Italy (Prosecco is a particular type of grape used to make this type of sparkling wine), a Cava or a California wine from the Anderson Valley. In the $50 to $75 price range, choose a wine from Champagne, avoiding the largest and most famous brands, because the smaller producers make some exciting products. In the case of a $100-plus bottle, a Champagne Millésimé—vintage Champagne—is your choice. In this case the big names still do the best in terms of consistent quality and charming appeal: Dom Perignon, Cristal, Veuve Clicquot Grand Dame, and Perrier Jouët Le Fleur.

Okay, let's break the bank! What are we looking at when the sky's the limit?

At that point you have the monumental wines that are meant to be enjoyed with the important moments in one's life. Vintage and size determine a price that can range into the thousands of dollars. For instance, Dom Perignon 1973 Enoteque for $1,500, with magnums selling at up to $6,000, or several vintages of Krug Clos de Mesnil at $1,000-plus. If that's not enough, look for the biggest bottle around, a Nebuchadnezzar, which holds the equivalent of 20 bottles and can cost up to $15,000.

you'll find some of the classic neon signs and façades —Stardust, Riviera, Sahara—and a sense of what Rat Pack-era Las Vegas looked like. Continue downtown—but not on foot, as this stretch of Las Vegas Boulevard goes through some rough areas—and take in the modern lighting extravaganza of the Fremont Street Experience and some of the historic signs displayed prominently at Neonopolis and around Glitter Gulch. Another option is to head to higher ground in northwestern Las Vegas or out toward Henderson and look back at the entire bejeweled strand, which is arguably humanity's greatest visual excess.

CASINO CRUISE

Las Vegas hotel-casino-resort construction is building for the sake of sheer spectacle with its rain forests in the desert, the Spice Road as shopping mall, jousting knights, casino change carts dressed up like Checker Cabs, and serenading gondoliers. An entire week could easily be spent just walking from joint to joint to joint, soaking it all in. The scene is so lusciously absurd.

FREMONT STREET EXPERIENCE

The "Experience" is downtown's must-see wonder, and luckily for you, it was totally reworked and kicked up several notches not that long ago. The guts of the matter are comprised of a concave metal grid that towers over a four-block stretch of pedestrian-only Fremont Street. The heart is a canopy studded with 12 million LEDs that produce a tableau of bright colorful images that race from one end to the other, synchronized with heart-pounding sound. The Experience alone is reason enough to venture downtown. Alternating shows play at 8:30 pm and on the hour from 9 p.m. to midnight.

SEE NATURE

Everything in the valley isn't supremely unnatural and hiking, biking, strolling, and gawking are all amply rewarded at Red Rock Canyon National Conservation Area or Valley of Fire State Park. The alpine refreshment of Mt. Charleston is not much farther away and the mountain's antithesis, Death Valley National Park, sits a bit more removed to the west. If you're really gung ho, three of the country's best national parks—Bryce Canyon, Zion, and the Grand Canyon—are each a reachable, but long day trip away. If you like your nature more contrived and a lot closer, yet no less spectacular, try Lake Mead and Hoover Dam. Although it's not exactly free (because you do have to get there and perhaps pay a nominal entrance fee), the act of communing with nature and experiencing the splendor of the great American West doesn't cost one thin dime.

SIRENS OF TI

Sin City purists scoff at the new show at TI (formerly Treasure Island, although that name is still on the building) and, yes, the "Sirens of TI" is not, repeat *not*, the rollicking sea battle that raged across Buccaneer Bay for 10 years. The ever-victorious pirates are gone, the 0-for-16,334 yet indefatigable British captain is gone, the *Hispaniola* is gone, and *HMS Brittania* is gone. It's now Captain Mac and his band of brigands facing off against the songstress Sin and her crew of temptresses.

The new show incorporates most of the old hardware (renamed and refashioned), flashier pyrotechnics, better lighting, sound, and water cannons, and lotsa new "software" (the Sirens). Following the requisite taunts—more risqué than those exchanged by pirate and Brit—stuff blowing up, and a ship sinking, the show doesn't end, but instead it further explodes as pirates and Sirens light up the deck of the appropriately named *Song* (the pirate vessel is the *Bull*) with high-energy song and dance. It's an oceanic bacchanal, to the extent allowed in a place that still attracts families like Disneyland, despite whatever racy ad campaigns are conceived. It's silly, but it's still fun and free. The show plays daily, weather permitting, at 7, 8:30, 10, and 11:30 p.m.

And while you're in the area, pop next door and catch one of the every-15-minute evening "eruptions" of the volcano at the Mirage. Sure, it looks nothing like any type of naturally occurring form of volcanism, yet well over a decade since its first burp, the volcano still packs 'em in. Like the Mirage itself, the volcano has defeated time.

A FEW BUCKS TO GET IN

One step removed from the freebies is an entire category of good stuff that won't set you back more than a few piddling hands at a blackjack table. Some of these pursuits border on the edge of serious kitsch and a few step right over the line without looking back. Heck, there's even a little culture thrown in.

ALONG FOR THE RIDE

The award for best roller coaster *on* the Strip comes down to a competition between the only two roller-coasters *on* the Strip, **Manhattan Express** at New York-New York (www.nynyhotelcasino.com or 702/740-6815) and **Speed: The Ride** at the Sahara (www.saharavegas.com or 702/737-2111). Both are fun rides, particularly when enjoyed at other than full price, although neither reaches the pinnacle achieved at the nation's best amusement parks. Manhattan Express loops around the replica Big Apple, giving up some great views of the Strip along the way. Speed loops around the Sahara's classic entryway and there's a tall vertical ramp that delivers a moment of weightlessness.

But the best in town just might be found behind Circus Circus, inside the candy-cane-pink edifice that is the Adventuredome Theme Park (www.adventuredome.com or 877/224-7287). The coaster is called **Canyon Blaster** and the draw here is a double-loop double-corkscrew maneuver. Three rides atop the Stratosphere Tower (www.stratospherehotel.com or 800/998-6937) play off the thrill of being affixed to the tallest freestanding structure in the American West. The coaster is a bore, but **Big Shot**, a vertical-launch/freefall attraction, is *not*—it's a true thrill ride.

Prices for the rides vary and discount coupons and two-for-one passes can often be found in casino funbooks and the many freebie entertainment magazines scattered about town; check out all-day and multi-ride passes for additional opportunities to save.

For a sedentary ride-along experience and a perfectly corny truly Las Vegas attraction at that, the Venetian offers short **gondola rides** upon the Grand Canal inside the second-floor shopping promenade and on the lagoon beside the Strip (www.venetian.com or 702/414-4500). Tickets are $15 and $12.50, respectively, for adults.

CRITTER COUNT

Sin City has long offered free animal attractions, from flamingoes and penguins at the Flamingo to white tigers at the Mirage. Mandalay Bay has taken the wild-kingdom theme and run wild with it in the form of **Shark Reef** (www.mandalaybay.com or 702/632-4555), an aquarium that is well worth every one of the 1,595 pennies charged as admission. Shark Reef is set within an ancient temple ruin, the tour through which begins above ground with various reptiles and other land-dwelling creepy-crawlies, and concludes with several underground walk-through aquariums housing dozens of species of shark and other fish, with seasonal visitors.

FOR THE ART CROWD

Checking out the art scene certainly isn't the first thing that comes to mind when someone asks, "What should we do in Vegas?", but art fans will appreciate the Bellagio Gallery of Fine Art (www. bellagiolasvegas.com or 877/957-9777) and the Guggenheim Hermitage Museum at the Venetian (www.guggenheimlasvegas.org or 702/414-2440).

Exhibits rotate throughout the year and recent showings have included "Claude Monet: Masterworks from the Museum of Fine Arts, Boston" and "A Century of Painting: From Renoir to Rothko." Admission to each museum is $15 for adults. Steve Wynn's personal collection is on display at Wynn Las Vegas.

NIGHT SHIFT

I'm not going to even attempt to corral all the dozens and dozens of nightclubs, dance hot spots, and lounges. Suffice it to say, every resort of any note has at least one place to carry it into the wee hours of the morning. Among the most popular spots are **Rain** and the **Ghostbar** at the Palms, pretty much the entire **Hard Rock**, **rumjungle** and the poolside **Moorea Beach Club** at Mandalay Bay, **Risqué** at Paris, **Studio 54** and **Tabú** at MGM Grand, **Light** at Bellagio, and the **Shadow Bar** and **OPM** within Caesars and its Forum Shops.

A FEW SHOWS WORTH SEEING

Las Vegas *is* entertainment. From the Rat Pack and Elvis to Liberace and Wayne Newton to Barbra and the Boss, if you performed for a living, you played Vegas, baby ... and some performers even called it home. Times have changed, and while headliners remain a staple, there's more than crooners, rockers, and Parisian revues to fill time and imaginations between rolls of the dice.

Celine Dion in A New Day ...
Caesars Palace
Tickets: $87.50, $127.50, $175, $225.
Times: Seasonal
877/4-CELINE
www.caesars.com/Caesars/LasVegas

The show is called *A New Day* ... and as trite as it may sound, the arrival of five-octave-range super-vocalist Celine Dion did mark a new day and chapter in Las Vegas entertainment history. Staged in Caesars Palace's gotta-see-it Colosseum—an airy acoustical cradle for 4,000-plus—and borne of the mind of *Mystère* and *O* producer Franco Dragone, *A New Day* ... is entertainment at its apex.

The stage instills a sense of infinity with its simple black wide lines rising away from the audience with several stair-step ledges. As with other Dragone productions, the musicians are integrated within the performance. Dancers, haunting background voices, mute "narrator-messengers" coming in and out, a "canvas" of varied dimensions—projection screens enveloping the set, performers who appear and vanish from any direction, preposterously sized instruments and notes that frolic across the sky—provide additional hints of a Cirque lineage. Yet the entire tableau ultimately serves as a vehicle for Celine, and that voice—one without weakness or limitation, one of range, depth, clarity, and strength, yet one so gentle.

Unlike some lesser divas, she never relinquishes command, performing for the duration of the show with songs in Italian, English, and her native French. The repertoire includes her own chart-toppers and tributary covers of Etta James, the Chairman of the Board, Roberta Flack, and Satchmo, amongst others.

Elton John: The Red Piano
Caesars Palace
Tickets: $100, $175, and $250.
Times: Seasonal
(888) 4-ELTONJ
www.caesars.com/Caesars/LasVegas

The Colosseum at Caesars Palace takes on an entirely unique look from Celine's show when arguably the greatest pop/rock performer of all time takes the stage. Elton John's show *The Red Piano* is a blockbuster production showcasing an artist we all should see at least once in our lifetime.

The show is vintage Elton John in every way—great lyrics, great musicians, great music—it's all there, except the over-the-top Captain Fantastic costuming of the days of Eltonian yore. The stagecraft is whimsical and deep in symbolism, verily screaming at the issues of sexuality, identity, and acceptance in a provocative entertaining way. The tunes are all there, from crowd raisers like "Benny and the Jets" and "The Bitch is Back" through moving personal tributes "Tiny Dancer," "Daniel," and "Candle in the Wind."

Elton John is a must-see. And with the intimacy afforded by the Colosseum, go for the best seats you can find; get close and feed off his majesty and love.

Mac King Comedy Magic Show
Harrah's
Tickets: $18.65
Times: 1 p.m. and 3 p.m. Tuesday through Saturday
702/369-5000
www.harrahs.com

In the town's never-ending process of reinventing itself, Las Vegas is offering more and more afternoon shows. While some of these daytime shows play as hollow fillers, the same cannot be said of Mac King, magician and comedian extraordinaire for the down-to-earth crowd.

King has a wry, easy wit, a hint of self-deprecation, and an ensemble of expressions and body language that could melt even the most cynical soul in the crowd. His sleight of hand is simple yet amazing, a feat made all the more unbelievable given the close proximity between King and the audience. A number of volunteers are pulled on stage and they appear even more dumbfounded by his magic, if for no other reason than they're hands-on participants. The show is suitable for the entire family. As an added treat, King takes time after the show to talk to the audience.

Discount and/or complimentary tickets are given to invited guests and new slot club members, and buy-one-drink-get-in-free vouchers are frequently handed out at the outdoor Carnaval Court.

Mamma Mia!
Mandalay Bay
Tickets: $45, $75, $100
Times: 7 p.m. Monday, Wednesday, and Thursday; 8 p.m. Friday; 7 p.m. and 10:30 p.m. Saturday; and 5 p.m. and 9 p.m. Sunday
877/632-7400
www.mandalaybay.com

Following the brief yet acclaimed run of *Chicago* a few years back, *Mamma Mia!* has brought the live musical production back to Mandalay Bay.

The storyline is about Sophie Sheridan, a young woman who invites three men she's never met to her upcoming wedding, convinced that one of them is the missing ingredient in her life—the long-lost father she never knew. Of course, her free-spirited mother is in the dark and the addition of mom's former paramours, along with two girlfriends from her days on stage, adds a nice touch of spice to the idyll of their Greek isle. It's all joyously woven around 22 ABBA songs, and it works.

Mamma Mia! is a story of love, friendship, discovery, and the chance to do it right the first time and all over again; who wouldn't want that? You will smile throughout, shed tears of laughter and joy, and likely be forced to make an admission you wouldn't have made just minutes before curtain call ... you really had missed those ABBA tunes.

Mystère
TI
Tickets: $95
Times: 7:30 p.m. and 10:30 p.m. Friday through Tuesday.
800/392-1999
www.treasureislandlasvegas.com

Mystère was the first of the many permanent Cirque du Soleil productions to hit Las Vegas, and 10-plus years later it is considered by a lot of people—including myself—to be the best of the bunch. The show, rather the experience, is a phantasmagoric journey of art and athleticism, color and sound. Scores of characters—vividly costumed birds and imps and babies and any number of creatures wild and imaginative, collectively adorned in vibrant colors that could redefine the color spectrum—take you through a metaphoric exploration of life's cycles. The music is celestial, haunting, driving, and at any moment a lyrical chant might give way to an assemblage of Taiko drummers descending from on high. The stage is multi-dimensional, allowing the performance to come at you from before, behind, above, and below. And it exists to showcase the artistry and the supreme balance and strength possessed by the show's ensemble of dancers, acrobats, contortionists, trampoline and high-bar aerialists, pole climbers and stilt walkers, flyers and dancers. *Mystère* is a singular exercise in sensory enjoyment.

Penn & Teller
Rio
Tickets: $75
Times: 8:30 p.m. Wednesday through Monday.
888/746-7784
www.harrahs.com

Few acts have successfully combined the genres of comedy and magic and none have done it in such a refreshingly *noir* way as Penn Gillette and his mute cohort Teller. Now signed to a multi-year deal in the Rio's comfortable Samba Theater, *Penn & Teller* dispense their particular brand of the dark arts on a human scale; forget disappearing helicopters, jumbo jets, and tigers. Using audience members and themselves, they mock the craft and several of its most renowned practitioners, exposing some of the inner workings of popular magic tricks like the "inescapable" straightjacket (that's conveniently missing a seam) or the "segmented" body trick with torso or limb or head moved here and there in a multi-part box suddenly stripped of its covering sides. Then they turn right around and mesmerize the audience, leading them to believe what the magicians openly challenge them not to believe. Their stock-in-trade gig is a stunt involving firearms and bullets caught between their teeth and one of their best tricks involves coins dropped into a clear empty bowl that instantly become goldfish.

The show is edgy, bold, and humorous—a real winner. And don't buy into the myth: Teller can talk.

Rita Rudner
New York-New York
Tickets: $60.50
Times: 8 p.m. Sunday through Thursday; 9 p.m. Friday; and
7 p.m. and 9 p.m. Saturday.
866/606-7111
www.nynyhotelcasino.com

Comedians are nothing new to Las Vegas—Jimmy Durante was part of the 1946 opening of Sin City's first paradigm-shift resort, the Flamingo. It is, however, newsworthy when one gets a show and a theater all her own.

Rita Rudner won't perform her trademark splits. But that's about the only thing she's not warmed up enough to tackle during her 90 minutes of stand-up at New York-New York's Cabaret Theater. Men, and our place in the female-male relationship, are an abundant spring into which Rudner frequently taps. The banter is playful, on target, and never chiding; she pauses often to assure the guys in the audience that they're okay (though I sensed that she and the female patrons still knew better). Her material continues through marriage, love, friendship, and just finding fun in the routine and the unanticipated in day-to-day life.

Rudner's is a refreshing voice in the roar of Las Vegas comedy, which features a steady rotation of the giants of the genre, numerous outlets showcasing the up-and-coming, and a whole bunch of volume and tone just for the sake of volume and tone. This author, actress, and comedian is charming, disarming, and packs the room with creativity and laughter. This show is one to which you'd not be ashamed taking your grandmother; although she might blush a bit, she'd not reach for the soap.

SHOPPING

For several years Las Vegas has marketed itself as the ultimate adult destination with its famous "what-happens-here-stays-here" campaign. But something that definitely should go home with you is a shopping bag or three. One glance around town and you'll find that shopping is as central to the modern Sin City experience as is dinner with a TV-star chef.

Nearly every major resort has some type of shopping promenade, although three have taken it to a nearly unfathomable extreme. The first to debut, and probably most recognized, is **The Forum Shops at Caesars Palace**. Opened in 1992 and twice-since expanded so that it now includes nearly 700,000 square feet of retail, dining, and entertainment space spread across 160 or so storefronts, the Forum Shops is a Las Vegas destination in its own right. Its theme is even more audaciously classical Roman than Caesars Palace, with toga-clad statues that move and talk, the roaring Fountain of the Gods from which spring Jupiter, Pegasus, Venus, Mars, and Diana, and a clouded "sky" that cycles from day to night every couple of hours. Wolfgang Puck and New York's Palm Restaurant provide some of the food. And shops from Armani to Versace leave little chance for the credit card to remain untouched. The Forum Shops has the highest sales-to-square-footage percentage in the nation and some 20 million people visit it on an annual basis.

Another part of Italy was replicated when the Venetian opened with its **Grand Canal Shoppes**. Located on the second floor of this grand resort, the Grand Canal Shoppes is named for the quarter-mile-long canal, complete with gondolas and singing gondoliers, that wends its way through the middle of the mall. The façades are wholly Venetian and the experience is centered on a replica St. Mark's Square (only this one stays dry at high tide). The line-up of shops and eateries hits about 100, with a more balanced mix between high culture and everyday shopping than over at Caesars Palace. A number of the resort's excellent restaurants overlook the canal and promenade.

Desert Passage at the Planet Hollywood breaks the Italian stranglehold on themed shopping. The experience here is decidedly more exotic, seeming to evoke a trip along the historic trading route that ran from Morocco across North Africa through the Near East and on to India; I love the theme and the look. If you aren't up for the excursion, pedicabs can take you from land to land (store to store), and if all the desert locales prove too arid, make sure to take in the indoor rain storm.

Despite its break-out-of-the-mold design, keeping shops and restaurants in this mall has been a challenge since its opening. The number now hovers around 140, with some nice higher-end stuff—Ann Taylor Loft, bebe, Sur la Table—tucked in with Build-A-Bear Workshop, alpaca woolens, and the like. Commander's Palace anchors one corner of the souk-like mall (the first time you get totally turned around in Desert Passage you'll understand my reference to an Arab market).

Although themes are fun, head directly to the **Fashion Show** mall for Las Vegas' singular shopping experience. (It sits at the corner of the Strip and Spring Mountain Road across from TI and Wynn Las Vegas.) Fashion Show ambles across just short of two million square feet of retail space. (That's about three Forum Shops.) Seven anchors—Neiman Marcus, Saks Fifth Avenue, Macy's, Dillard's, Robinsons-May, Bloomingdale's Home, and Nordstrom—pin the corners and something like 300 shops and restaurants fill in the middle. The silver spaceship-looking thing out front is The Cloud. It functions as something like the world's largest sunshade and a multimedia advertising vehicle with its four massive video screens. Inside, the mall's Great Hall hosts fashion shows and other events.

Malls of a smaller more typical size, sporting the customary national retailers, can be found on the west and east sides of Las Vegas: the **Meadows Mall** at Valley View Boulevard and U.S. Highway 95 and the **Boulevard Mall** at Maryland Parkway south of Desert Inn Road. The **Galleria at Sunset** in Henderson is handy if you're staying at Green Valley Ranch or the Lake Las Vegas resorts.

Finally, outlet mall fans won't have to go without. The new Las Vegas Premium Outlets on Charleston Boulevard at I-15 is convenient to both the Strip and downtown, the Las Vegas Outlet Center (formerly the Belz Outlet Mall) at Blue Diamond and the far south end of Las Vegas Boulevard is just minutes from the heart of the Strip. The poorly named Las Vegas Premium Outlets is located 40 miles away in Primm on the California-Nevada state line.

SPAS

Of all the diversions available in Sin City, nothing says "vacation" to me like a day (or several) at the spa. Though day spas are popping up all over the place and it's convenient to partake of treatments back in the real world, how many of us ever get around to doing that? For some reason, it's easier to indulge in such pampering away from home and a facial and a massage just seem to go hand in hand with a stay at a resort.

Most major hotel-casinos along the Strip feature a spa (and more than likely, a gym and salon), as does the Golden Nugget downtown. Away from the Strip and Glitter Gulch, the JW Marriott, Rio, Palms, Orleans, Green Valley Ranch, Hyatt Regency, and Ritz-Carlton can take care of your rub, fluff, and primp needs.

If you've never visited a spa and you're intimidated or anxious about what to wear or how to behave, for instance—don't be. Going to a spa is all about being pampered and relaxing, so fret not.

As with restaurants and shows, there's seemingly no limit to the number of spas in Las Vegas. All can take care of your basic needs—a place to change and shower, an array of services from pedicures and facials to wraps and various types of massage, treatment rooms, and therapists. Some spas have a long and distinguished pedigree in other locales, like Canyon Ranch (at the Venetian). Some look like an after-the-fact addition, which is what happens when management realizes the place was being left in the dust because the competition offered a spa and spa services. Yet it's all, ultimately, highly personal, as it's all about what makes us comfortable, and that certainly won't be the same for everyone. Following are reviews of three spas I've have used several times; repeat business is a telltale sign of a worthy establishment.

Aquae Sulis Spa—JW Marriott Las Vegas
221 North Rampart Boulevard
702/869-7807
http://www.gowestmarriott.com/lasvegas/

This is my pick for the best spa in Sin City, and as you know, I don't toss "best" around lightly. Since the day of its conception, this spa has always been about one thing: therapeutic pampering. And with 40,000 square feet of space, there's absolutely none of that claustrophobic three-closets-and-a-tub sense that a lot of older or less purposeful spas evoke.

The spa is named after the Roman goddess of water, and it shows. Both the men's and women's ritual rooms offer hot and cold plunges, steam, sauna, whirlpool, a warm flotation pool, and inundation shower. There're also co-ed whirlpool, steam, and sauna facilities and a spa-guests-only pool located within a garden setting. The spa pool is unique in that it features six hydrotherapy chambers—think of them as alcoves where jets massage different parts of your body. The spa also features a full gym and fitness center that overlooks the hydrotherapy pool and the resort's lush grounds.

I'm a fan of massage over other types of treatments and the Aquae Sulis therapists administer killer cranial sacral and Shiatsu therapies, in addition to other modalities. Signature body treatments include a green tea-ginger "ultimate body facial" (a two-hour indulgence), firming body mask, chamomile, thermal-mineral, and Turkish-salt scrubs, and an essential-oil wrap with acupressure facial/scalp massage.

The Palms Spa—The Palms
4321 West Flamingo Road
866/942-7777
www.thepalmslasvegas.com

I've recommended the spa at the Palms to several friends/spa neophytes and the tip has worked like a charm every time; this spa has about the lowest intimidation factor in town and that works out well for some folks. (Although you really shouldn't be made to feel intimidated at any spa, it does occasionally happen.)

The facilities are complete, yet not overwhelming when it comes to decoration or size. The staff and clientele are typically younger and a bit more talkative and outgoing than the folks you'll find at most spas and there's little hint of pretension—just the occasional Hollywood wannabe who attempts to impress with her Clooney's-hairdresser-told-my-trainer shtick. The Palms Spa offers a long but not exhaustive list of services, so if you're looking for an Icelandic lava dust and Lapland lichen exfoliation, look elsewhere. If, however, a soothing and more typical facial, body treatment, or massage is your ticket, at a very reasonable price, you're covered.

This spa's strong suit is its personnel—young, hip, energetic, personable, and in many instances, former employees of Aquae

Sulis. I've been told that members of the Maloof family, owners of the Palms and pro basketball's Sacramento Kings, spent some time at Aquae Sulis between casino gigs and appreciated the skill and personalities of some of the people who are now Palms spa therapists and managers.

Check the resort's Web site for spa specials and package deals (usually offered seasonally). Also, *Las Vegas Advisor* members can use their Pocketbook of Values coupon for up to $50 in savings, or about half the cost of a typical treatment.

Spa Vita di Lago—Ritz-Carlton Lake Las Vegas
1610 Lake Las Vegas Parkway
702/567-4700
www.ritzcarlton.com/resorts/lake_las_vegas

One of Las Vegas' newest resorts and in some sense its most stunning, the Ritz-Carlton also offers one of the finest spas around. While some spas go for the frill factor, a look or an air that exists for what seems like the sole and express purpose of making sure you don't somehow "miss" the facility, Spa Vita di Lago is built around tranquility. Yes, all spas should be soothing and calming, but all aren't; sometimes there's too much hustle 'n bustle, noise, or activity.

The Ritz-Carlton's spa is centered on a private courtyard, which is a wonderful spot to read a book, veg in the sun between treatments, or eat a lunch served up healthy and tasty by the spa's cafe. Arrayed around the courtyard are the spa's 24 treatment rooms and its fully equipped men's and women's facilities. The resort's main pool is adjoining, with a fantastic view of the hotel and Lake Las Vegas, and a second lake-style pool sits behind the spa. A fitness center, salon, and boutique round out the amenities.

The spa's signature treatment, *La Culla—Dalla Testa al Piede* (Italian for The Cradle—From Head to Toe), requires an entire room, *La Cabina Benessere* (The Room of Health) and a special wet/dry therapy table. The process combines light, sound, color, and aromatherapy with an array of services including a facial and massage; it's almost too much to comprehend. And I can't say enough about the Sports Regimen, a combo wrap/Vichy shower/massage treatment. The treatment starts with a quick exfoliation followed by a slathering of cooling peppermint- and eucalyptus-oil clay; then you're trussed up in what looks like industrial-size wax paper and in a process best equated to cold-smoking, you stew or perhaps marinate while head, face, and scalp are massaged. A Vichy shower follows and the service concludes with a quick sports massage. Unlike more typical wraps, the Sports Regimen has a decidedly cool aspect to it, with the tingling refreshing clay standing in contrast to the more typical mud-and-heat-lamp wraps. The clay wrap is designed to draw out toxins from the body and induce relaxation. It works. Really.

GOLF COURSES

Las Vegas now exceeds almost every other famous golf destination in one important way—price; it's damned expensive to play golf in Sin City. The good news is that it is some of the best golf that money can buy. And it's in Vegas. How fun is that?

The course count stands at something like 60 now, including publicly accessible and private tracks. Several older, classic, parkland-style courses remain in the urban core and Strip-side golf has returned with a vengeance with visually stunning yet exceedingly overpriced Bali Hai Golf Club and the much-anticipated course at Wynn Las Vegas. Yet, like development of the valley itself, nearly all the new course construction is taking place on the edges of town and that's where you'll find most of the hottest plays.

Outlined below are a handful of some of Las Vegas' must-play golf courses. That other equally worthy tracks aren't included simply reinforces that this is a wedding book, not a golf guide. The courses listed are personal favorites, and whether you play or simply want to get rid of him for the day, I'm confident at least one of you will agree with my selections.

Bear's Best Las Vegas
11111 West Flamingo Road
866/385-8500
www.bearsbest.com
$85-$245

Bear's Best is located in Summerlin on the west side of town. This track features holes chosen by the Golden Bear himself from his more than 200 worldwide designs, with an eye toward examples suited to the lay of the land, the altitude, and the climate in Las Vegas. (Designs for all but one hole are taken from Nicklaus-designed courses in Arizona, Baja California, and the Rocky Mountains states.) From a player's perspective, you get a routing without any weak links and many of the holes give you a gypsy-in-the-palace chance for a taste of the action behind some rather private gates.

As a player, Jack Nicklaus brought a ton of power to the game, and it shows at Bear's Best if you step up to the wrong set of tees. Yet it was the way he thought himself around the course that made Nicklaus (still) the greatest. If the pin's tucked, don't be a sucker. If the most direct route off the tee takes you uncomfortably close to a bunker or hazard, the approach shot will be through the green's most exposed flank. Use your head, play your game, and like a true professional heed the forecaddie (one is provided to each foursome). When told to hit over the left-center-of-fairway bunker on 16, for instance, do it, even though you believe in your heart of hearts that the route surely leads to *terra incognita*.

And tip the caddie too.

The Falls Golf Club—Lake Las Vegas Resort
101 Via Vin Santo, Henderson
877/698-4653; 702/740-5258
www.lakelasvegas.com
$120 to $260

Tom Weiskopf's first Las Vegas design—the Falls Golf Club—is a bit like Sin City itself—softly seductive one minute, sensorially overloading the next. The course's front nine plays atop a tilted expanse of desert framed and bisected by *barrancas* (ravines) and sprinkled with water hazards. In typical Weiskopf fashion, fairways and approaches appear ample and inviting, but beware what lurks at the edges, as closely mown grass gives way instantly to desert rock and gully.

From the tee of the par-3 8th, the falls that give the course its name come into view, cascading over the black-, red-, and buff-colored escarpment that you now start to suspect might harbor the inward nine. The climb up and into the rocks—literally desert bighorn sheep country—begins innocuously enough. But by the time you reach what looks like the Continental Divide on 12, a long par 5 shaped like an inverted "V" with perhaps the most blind blindshot in golf, you realize the Tuscan-style clubhouse (with vineyard) is a couple of hundred feet below and that the entire Las Vegas Valley is stretched out before you. Cool. The signature dogleg-right downhill-then-uphill par-4 13th drops 150 feet from the tee and with a Mojave "breeze" working, even the most astute trigonometry student will have difficulty choosing between draw and fade, and exactly how much of the desert to borrow to make the angles work. Another stair-step hole brings you back to the flats and the chance to negotiate closing holes that bring into play all that water that's tumbling down the mountain.

The Falls is the kind of course that just brings a smile, no matter the score on the card.

Las Vegas Paiute Golf Resort
10325 Nu-Wav Kaiv Boulevard
800/711-2833; 702/658-1400
www.lvpaiutegolf.com
$95 to $195

Las Vegas Paiute Golf Resort offers three courses in one spot and not a weak one among them. Located on tribal land in a long broad valley bracketed by mountains about a 30-minute drive northwest of Glitter Gulch, the Paiute's golf resort is the largest in greater Las Vegas.

Pete Dye designed the three courses, although from a design and visual standpoint, there are in essence two styles. The first two courses, Snow Mountain and Sun Mountain, opened in the mid-1990s and are decidedly kinder gentler Dye routings. Both courses hug the land, with a generous mantle of rolling fairway edged by native vegetation and a seasonal riot of wildflowers. Forgetting for a second the fact that turfgrass is antithetical to the desert, these are the most "natural" golf courses in Sin City. Forced carries are minimal and the deep bunkers and shouldering waste areas for which Dye gained fame (at PGA West and Sawgrass) give way to subtle yet effective dog-legging, the natural rise and fall of the land, and the use of constricted landing areas as the means to put some bite into the courses (and with ratings pushing 74, there are plenty of teeth out there). More amazing is his incorporation into the design of traditional architectural features: multiple drive and approach angles—shorter more aggressive interspersed with longer more forgiving—shallow-bottom bunkering that "looks" like it belongs with the course, and green openings that put chipping back in the game. It's strategic, not simply heroic or penal, golf. I've played a lot of Pete Dye courses and these are about the most enjoyable.

The newer Wolf Course, which opened in late 2001, looks even less like a "Dye" course than its Las Vegas Paiute siblings. Sure, there's a hit-or-die island green and one or two building-swallowing traps, but that's about it. The course is situated on a higher portion of the property with fewer elevation changes, but with a seemingly endless supply of mounds and hummocks that give each hole a feeling of isolation (like some of Nicklaus' flatland courses, but with less artifice). You just *know* a lot of dirt was moved here, but exactly where?

With the ever-present winds and middle tees set at 6,500 yards (the tips are 7,600), this wolf can howl without sending a chill down a golfer's spine.

Reflection Bay Golf Club—Lake Las Vegas Resort
75 MonteLago Boulevard, Henderson
877/698-GOLF; 702/740-GOLF
www.lakelasvegas.com
$120 to $260

Reflection Bay Golf Club is one of two Jack Nicklaus designs at Lake Las Vegas (the other is private and wends through Celine Dion's neighborhood), and the sister course to the Falls (and a pending Tom Fazio track). Reflection Bay is less desert-austere than the Falls, with more grass, yet enough rocks and thorn-nasties that there will be no mistaking the environment for North Carolina.

And given that the Golden Bear had a lake and a more varied topography with which to craft, Reflection Bay feels more diverse, with holes along the lake, on the flats, skirting plateaus and arroyos, and within a box canyon. Despite the fact that four holes play along the wholly artificial-in-the-desert Lake Las Vegas, Reflection Bay has an organic feel to it. And while gobs of dirt had to be moved to accommodate the adjoining (and properly set-back) housing, it just appears that Nicklaus moved much less of the Mojave than is the norm with many of his other courses.

The lakeside holes dominate photos of the place, but I'm as taken by a three-hole stretch on the front—five through seven, where players have to contend with both an encroaching arroyo on every full swing and plenty of chances to play hero or goat depending on the interplay of brain and brawn off the tees—and 15, an air-it-out par 5 with a forced carry and a go-for-it second shot that can yield eagle or bogey as easily as the lay up produces par.

Don't get me wrong. The water's fun and there's really not an abjectly weak hole on this course—a claim not many courses can stake. That's a testament to the designer, the developer, and the land.

Tournament Players Club at the Canyons
9851 Canyon Run Drive, Las Vegas
702/256-2000
www.tpc.com/daily/the_canyons
$65 to $250

TPC at the Canyons has hosted the PGA Tour's best on several occasions, and the fact that the big boys fare more than considerably better than I do does not diminish my enthusiasm for this exhilarating track with the knockout views. Much of this Summerlin-situated course is comprised of slim ribbons and small patches of green stitched alongside a canyon that runs from narrow and deep to freeway wide. The outward holes play through and around a gentle arroyo, green strands of fairway woven through the rocks, yuccas, and coyotes of the Mojave. You play downhill for several holes until just before you reach the JW Marriott. Desert trees take over on the return—mesquite, palo verde, ironwood. Other than the first hole, which is a tad pedestrian, I adore the front nine and its desert aesthetic.

The second hole gets a lot of attention, with good reason. It's an island par 3, similar to the 17th at the Players' Championship, but without gators and water and with more yardage. The green would, however, become engulfed in a flash flood (during which I would be inside, perched at a video poker machine).

You truly get an appreciation for the canyon in the club's name on TPC's home nine. It comes into play as the to-be-avoided area at the mesa-topped par-3 12th, and it's your constant companion until you reach the safety of 16. If playing from the forward tees, do yourself a favor on 13 and tee off from one of the markers pasted to the canyon floor. There is a rock on the far rim that guides your aim. Trust it.

Appendix I

PRENUPTIAL

Although this book is the most exhaustive, complete, and independent-of-wedding-industry-influence Las Vegas wedding guide on the market—heck, perhaps the only one that meets those criteria—there's lot more to a neon nuptial than the nuptial itself. For advice and suggestions beyond this book's coverage of great places to wed, stay, eat, and play, and for insight on a host of other Sin City goodies, check out some of the resources below.

Bob Sehlinger, *The Unofficial Guide to Las Vegas 2005*, Wiley Publishing, Inc. If you only have the time, interest, or wallet to buy one general Las Vegas travel guidebook, this is it. In fact, even if you're a bazillionaire and want to buy 23 books, don't bother. It contains commercial-free, no-holds-barred, honest, and complete reviews of restaurants, shows, hotels, attractions, and other entertainment venues; great tips on how to plan and book a trip and how to get around town; practical information on gambling; and much more. In short, a must-have in your Las Vegas travel bag.

lasvegas24hours.com. You know that "what happens in Vegas ..." spiel? Yep, came from these guys: the Las Vegas Convention and Visitors Authority. The Web site is complete, with info and links to pretty much every bit of boilerplate you'd ever need when contemplating a Sin City getaway. The local governments and the travel and tourism trade fund this outfit, so keep that in mind.

LasVegasAdvisor.com. This Web site is the online counterpart to the *Las Vegas Advisor* newsletter. Both are invaluable resources. The monthly 12-page newsletter is all about the latest Las Vegas news, particularly information on maximizing value in Sin City, from food and drink to shows and gambling. The Web site offers hotel, chapel, golf, and show booking links; the latest and greatest deals available across town; breaking news; and—my favorite thing about the whole shebang—a variety of message boards that are likely the most active and the most informative of any of the many on the Internet. Full and online memberships cost $50 and $37, respectively (the latter provides you with the newsletter in an electronic format only), and come with the Pocketbook of Values, a dynamite package of coupons that can easily save you hundreds of dollars.

lvchamber.com. The Las Vegas Chamber of Commerce's Web site features wedding and visitors' guides. The listings are complete if not exhaustive, and of course most of the links are to commercial enterprises; big surprise, it's a business-representing organization. An advantage of the chamber over other content providers is that the featured businesses are chamber members. This doesn't guarantee you fool-proof service—I guarantee that some of the chapels that absolutely blew me off have the chamber sticker proudly displayed in their windows—but it will provide a sounding board if you have a problem. For a more consumer-oriented resource, check out vegasbbb.org below.

theknot.com. As with other bridal/wedding Web sites —ultimateweddings.com comes to mind—theknot.com is helpful for getting info and articles of a general how-to nature, like what to look for in a dressmaker, floral and florist pitfalls to be avoided, digital versus film photography, etc. Within the Web site, look to "Local Resources," then key the "Las Vegas-Reno-Tahoe" tab. You'll find all sorts of links to chapels and wedding-services providers. This is a commercial venture, so the links are not of an independent reviewing nature. But sign up for the free service, dive into the message boards, and converse with other brides (and some grooms) who have or are taking the neon-nuptial plunge.

unlv.edu/Tourism/vegas.html. This site is known as "All Things Las Vegas!" and that it is. Sponsored by the hotel administration school at the University of Nevada-Las Vegas, it presents a ton of Las Vegas-specific content and links to fun, funky, and practical information.

vegasbbb.org. The good folks at the Better Business Bureau will tell you which love palaces abide by BBB guidelines and which don't respond to consumer complaints. And if you have a problem with your chapel, the BBB can help.

wizardofodds.com. Odds are, you're going to gamble in Las Vegas—even if it's just a little. Forget what your Aunt Freda said about using the quintuplets' birthdates on a five-spot keno card; there are no guarantees in gambling. The site is run by Michael Shackleford—bean counter, math whiz, and superstitions-be-damned gambling expert. Look through the "Advice & Strategies" section on the homepage, take it to heart, and you'll be a big leg up on most everyone else in the casino. Sure, you probably won't win, but you should lose less than you would've without the wizard's guidance.

Appendix II

CHAPEL-RATINGS CHARTS

Standalone Chapels & Facilities—4+ Ratings	
Romance Quotient	**Fresh Test**
Hartland Mansion-4 Las Vegas Weddings at the Grove-4 Little Chapel of the Flowers-4 Little Church of the West-4 Mon Bel Ami-4	Little Chapel of the Flowers-5 Mon Bel Ami-5 Victoria's Wedding Chapel-5 Vegas Wedding Chapel-4.5 Always and Forever-4 Chapel of the Bells-4 Las Vegas Weddings at the Grove-4 Shalimar-4
Comfy/Cozy Test	**Kitsch Factor**
Little Chapel of the Flowers-5 Cupid's Wedding Chapel-4 Las Vegas Weddings at the Grove-4 Mon Bel Ami-4 Secret Garden-4 Vegas Wedding Chapel-4 Victoria's Wedding Chapel-4 Viva Las Vegas-4 Wee Kirk o' the Heather-4	Graceland-5 (with Elvis) Hartland Mansion-5 Hitching Post-5 Las Vegas Garden of Love-5 Little Church of the West-5 Little White Wedding Chapel-5 (drive-thru) Monaco Wedding Chapel-5 San Francisco Sally's Victorian-5 Viva Las Vegas-5 Wee Kirk o' the Heather-5 Candlelight-4 Chapel of Love-4 Heavenly Bliss-4 Special Memory-4 Stained Glass Wedding Chapel-4

Standalone Chapels & Facilities

Chapel Name	NN Best-of Facility
Always and Forever	
Candlelight Wedding Chapel	
Chapel by the Courthouse	
Chapel of Love	
Chapel of the Bells	
Chapel of Dreams	
Cupid's Wedding Chapel	
Elvis Chapel	
Graceland Wedding Chapel	Chapel - 5
Hartland Mansion	
Heavenly Bliss Wedding Chapel	
Hitching Post Wedding Chapel	
Hollywood Wedding Chapel	
Las Vegas Garden of Love	
Las Vegas Weddings at the Grove	Outdoor - 4
Little Chapel of the Flowers*	
Little Church of the West	Chapel - 4
Little White Wedding Chapel	
Monaco Wedding Chapel	
Mon Bel Ami Wedding Chapel*	
San Francisco Sally's Victorian Wedding Chapel	
Secret Garden at the Las Vegas Racquet Club	
Shalimar Wedding Chapel	
Special Memory Wedding Chapel	Chapel - 3
Stained Glass Wedding Chapel	
Sweetheart's Wedding Chapel	
Vegas Wedding Chapel	Chapel - 2
Victoria's Wedding Chapel	Chapel - 1
Viva Las Vegas Wedding Chapel*	
Wee Kirk o' the Heather*	

*As noted elsewhere, several chapels that ranked high enough under this system to warrant best-of distinction didn't because of unsatisfactory ratings from the Better Business Bureau.

Standalone Chapels & Facilities—Continued				
Chapel Name	Kitsch	Romance	Fresh	C/C[1]
Always and Forever	3	3	4	3
Candlelight	4	3.5	3.5	2.5
Chapel by the Courthouse	3	1	1	1.5
Chapel of Love	4	2.5	2.5	3
Chapel of the Bells	2	2	4	2.5
Chapel of Dreams	2	1	3	2
Cupid's Wedding Chapel	2	2	2.5	4
Elvis Chapel	2	2	3	3.5
Graceland Wedding Chapel	5 (3)	3	3.5	3
Hartland Mansion	5	4	3	3
Heavenly Bliss	4	3	2	2
Hitching Post	5	1	1	1
Hollywood	3	2	2	2
Las Vegas Garden of Love	5	1	1	1
Las Vegas Weddings (Grove)	2	4	4	4
Little Chapel of the Flowers	3	4	5	5
Little Church of the West	5	4	3	3
Little White Wedding Chapel	2 (5)	2	3	2
Monaco Wedding Chapel	5	1	1	1
Mon Bel Ami	2	4	5	4
San Francisco Sally's	5	1.5	1.5	1.5
Secret Garden	2	3	3.5	4
Shalimar Wedding Chapel	2	2	4	1
Special Memory	4	3.5	3.5	3.5
Stained Glass	4	3	2	1
Sweetheart's	1	1	1	1
Vegas Wedding Chapel	1	3	4.5	4
Victoria's Wedding Chapel	2	3.5	5	4
Viva Las Vegas	5	3	3	4
Wee Kirk o' the Heather	5	3	3.5	4

[1] Comfy/Cozy

Hotel-Casino Chapels & Facilities—4+ Ratings

Romance Quotient	Fresh Test
Bellagio-5	Bellagio-5
Caesars Palace-5	Caesars Palace-5
Lake Las Vegas Resort-5	Four Seasons-5
Luxor-5	Imperial Palace-5
MGM Grand-5	Lake Las Vegas Resort-5
Star Trek: The Experience-5	Luxor-5
Stratosphere-5	MGM Grand-5
TI-5 (pirate wedding)	Paris Las Vegas-5
Venetian-5	Planet Hollywood-5
Excalibur-4	Rio-5
Flamingo Las Vegas-4	Sam's Town-5
Four Seasons-4	Star Trek: The Experience-5
Mandalay Bay-4	Texas Station-5
Paris Las Vegas-4	Venetian-5
Sam's Town-4	Mandalay Bay-4.5
Texas Station-4	Excalibur-4
Tropicana-4	Flamingo Las Vegas-4
	Monte Carlo-4
	TI-4

Comfy/Cozy Test	Kitsch Factor
Bellagio-5	Bellagio-5 (terrace)
Caesars Palace-5	Caesars Palace-5
Four Seasons-5	Greek Isles-5
Lake Las Vegas Resort-5	Paris-5 (variable)
MGM Grand-5	Sam's Town-5
Star Trek: The Experience-5	Star Trek: The Experience-5
Texas Station-5	Stratosphere-5
Flamingo Las Vegas-4	TI-5 (pirate wedding)
Luxor-4	Tropicana-5
Mandalay Bay-4	Venetian-5 (gondola)
Paris Las Vegas-4	Flamingo Las Vegas-4
Rio-4	
Sam's Town-4	
Stratosphere-4	
TI-4	
Venetian-4	

Hotel-Casino Chapels & Facilities

Venue Name	NN Best-of Facility
Bellagio	Hotel-Based Venue - 2, Outdoor - 3
Boardwalk	
Caesars Palace	Best Overall, Outdoor - 5
Circus Circus	
Excalibur	
Flamingo Las Vegas	Outdoor - 2
Four Seasons	
Greek Isles	
Imperial Palace	
Lake Las Vegas Resort	Outdoor - 1
Luxor	Hotel-Based Venue - 3
Mandalay Bay	
MGM Grand	Hotel-Based Venue - 1
Monte Carlo	
Paris Las Vegas	
Planet Hollywood	
Plaza	
Rio	
Riviera	
Sam's Town	Vegas Personified - 3
Star Trek: The Experience	
Stratosphere	Hotel-Based Venue - 5
Texas Station	Hotel-Based Venue - 4
TI	Vegas Personified - 1
Tropicana	
Venetian	Vegas Personified - 5

Hotel-Casino Chapels & Facilities—Continued				
Venue Name	**Kitsch**	**Romance**	**Fresh**	**C/C[1]**
Bellagio	5	5	5	5
Boardwalk	2	2	2.5	1
Caesars Palace	Up to 5	5	5	5
Circus Circus	3	2.5	3	2
Excalibur	3	4	4	3
Flamingo Las Vegas	4	4	4	4
Four Seasons	1	4	5	5
Greek Isles	5	3	3	2.5
Imperial Palace	2	3	5	3
Lake Las Vegas Resort	1	5	5	5
Luxor	1	5	5	4
Mandalay Bay	1	4	4.5	4
MGM Grand	1	5	5	5
Monte Carlo	2	3	4	3
Paris Las Vegas	Variable	4	5	4
Planet Hollywood	3	3	5	3
Plaza	2	2	2	2
Rio	2	3.5	5	4
Riviera	2	2	2	3
Sam's Town	5	4	5	4
Star Trek: The Experience	5	5	5	5
Stratosphere	5	5	3	4
Texas Station	1	4	5	5
TI	1 and 5	3 and 5	4	4
Tropicana	5	4	3	3
Venetian	1 and 5	5	5	4

[1] Comfy/Cozy

INDEX

About the Author

Ken Van Vechten is a native Southern Californian and a historian by training. He's a regular contributor to *Alaska Airlines*, *Midwest Airlines*, *Nevada*, and *Westways* magazines. *Neon Nuptials* is his first (but assumed to be far from his last) book. The 40-something-year-old previously toiled in the worlds of retail sales, taverns, newspapers, politics, and soulless corporations before embarking on his unique version of a mid-life crisis: becoming a freelance travel and golf writer. His "crisis," such as it is, is abetted by his understanding, indulgent, and wholly supportive wife of seven years, Teresa.

About Huntington Press

Huntington Press is a specialty publisher of Las Vegas-
and gambling-related books and periodicals, including the
award winning consumer newsletter, *Anthony Curtis' Las
Vegas Advisor*. To receive a copy of the Huntington Press
catalog, call **1-800-244-2224** or write to the address below.

Huntington Press
3687 South Procyon Avenue
Las Vegas, Nevada 89103